Praise for *Amazonia*

"An exquisitely written literary delight. . . . Marcus takes a story that most of us already know—the giddy euphoria of the late '90s stock market—and turns it into a riveting, personal document."　　　—*Salon.com*

"One of the first really good books to be written about the dot-com boom. . . . The contrast with some of the more foolish examples of journalism and blockbuster titles, published at the height of the boom, could not be more pronounced. . . . And his literary skills, and sense of humour, were left intact, as this beautifully written book confirms."

—*Financial Times*

"James Marcus and his *Amazonia* enter the [dot-com] fray with notable distinction . . . a clear-eyed, first-person account, rife with digressions on the larger cultural meaning throughout."　　　　　　—*Newsday*

"[*Amazonia*] offers sharply drawn insight into the company's early years and shows what it was like to be on the intense and chaotic front lines . . . a print complement of sorts to 1999's *Office Space.*"　　—*Los Angeles Times*

"A truly engaging, amusing dot.com memoir . . . probing middle management, stock splits, and bizarre business strategies. . . . Marcus is a wonderful writer who should win over even the most jaded dot.com vets with his swift, clever, and intelligent rendering of their history."

—*Seattle Weekly*

"An utterly beguiling book. *Amazonia* has the shapeliness and intensity of a novel . . . but it's the tone of Marcus's writing that enthralls: rueful, disenchanted, often very funny, he is nevertheless able to infect the reader with the dizzy euphoria of an age that now seems hardly less distant than that of the robber barons of the century before last."

—Jonathan Raban, author of *Bad Land*

AMAZONIA

JAMES MARCUS

THE NEW PRESS

NEW YORK
LONDON

Requests for permission to reproduce selections from this book should be mailed to:
Permissions Department, The New Press, 28 Greene Street, New York, NY 10013.

Published in the United States by The New Press, New York, 2005
Distributed by W. W. Norton & Company, Inc., New York

LIBRARY OF CONGRESS CATALOGING-IN-PUBLICATION DATA

Marcus, James.
Amazonia : five years at the epicenter of the dot.com juggernaut / James Marcus.
        p.   cm.
ISBN 1-56584-870-5 (hc.) ISBN 1-59558-024-7 (pbk.)
    1. Amazon.com (Firm)—History.   2. Marcus, James.
        3. Internet bookstores—United States—History.
    4. Electronic commerce—United States—History.   1. Title.

Z473.A485M37   2004
381'.45002'02854678—dc22   2003066505

The New Press was established in 1990 as a not-for-profit alternative to the large,
commercial publishing houses currently dominating the book publishing industry.
The New Press operates in the public interest rather than for private gain, and is
committed to publishing, in innovative ways, works of educational, cultural, and
community value that are often deemed insufficiently profitable.

www.thenewpress.com

Composition by dix!

Printed in the United States of America

2   4   6   8   10   9   7   5   3   1

For Nina

The history of the Victorian Age will never be written: we know too much about it.

—Lytton Strachey, *Eminent Victorians*

1

ONE FINE SPRING DAY IN 1996, I took off from Portland, Oregon, in a prop plane the size of a toy, which seemed to touch down in Seattle only minutes later. At the airport I rented a car. Then I drove to a low, inauspicious building south of the downtown, next to a barbecue joint whose vinegar-scented fumes I could smell the moment I hit the sidewalk, and made my way inside.

Since I was there for a job interview, I had donned a jacket and tie before entering. At once I had the sensation of being the most formally dressed guy in the building, not to mention the oldest, and let's recall that I was only 37—sufficiently elderly, that is, to play Father Time in Amazon.com's winter pageant. To my right sat a half-dozen employees, answering phones and papering their computers and crude wooden desks with yellow Post-it notes. Directly in front of me was a receptionist seated at another crude wooden desk. Yet the atmosphere of the place was so anticorporate that she seemed merely decorative, and it struck me that a toddler could have breached the security cordon.

"Are you James?" a woman said, approaching me. I recognized Susan Benson's voice from our telephone conversation: an East Coast accent with a slight Californian deceleration at the end of her sentences. She shook my hand warmly and ushered me into what looked like the only bonafide office in the place. Jeff, she explained, would be interviewing me first.

And here he was. At this point Jeff Bezos hadn't yet become a figure out of American folklore, hadn't yet been celebrated as the only begetter of e-commerce or vilified as a purveyor of virtual snake oil. His explosive laugh, which first erupted about sixty seconds into our conversation, was still an unknown quantity. He was a small, sandy-haired man seated at a messy desk, reading my clips.

"I like these," he said, brandishing the manila folder. "I like your first sentences."

I thanked him. Although I had flown, we spoke for a moment about the surprising dullness of the drive between Portland and Seattle, which tended to peak around the time you crossed the Nisqually mud flats. I was in the rare and enviable position of not caring if I got the job, which made me relaxed, tie or no tie. Jeff was wearing baggy khakis and a blue Oxford shirt, and his demeanor was so low-key that he seemed at some moments to be moving in a kind of affable slow motion. He asked me how I would feel about working sixty hours a week.

"I'm not wild about the idea," I said, wondering if this was the good or bad kind of honesty. "But if I love the work I'm doing, I don't think I'd mind as much."

"What I'd like you to do," he said, putting these nuts-and-bolts matters firmly behind us, "is explain a complicated process in as simple a manner as possible."

Later I discovered this was the Bezonian curveball, which in some shape or form was lobbed at every job candidate. In many cases the trembling applicant was asked how many gas stations were in the state of Texas, or how many windows there were in New York City. Nobody was expected to cough up the right answer. You *were* expected to demonstrate some conceptual shrewdness in how you arrived at the number, though, and I suppose my own answer supplied a similar window into my mental processes.

It was easier, of course, since Jeff had let me select my own brain-teaser. I chose to explain how I had translated the florid Italian cursing in Oriana Fallaci's novel *Inshallah* into florid American cursing.

"How was that complicated?" he asked.

"Usually a word-for-word translation of an idiomatic expression doesn't work. What sounds blasphemous in one language sounds dopey in another. But it's simple, too, in the sense that you just sit down with a dictionary and a pad and some sharpened pencils and get it done. One sentence after another."

I gave Jeff some examples, and he seemed satisfied with the way I juggled simplicity and complication, laughing at my potty-mouthed equivalents for *cazzo d'un cazzo stracazzato*. Then, looking embarrassed, he asked me what my SAT scores had been. "I know it's been a while since you took them," he said, "but if you could remember at least your approximate scores . . ."

I took a guess, and here too he seemed satisfied, noting the numbers on a piece of paper. In retrospect this would be my first taste of the company's mania for quantification, for its immersion in what was grandly called the Culture of Metrics. It was obvious that my performance on those tests, which had taken place a generation ago, had little bearing on my current abilities. Still, Jeff jotted down my scores with evident relish.

"Would it bother you to be working for a store rather than a newspaper or magazine?" he said.

"That depends," I replied. "I understand that you're not running a philanthropic service here: you're selling stuff. But is the idea that I pretend to like everything?"

"Not at all. We'd be hiring you for your abilities as a book critic.

The idea is to seem smart and authoritative—to become not just a store but a *destination*." He gave this last word an almost theological stress.

We batted around favorite books for a moment. It turned out that we both had a weak spot for Frank Herbert's Dune trilogy, and we spent a minute or so dissecting the desert ecology of Arakis and the sublimely evil Baron Harkonnen—the sort of villain who chuckles a lot. Then Jeff turned the tables.

"What about you?" he said. "Is there something you'd like to know?" He leaned back in his chair and seemed to be girding himself for an assault. He needn't have bothered. I had already succumbed to his brand of anticharismatic charisma, which would have mortified a Great Man of a century ago but seemed just right for our nerd-driven meritocracy. Jeff, it should be stressed, was a likeable and normal person. He had none of Bill Gates's pasty paranoia, nor would he be likely to build a floating Xanadu in the manner of Larry Ellison. No doubt he was, and is, as ambitious as either of these empire builders. Yet the habit of humorous self-effacement kept his Napoleonic side under wraps.

"Yes, there is. What's a hedge fund?" According to a *Wall Street Journal* article I had read, this had been Jeff's bread and butter at D.E. Shaw, and the term meant nothing to me.

"Good question," he said. Sketching a graph on a piece of scrap paper, he explained that it was possible to track the diverging and converging fortunes of certain industries—airlines and oil, for example—and, once you understood their peculiar rules of attraction, to make scads of money. Here he hit the Bezonian curveball out of the park. He made the mind-bending complexity of running a hedge fund seem so simple that I thought I could run out and start my own. But now Jeff escorted me back downstairs to Susan. "We had a *great* conversation!" he told her, and then asked her to show me the warehouse.

Although Amazon had been selling books for less than a year, it had long since outgrown its original quarters in Jeff's Bellevue garage, and the current location was basically a warehouse with (very) ad-hoc offices. Susan led me down a short corridor and into a large room with row upon row of metal shelves. On each shelf was a pile of books. The place might have resembled a library, except that each pile represented an individual order. And if the high chilly room with its Home Depot hardware was an impersonal space, the books themselves were all too personal. Indeed, the more you trawled up and down the aisles and examined the rubber-banded merchandise, the more you felt yourself surrounded by Rorschach blots. In one pile Stendhal cohabited with *Pat the Bunny*. Another included Tolkien, a vegan cookbook, and a guide to field-stripping and cleaning your .22 rifle. It was dispiriting to find a shrinkwrapped copy of *Mein Kampf*, but at least somebody one aisle down was investing heavily in Wallace Stevens.

This being an Internet bookstore, there were plenty of geekish tech manuals: Perl and HTML and C++ seemed to be the flavors of the month, although here and there you saw an antediluvian primer on COBOL or (heaven forbid) BASIC. Clearly many customers were prepping for the MCSE exam. And clearly many, encouraged by the blessed anonymity of the online experience, were indulging their private pastimes. Forget heterosexual, plain-vanilla porn (of which there was a great deal). Trotting up and down the rows with Susan, I came across tutorials on spanking, fisting, flogging, and shagging, not to mention a saucy bit of Victoriana called *Furtling: The Rediscovered Art of Erotic Hand Manipulation*. There were books for the Man from NAMBLA. There were stashes of lesbian erotica, much of it involving vampires or motorcycles or both. In cyberspace, I could see, there was no love that dare not speak its name—instead there was a refreshing sexual cacophony, which suggested neither Sodom nor Gomorrah but fin-de-siècle America, where the pursuit of happiness was a matter of individual taste. *Trust thyself: every heart vibrates to that iron string.* Yes, Emerson would be spinning in his grave. Yet perhaps the world-spanning, mind-melding Web would it-self offer the best escape from what he called "the stern fact, the sad self, unrelenting, identical."

Up and down the aisles we went. Warehouse workers circulated around us, snatching from the shelves Dover paperbacks at a dollar a pop, *The Cat in the Hat,* Hölderlin, a history of duct tape, and (I no-ticed as Susan led me out) many, many copies of Thomas Kuhn's *The Structure of Scientific Revolutions.* The author had died not long be-fore, which might have contributed to a momentary boost in sales. But surely Kuhn's sermon on the New Paradigm—the process by which one conception of the universe supplants, and swiftly eradi-cates, another—had a very Amazonian ring to it. Call it wacky, call it hubristic, but the employees of what was then essentially an online catalogue-and-fulfillment operation were intent on changing the world. Their sense of having grabbed history by the horns was al-most palpable. It made them slightly giddy and enormously tired.

Or so it seemed as we adjourned to the Starbucks world headquar-ters across the street, where there was a shiny new cafeteria. I had put on my jacket as we crossed First Avenue and once again resembled an Evil Businessman sent over from Central Casting. My future col-leagues, on the other hand, looked like they were about to attend a clambake.

There was Jonathan, a rumpled guy in a fez who had studied ge-netics, sociobiology, and programming, and had written one of the first books on the Internet—a kind of Mensa poster boy. There was Barrie, quite literally a rocket scientist, who used to work at the Jet Propulsion Lab down in San Diego and seemed the most unruffled of the entire crew. Compared to these two I felt like a seedy little hu-manist. But Tod, with his shock of bleached hair and elaborately shabby clothes, was more of a kindred spirit. Like me, he had gotten a graduate degree in writing and kept himself just above or just below the poverty line by dint of freelance journalism.

"Not that I've been doing much writing of any kind," he said as we carried our trays to the table. "Ever since the *Wall Street Journal* article came out, we've all been swamped with customer service. Jeff's supposed to be hiring a ton of CS people. Until then we have to hold down the fort."

Jonathan daintily rearranged his fez: as I would later learn, he never exposed his scalp in public. "What I'm interested in right now is collaborative filtering," he told me, taking a sip of soda. "I've not seen anybody really using the technology we have, let alone what we'll have in six months."

We chatted, the five of us, and sized each other up. Barrie said little, although it did come out that she'd been a National Spelling Bee Champion as a girl. Jonathan delivered a measured, Pepsi-fueled critique of Stephen Jay Gould, whose views of evolutionary history he found archaic. Here I was out of my league. But Tod asked me what I thought of the latest Richard Ford, then moved on to what would prove to be an eminently practical question.

"How long does it take you to write a book review?" he asked.

"Depends on the length. A short one, maybe two hours," I said, shaving off the odd minute. "A longer piece, like the Albert Murray thing I sent Jeff, could take a day or so."

"How fast could you review one hundred books?" Tod said.

I paused. I already understood from my talk with Jeff that literary criticism at Amazon would be a wholesale rather than a retail business. Still, the number was daunting. It sounded less like reviewing and more like a pie-eating contest. But there were precedents, weren't there? Samuel Johnson dictating the *Rambler* essays directly to the printer. Balzac with his coffee, Kerouac with his speed. I chuckled

like the incipient hack I was and said, "How long would you *like* it to
take?"

"An afternoon," he replied, and although we all laughed, it wasn't
clear exactly how hyperbolic his answer was.

After an obligatory dose of the Brew of the Day, we headed back
across the street. The breeze had shifted and the barbecue fumes were
again in evidence. We shook hands, Susan assured me that she would
be in touch soon, and I found myself on another flight to Portland. To
the east, across the aisle, I could see the tops of the Cascades. To the
west the sun was setting, and for another fifteen minutes, until its fiery
disappearance behind the Olympics, we were in the midst of a temporary golden age, which made us squint.

I ate the pretzel nuggets I'd found in the seat pouch. I mulled over
the day's events. I flipped through the book in my briefcase, whose
pages appeared to be gilded by the pyrotechnic display outside. At
the time I was interested in writing an essay on being Jewish—a relatively rare condition in the Pacific Northwest, with its heftier complement of black bears and white supremacists—and was looking for
material. As we approached the Columbia River I read the following
bit from Martin Buber: *The life-story of a people is, after all, basically
nothing more than the life-story of any member of that people, in large
projection.* This was either a killer insight or an eerie anticipation of
the Me Generation, I wasn't sure which. In any case, it made me wonder whether my lunch companions would be making history on the
scale they imagined, and whether I should join the party, if invited. I
still hadn't decided when the plane made its final descent.

2

"Everybody was so *excited*," I said, for the second time. I was sitting on the edge of the bed with my wife. The window was open, because our cat was on the roof and we were waiting for him to come back inside.

"I think you should consider it," she said. "You keep dismissing it, but I can tell you're interested. The minute you came in the door you said it was a pity we couldn't move up there. Why couldn't we?"

"It's not just moving to Seattle. It seems like an admission of defeat to me. I couldn't make it as a writer, so I'm becoming a clerk in an electronic bookstore. I'm pimping for literature via the Internet."

"That's not what Jeff told you." Already we were on a first-name basis with the guy, whose high-impact laugh I had tried and failed to imitate for Iris. "He said they wanted to hire you for your talent."

I got up and poked my head out into the cool air. "Dinner time, Al," I called. A lie: he remained where he was, a black-and-white shape curled up next to somebody's TV antenna. I sat down again and sighed. "Look, there's no guarantee they want to hire me for anything. Maybe it'll just be a freelance gig, where they pay me a nickel a word and I get to keep the books. We'll see. Susan said she would get back to me."

Despite my reservations—which kicked in the moment my plane hit the tarmac in Portland—the interview at Amazon had occurred in the nick of time. Two years earlier, in 1994, I had fled New York City with my wife and infant son. The idea was to live cheap in the Pacific Northwest, where I would pursue my career as a writer, and Iris, as soon as she leaped the hurdle of the Oregon Bar Exam, would practice law. We found a tiny apartment in a nice part of town. We developed a tolerance for rain and semi-perpetual cloud cover. Buckling our son into his stroller, we wheeled him over to charming neighborhood playgrounds, where the absence of used condoms and empty crack vials signified a kind of anti-Manhattan, and where half the toddlers in the sandbox seemed to be named Cody.

The problem was that we were broke. No matter how rapidly I wrote—and if you were juggling not only book reviews but also articles on jealousy, dental malocclusion, writer's block, hypnosis, and aluminum smelting, you wrote *fast*—I couldn't make enough money to keep us above water. As for Iris, she had snagged a job with the family law unit at Multnomah County Legal Aid. This was admirable and necessary work, and the level of human misery she encountered each day had a chastening effect on us: when it came to happiness, at least, we turned out to be not paupers but princes. Yet the job paid next to nothing, which meant that in all other respects we were paupers. We had no savings, a twelve-year-old car my parents had sold us for a dollar, and an assortment of yard-sale furniture. Yes, ours was a middle-class sort of poverty, but it was taking on a feeling of dreary permanence, especially as our Mephistophelian bargains with Visa and American Express began to catch up with us.

In early 1996, in fact, things had gotten worse than ever. Iris's sister had asked whether we wanted to vacate our place in Northwest Portland and move into her attic. It was a nice attic, and a nice offer, but the injury to my pride was so great that I could hardly bear to talk about it, or even to visualize us encamped under the slanting eaves, penniless and shivering. I put off any final decision, and put it off some more, praying for some deus ex machina to bail us out—and amazingly, one materialized, in the form of a telephone message: *This is Susan Benson calling from Amazon.com Books. I wanted to talk to you about doing some work for us.*

Not that I recognized her message as such. Amazon had opened its (virtual) doors the previous July, and while business had picked up impressively, it hadn't been so long since a bell had rung in the office each time somebody made a purchase. By now the company was shipping perhaps 2,000 books each day. Still, I knew almost nothing about it. The name was familiar to me only because of a shrewd gimmick: the company had taken to buying the miniscule advertising slots on the front page of the *New York Times.* There at the bottom, in eyeball-punishing type, the ads wished Saul Bellow or Anne Tyler a Happy Birthday and urged customers to visit the largest bookstore on the World Wide Web.

Few did. Certainly I hadn't—and at that point, in the olden days of 1996, this was no surprise, because the Web was still mostly the province of geeks, technicians, New Age nuts, scientists, and academics of the racier sort, who had been nudged online by their institutional overseers. Several million other people, myself included, had taken the first step of getting an email account with CompuServe or risible, crash-prone AOL. Thanks to the miracle of high-speed packet routing, we were now able to send and receive trivial messages almost *instantaneously.* We had even begun to adjust to the breathless, ungrammatical texture of email, with its peculiar eroticism (it always made me think of the low-tech Ford Madox Ford, whose ideal form of communication was a "long monologue spoken by a lover at a little distance from his mistress's ear"). Yet the Web itself was still something of a puzzle to mainstream America. What was the point of it? Who could remember those endless addresses, the dots and colons and backslashes? Why sit around twiddling your thumbs while your modem struggled to load the pages?

But when Susan left her message, I fired up Mosaic—already the Model T of Web browsers, which I had installed when I began writing for *Salon*, meanwhile hoping that the magazine would revert to a sensible, ink-and-paper format. I typed the address into the window and waited. Somewhere out in the ether, mysterious bits of information were conveyed back and forth, and the site appeared on my screen. To be honest, there wasn't much there. An assortment of lists, most of them notable for their kooky eclecticism. A crude graphic of a bookshelf, the spines facing out, the titles not entirely legible on my computer. I experimented with the search box. In several cases, customers had chimed in with reviews of their own—a nice innovation, I thought, although many of them weren't too strong in the grammar department. I considered buying something, just to see how the process worked, but my cheapskate instincts rebelled, and in any case my credit cards were maxed out or suspended.

The whole thing resembled a science project executed by the smartest kid in the class. And that, in fact, was what the company seemed to be, at least to judge from the slender sheaf of articles Susan sent me soon after her initial call. There was the *Wall Street Journal* piece ("How Wall Street Whiz Found a Niche Selling Books on the Internet"), which played up the Tom Swift aspect of Jeff's personality, and a squib from *Newsweek*, plus an agitated-looking article in Japanese, with the Wall Street Whiz wearing some kind of aviator glasses.

I remained skeptical, then, until my interview, when the pixilated atmosphere of the place got to me. There was something irresistible about Jeff, and about the Mod Squad of potential colleagues I met at lunch, not to mention my bedazzled tour of the warehouse. Wasn't the future in Seattle? Once I got back to Portland, I could no longer tell. Sitting at my desk and revising my jealousy article (the two psychologists I interviewed had jealously badmouthed each other's work), I went back and forth. Should I stick to my career as a freelancer or make that leap into the e-commerce void? I wasn't sure.

Nor, it turned out, was Amazon. When Susan called, it was to summon me back to Seattle for a second round of interviews. Had there been some problem the first time? "Oh, no," she reassured me. "Everybody *really* liked you. We thought you should talk to Leslie Koch, that's all. She's our vice-president for marketing, and she's signing off on all editorial hires."

Leslie, whose hand was warm and whose hair was dangerously cantilevered forward over her brow, occupied the only other bonafide office at the First Avenue South headquarters. She had come to Amazon from Microsoft, where, I was told, she had already made a substantial pile. In a sense she represented the wave of the future: the company would end up importing plenty of people from the managerial spawning grounds in Redmond. For now, though, her tenure at Microsoft seemed like a good (and novel) omen—or so I thought as I settled into a chair, having left my jacket and tie back in Oregon. She and I went over much of the same ground I had covered with Jeff and Susan back in June. In fact, I began to wonder why we were even having this cordial, superfluous conversation, when I hit my first and only speed bump.

"Let's say you were working here," Leslie said, making it sound a little too hypothetical for my taste. "If you wanted to find out which books to feature—what the buzz was all about, I mean—what would you do?"

"What I already do as a journalist," I said. "I'd read the catalogues and the trades, especially *Publishers Weekly*. Talk to publicists and editors I know. I've been doing this for a long time, and my instincts are pretty good."

She didn't look satisfied. "Anything else?"

"Well, I'd probably scour the magazines and newspapers, too. And hit the trade shows—the ABA and some of the regional ones. Other than that, I think it's mainly a matter of keeping your ear to the ground."

"Nothing else? You're sure?"

This was perplexing. Obviously I was overlooking something, but even when I ran the question through Jeff's simplicity-and-complexity wringer, I came up with zero. Leslie appeared disappointed as she escorted me from her office, then called Susan over for a brief confabulation behind closed doors. For the next hour, while I lunched with Susan and the crew at Pike Place Market, I was dying to hear what my blooper had been. She said nothing. We moved on to the new, vacant offices in the nearby Columbia Building—which everybody clearly viewed as a step up from the light-industrial squalor of the warehouse—and rode up and down in the elevator, and still she said nothing. Finally, just before we were due to return, she took me aside and supplied me with the missing answer.

"She meant newsgroups," she said.

"What?"

"Newsgroups," she said. I felt like Benjamin Braddock in *The Graduate*, being apprised of his future with a single, encapsulating word. Not plastics, in this case, but those online conversation groups devoted to every topic under the sun, and then some. I had joined a couple, including one particularly ardent cenacle devoted to Duke Ellington, and had found it a mixed bag. For every intelligent comment, there was at least one crazy insisting that he be buried with his Sophisticated Lady cufflinks, *or else*. It hadn't even occurred to me to turn to this disembodied peanut gallery for advice on books. But the Web was a democratic affair, and during my chat with Leslie I had made a real mistake: I hadn't listened to the guy in his underwear in

Akron, Ohio, eating macadamia nuts and sounding off on metafiction. It wouldn't hurt me to try, though.

"Well, sure," I told Susan. "That's an excellent idea. I could join two or three groups and scan through the postings once a week."

"Great," she said. "Would you like to go back and take another swat at that question?"

"With Leslie, you mean? But wouldn't she know you told me the answer?"

"I think she'd like to hear it from you."

Coming from a person as sane as Susan, this was surprising. Did she really want me to make an encore appearance in Leslie's office and, on cue, say the magic word? I told her I was willing, and we drove back down to headquarters, where Leslie proved to be unavailable. "Maybe we could speak on the phone," I said. Susan shook her head and suggested a tour of Seattle, and for the rest of the afternoon she kindly chauffeured me from Belltown to Fremont, Queen Anne to Green Lake, Magnolia to Phinney Ridge. Studying the dramatic tilt of the terrain, the endearing, expensive bungalows, the potholes and the flowering shrubs, I tried to put the word *newsgroups* out of my mind. I couldn't help but notice that compared to Portland, much of Seattle seemed ramshackle, as though it had been hastily erected for the 1962 World's Fair and then abandoned to the elements (i.e., rain). Once you left the tonier neighborhoods, everything needed a coat of paint. The traffic was a mess. The Space Needle, the city's primary architectural icon, resembled a swizzle stick. It didn't matter. I was won over. Susan was showing me the sights because she wanted me to say *Yes*—it had somehow slipped her mind that this was the only word in a freelance writer's vocabulary.

To get *there*, however, required a few more conversations on the phone. Friends and family urged me to play hardball when it came to salary, not to mention the stock options that were, as Susan said, "part of the package." Once she and I began to bat numbers around, I told her I couldn't consider doing the job for less than $50,000—chump change, really, when you took into account that we'd be losing Iris's income and relocating to a pricier city. "Oh, that's not possible," she said. An image of my sister-in-law's attic, comfy and low-ceilinged and with that missing banister on the staircase, flashed through my head. "I see," I said. The hardball portion of the negotiations came to an end. We agreed that I would be paid $44,000 and that I would receive options to buy 1,000 shares of Amazon stock at a dollar a pop. The latter struck me as a kind of play money, especially once Susan got rolling with the caveats. "It's always possible that the company will never go public," she confided, "in which case the options won't be worth a dime." It sounded like (to use a favorite phrase of my father's) a sucker's paradise. Perhaps it would produce the equivalent of a Christmas bonus, I told myself, and since I had never received such a bonus in my life, that seemed just fine. I could buy a nice suit or a new sofa and count myself lucky.

In due course a ten-page work agreement arrived in the mail, to be signed by Jeffrey P. Bezos, President, and James Marcus, Editor. The latter bit of language came as no surprise. When I had asked Susan what my job title would be, she responded with her customary tact: "Officially you're an editor, but of course we'll think of you as Editor Extraordinaire." I *liked* the sound of that, as Wile E. Coyote used to say. But as I would learn, the company was leery of titles in general, both because we were one big happy family and because the frantic rate of Internet evolution was supposed to make your title obsolete long before the ink dried on your business card.

And the agreement itself? Most of it consisted of HR boilerplate, giving the employer an enlightened whip hand in any dispute, but there were a few elements that were new to me. For starters, there was a vesting schedule for my options, which would be doled out to me over the next five years, despite the fact that they wouldn't be worth a dime. There were a number of confidentiality clauses, clearly intended to keep any solid-gold algorithms close to the corporate chest (and around which I will be tiptoeing for the duration of this book). But my favorite part addressed the sticky issue of "Job-Related Stress," and made it clear that for better or worse, I was entering a brave new world. Let me quote from Paragraph 9, Clause (a):

> The Employee acknowledges that he has been informed of the nature of the Company's business activities and recognizes that his position may involve a high degree of job-related stress. As a condition of his employment, the Employee agrees that he will not bring an action against the Company for the recovery of any damages alleged to have resulted from such job-related stress, and will indemnify the Company and hold the Company harmless against any such claims by any of the Employee's relatives or by other third parties.

Strip away the legalese and what remains is a fairly colorful stipulation. Namely: if you go crazy on the job, the company won't pay to patch you up. Given how small the place was then, this didn't strike me as unreasonable. It did make me wonder exactly what was supposed to drive you around the bend. Was it the frenetic pace? The electromagnetic radiation? Or was the psychic strain of making history too much for an average human to bear? I hesitated for a few seconds over the whole paragraph. But there was something faintly thrilling, too, about thrusting yourself into a high-tech hothouse—a suspicion that it might reconfigure your personality along sleeker, speedier lines—so I stopped worrying and signed the agreement with my most rakish signature and sent it back to Seattle. I had joined the party after all.

3

I WAS SLATED TO START at Amazon on September 9. Since Iris needed to wrap up a number of cases in Portland, my brother-in-law Chris offered to put me up in suburban Bothell until the end of the month. There in his bachelor pad, with its refrigerator full of beer and its formidable home theater system, I spent the weekend preparing for my first day of work. Chris, who had been negotiating the corporate chutes and ladders at Allstate for decades, gave me some pointers on my wardrobe (too swishy) and my deodorant (too blue-collar). Watching *Dumb and Dumber*, which we did several times, he also told me that it was no use hiding my New York background: "You might as well try to think of it as an asset."

At last it was Monday. Chris gave me a lift to the bus depot, sniffing and shaking his head in sorrow: "I can smell that Speed Stick. You just wouldn't listen to me, would you?" His day began on the early side, which meant that mine did, too, and I hit the city before 8:00 A.M. It seemed like an indecent hour to show up—I imagined that even the most ardent programmers were still asleep at their desks, clutching empty Jolt bottles or Pringle canisters. But after circling the block a couple of times I paused in front of the Columbia Building and studied the defiantly grubby establishments across the street:

there was a wig store, and a needle exchange, and an open-air parking lot with a pay phone, which was already being pressed into use for some furtive transaction. Seattle's downtown—what civic boosters would soon be describing as the "gilded retail corridor"—was well on its way to gentrification, but Jeff had chosen one of the seedier pockets for his world headquarters. No doubt the rent was more reasonable, and in any case, the neighborhood was a good match for the company's lean-and-mean aesthetic.

I ventured into the lobby and took the elevator to the fourth floor. Nobody seemed to be around, and I wandered the corridors in search of a familiar face, trying to look like I belonged there. Finally, next to some steel shelving piled high with office supplies, I ran into a cheerful young woman with the sort of rosy cheeks you see on a Hummel figurine. This was Rebecca Staffel, who had been hired out of a graduate program in library science to do . . . something. She was, like me, an editor, and had no idea what that meant, which I found very heartening.

"We might as well grab your supplies," she said. She loaded me up with the usual office crap—nothing high-tech here—and an Amazon mouse pad imprinted with several dozen book titles. Then she led me to the windowless room I would be sharing with Tod. My desk, the standard model made out of an unfinished solid-core door, was propped up on its side. "I'm sure Tod will be here any minute," Rebecca told me. "In the meantime you can set up your stuff. If you need any help, I'll be down the hall listening to *Shakin' the Shack*."

I grabbed the edge of the desk, which was heavy, and wrestled it into position. At that point Tod sailed in, and after greeting me, he began to explain the computer system.

"Jeff's dream is to have everybody on the same operating system: programmers, editors, customer service, inventory, you name it. That means we all use a UNIX box," he said, at which point he lost me. I was a thumb-sucking Macintosh owner, used to being coddled by my computer. "Don't worry," he continued, noticing my distress. "I'll show you the ropes."

We hooked up my terminal to a network cable, and for the next couple of hours he taught me UNIX commands. I wrote down every single word he said, as if I were some crazed court stenographer. Like so much of the knowledge I would accumulate at Amazon, this turned out to have a half-life of about four months, at which point the editors were all moved off the UNIX platform and issued old-fashioned Windows machines. But on my first day I dearly wanted to seem like a quick study. I scrawled, I scribbled, I tapped out the commands on the keyboard, mentioning that I had originally learned to type on an ancient Olivetti.

"How old are you, anyway?" Tod said.

"I'm thirty-seven. What about you?"

"Thirty-two." He studied me for a moment. "You're very well preserved," he decided. With his smooth skin and cropped hair—which looked a little more metallic than it had in June—he looked at least five years younger, but at least I wasn't being written off as a golden codger.

Now Tod waded into the arcana of Obidos, which was the name given to Amazon's proprietary software. I didn't need to know a thing about the guts of the program, which had been created by Shel Kaphan, a grizzled, agreeably cranky veteran of innumerable high-tech flops. I did, however, need to memorize a few crucial tags: long strings of characters that would direct the computer to fish this or that piece of information out of the bibliographical database. Most of the tags included an ISBN (International Standard Book Number), and all of them, perhaps meaningfully, included a dollar sign. Tod dictated, I typed. He was very patient. Still, by the time we took a break for lunch, I was beginning to get discouraged. I wandered through the parking lot, where a Green Tortoise bus was disgorging a load of stoners from the East Coast, and got myself a falafel. Hadn't Jeff hired me for my talent? Wasn't I going to preach the gospel of literature from the Internet pulpit?

Luckily, things improved after lunch, when I got to make like a man of letters—sort of. While Tod and I were hanging the compulsory whiteboard in our office, Susan ambled in with a tall stack of paperbacks, which she deposited on my desk.

"Are you familiar with Patrick O'Brian?" she said.

"Vaguely," I said. He was, I knew, the author of a multi-volume maritime epic, which by now had tacked quite comfortably into the mainstream: I had flipped through one episode in a bookstore, saw a great deal of talk about fo'castles and yardarms, and moved on.

"He's a big seller for us," Susan continued. "And guess what's coming out this month? *The Yellow Admiral.* Number Eighteen, I think."

"They're excellent," Tod said. "Surprisingly gory, too. There's a great scene where Jack Aubrey cuts off a guy's head during a fight and kicks the thing overboard like a soccer ball."

"We need some content for the previous volumes in the series," Susan told me. "Can you do them this afternoon?"

"You mean review them?" Given my conversation with Tod back in June, I had no right to be alarmed, but the stack of pages Susan had plopped in front of me was two feet high. She was quick to reassure me. These would be unsigned squibs, only a notch or so above flap copy in the promotional food chain: until now, in fact, the company had been *using* flap copy, but Susan was eager to draw an editorial line in the sand, and I was going to help her draw it.

Down to business. I thumbed through *Master and Commander,* got a dose of the author's crisply archaic prose, chatted with Tod about the series, and came up with a bit of effusive triangulation. I wrote:

The opening salvo of the Aubrey-Maturin epic, in which the surgeon introduces himself to the captain by driving an elbow into his ribs during a chamber-music recital. Fortunately for millions of readers, the two quickly make up. Then they commence one of the great literary voyages of our century, set against an immaculately detailed backdrop of the Napoleonic wars. This is the place to start—and in all likelihood, you won't be able to stop.

No, it's not something I'd want chiseled on my tombstone. Perhaps if I'd had only nine volumes to do that afternoon instead of seventeen, I would have come up with a more discriminating paragraph. Alas, there wasn't time. (Two years later, when *The Hundred Days* came out, I tried to atone for my sins by reviewing the book *and* interviewing the author, but couldn't overcome the accumulation of bad karma: O'Brian, speaking from his vineyard in the South of France, answered my questions with crisply archaic monosyllables.) "Now you're a published author on the Web," Tod told me, as he dumped my hasty efforts into the database. I had made my Amazon debut.

An admission: I've never lost any sleep over this whorish trial by fire. I had delivered the anonymous and expedient stuff that Susan requested. The real work would come soon enough. Over the next five years I would write thousands of reviews, articles, interviews, and miscellaneous bits of copy for Amazon, and was proud to sign my name to just about all of it. Still, there's something poignant, and telling, about the fact that I spent my first afternoon there engaged in hack work. For even as the company blew millions and millions of dollars on content—even as Jeff hired an editorial staff larger than that of most magazines, and gambled that this SWAT team of eggheads would be good for *something*—it was clear that art and commerce weren't necessarily the comfiest of bedfellows. You could, like

me, ignore the potential friction. You could aim your work at some
ideal, book-besotted reader and let retail take care of itself. But when
you were writing something for Amazon—where, incidentally, nobody ever told me to make nice to a single title—you couldn't avoid
the suspicion that your opinions were succumbing to the gravita-
tional tug of the marketplace. You worried about it even when it was
obviously not the case. This didn't mean you were corrupt: indeed, it
sometimes led to a strange, neurotic vigilance about the purity of
your enthusiasms. Meanwhile, if you didn't consider yourself a shill,
most of your readers did, and not without a certain logic: what kind
of salesman would point out the defects in his own merchandise?
Even for Amazon, with its glittering surround of utopianism, that
would seem to be the road to commercial ruin.

None of this, however, was troubling me on that September afternoon. Nor would it, in any substantial way, for the next couple of
years, when there was still a delightful uncertainty about what the
company *was,* when it could be taken for a bookstore or bulletin
board or electronic agora, a revolutionary enterprise or (as Jeff continued to say, perched high on his peculiar Mount Nebo) a destination. All I had at the time was a case of first-day jitters. Even these
faded as the afternoon wound down and Tod switched off his computer. "You did great," he said, and went off to meet his girlfriend, or
one of them, for a drink.

I climbed aboard the bus to Bothell in a state of elation. When
we crested the floating bridge across Lake Washington, I could see
the extravaganza that was Bill Gates's future home—which at that
point resembled a bombed-out strip mall—and, far to the south, the
melted-ice-cream profile of Mount Rainier. I decided that relocating
to Seattle had been a great idea. I was eager to tell Chris, since he had
lobbied for us to make the move, but when I got to Bothell I recalled
that he would be out most of the evening at his step aerobics class. I

called Iris: nobody home. Stewing with happiness, I made myself a turkey sandwich and sat on Chris's deck, looking beatific enough to scare the neighbors.

"I wouldn't wear that orange shirt if I were you," he told me the next morning as he drove me to the bus station. Again I got to Seattle early, again I found a virtual ghost town on the fourth floor of the Columbia Building. As I would discover, the company allowed for very flexible hours, tailored to both diurnal types (i.e., me) and nocturnal ones (i.e., Jonathan, who often napped under his desk at sunrise, miraculously keeping his fez on the whole time). This didn't surprise me. What did surprise me, over the next few days, was the sporadic nature of the work itself.

Tod continued to tutor me, and we mapped out projects on our whiteboard, and on Thursday I attended my first editorial meeting in Susan's office: a quick progress report, where everybody agreed that I was coming up to speed. There was a general feeling of haste—the very air seemed oxygenated with it. Meanwhile, there was nothing to do half the time. We were both frantic and indolent, a puzzling simultaneity that was actually due to the chaotic state of the company itself. Jeff was making the whole thing up as he went along, and he hadn't quite wished us into existence yet.

This didn't bother Tod. He had plenty of other things to do with his time, like dodging creditors on the phone or writing articles for the *Inlander*, an alternative paper in eastern Washington. He also filled me in on his Horatio Alger–like ascent at Amazon. Having fled a bad marriage and a wretched job market in Spokane, he had answered an ad for seasonal help the previous Christmas and found himself packing books in Jeff's suburban garage. That made him Employee Number 7. (I, by comparison, was Number 55—and two years later, after a mind-bending growth spurt, the payroll would expand to nearly

8,000.) For several months Tod had distinguished himself as a speed demon with a Jiffy bag. Then, at the first mention of an editorial department, he leaped into the breach. Gone were the days of squatting on a concrete floor with a tape gun and a massive copy of the *Physician's Desk Reference* (gone for the moment, anyway). On the other hand, there were plenty of noneditorial tasks that still needed doing, one of which he dropped in my lap on Friday afternoon.

"I'm taking off now," he said, removing his sweater from the doorknob. "You'll have to flip the site before you leave."

"Wait a minute! I can't do that."

"Sure you can. Ask Rebecca, she knows how. It's a cinch."

Back then there were two versions of the site, one online and one offline. If you wanted to modify the home page, or add reviews, or tinker with the discount on a title, you made those changes to the offline site. Then the two were flipped at the end of the day. Tod hadn't explained the routine to me, nor was I eager to try it, since I didn't want to risk destroying the entire business with a single keystroke. Later on, of course, an editor would never be allowed within a mile of such a procedure. But in that era Amazon was still a seat-of-the-pants operation, which meant that the site itself—the elan vital of the place—was entrusted on a daily basis to beginners like me.

"The scripts are in Jonathan's directory," Rebecca told me. "Not a problem."

I typed what she told me to type. The whole effort made me hyperventilate, a source of mild amusement for Rebecca. During the final keystrokes I felt like one of those guys defusing a bomb in an action movie: *first cut the blue wire, then the red wire, then the yellow wire.* "Geronimo," Rebecca murmured as I hit the Enter key. What happened? Nothing, really. The two sites did an invisible soft-shoe and changed places, a climax and an anticlimax, which was, for Amazon, business as usual.

4

FOR NEARLY A MONTH I lived with Chris up in Bothell. We didn't see much of each other: step aerobics still consumed most of his free time, and when he wasn't mounting and dismounting that little plastic pedestal, he was out on a date. But late at night or early in the morning, while he drove me to the bus stop, he offered me more advice on corporate survival tactics. "Whatever you do," he said, "don't sell your stock right away so you can buy some idiotic home theater system. I made that mistake with the stuff they gave me at Allstate." He nodded sadly at his own quadraphonic folly, which made me wonder whether the continuous showings of *Dumb and Dumber* amounted to a kind of confession.

By October, in any case, I was gone. Susan and her husband, Eric—a tall, pale, humorous programmer who had plied his trade at failed ventures (like Kaleida) and successful ones (like Netscape) but hadn't yet hit the Silicon Valley jackpot—were buying a jazzy blue house in Queen Anne. That meant they would be moving out of their rental. The place was something of an oddity: a rectangular green structure that the neighbors kept comparing to a bait shop. Near the entrance two Douglas firs blotted out the sky, and behind them was a narrow garden plot, choked with sword ferns, creepers, and banana slugs. We took it.

I drove a fourteen-foot diesel truck up from Portland with our belongings. By now it should have been overcast in Seattle—the cloud cover typically kicked in at the end of September—but as I circled the cemetery at the top of Queen Anne Hill, the sun was shining brightly through the canopy of evergreens. This seemed like a confirmation: we had made the right move by transplanting ourselves. Susan and Tod came by to help us lug our stuff inside, and in the crisp yellow light even our beat-up furniture had a reassuring sheen of prosperity.

Meanwhile I continued my education at the office. After eight weeks, the place struck me more than ever as a strange fusion, half science lab, half mom-and-pop grocery. Sure, the company had a high-tech backbone and was hiring programmers as fast as they could be found. Yet the editorial department functioned more like a lemonade stand, or one of those youthful productions Mickey Rooney and Judy Garland were always throwing together out in the barn. In early October, for example, Susan asked me what sorts of content I thought we could add to the site. At that point, *content* had a talismanic ring to it. Words on a printed page were old news, but words on a cathode ray tube were a glorious novelty, a Platonic triumph.

And for the moment, anyway, they were in very short supply at Amazon. Customers had their pick of more than a million titles, but in most cases there was no real information about the book in question—just bibliographic details, most of them gleaned from the database of the nation's largest book distributor, Ingram. If you knew exactly what you wanted, fine. However, if you needed to figure out which Edith Wharton novel featured a happy ending (none of them), or whether *The Coloring, Bronzing, and Patination of Metals* included a section on brass (it did), you were in trouble. This wasn't a matter of spackling in the odd bit of information. The entire site was essentially devoid of words. It was a blank slate of nearly biblical proportions, and now Susan was asking me what we should be scribbling on it.

"How about some author interviews?" I said. We already featured an automated Q-and-A: a generic list of questions that any author could answer online, then have linked to all of his or her titles. Still, the Luddite in me figured that it would be easy to beat the pants off this robotic process.

"Sounds good," Susan said. "Who do you want to start with?"

I suggested Scott Turow, whose new novel *The Laws of Our Fathers* would be hitting the shelves in a couple of weeks. A combination of brains and bestselling brawn, he seemed like a perfect choice, and Susan agreed at once: "Go do it."

"We have a design for a feature like this, don't we? I'd like to get a look at that before I go ahead with the interview."

"Oh, no. You'll have to make it up yourself. Maybe Chris Mealy can help you with the HTML."

This was less forbidding than it sounded. Hypertext markup language, like so many of the acronymic delights of the age, was basically old-fashioned technology with a cutting-edge twist. If you could operate a typewriter—hell, if you could operate a pair of *scissors*—you could insert HTML code into a document.

As for the design itself, that was a no-brainer. Online magazines such as *Salon*, *Slate*, and *Suck* had already made an elementary discovery: a reader staring into the equivalent of a thirty-watt bulb didn't want to confront thousands of words. The medium required a little extra white space, a sort of oasis for the optic nerve. The copy, then, tended to snake down the page in a narrow column, and I followed suit. Nor was there any question of fancy graphics or animation. Most people were still accessing the Web at a relative crawl, and even the most ardent Scott Turow fan might be unwilling to wait twenty-five minutes for his smiling face to materialize on-screen. As an exile from print journalism, though, I longed for some kind of visual pizzazz. So I made the Microphone.

I suppose I could have found an appropriate piece of clip art. But this was Amazon, where everything had to be invented from scratch, and besides, I wanted something very specific: one of those boxy, 1940s-era microphones, which would catch your eye and also make an ironic comment on the site's futuristic vibe. I located just the item in a volume of old jazz photographs. All I needed to do was scan in the image and erase every other thing in the photo: the musicians, the instruments, the nightclub patrons, the liquor and lipstick and wide lapels, the very smoke in the air. With this in mind, I scuttled around the corner to the scanning room, where the company was already laying the foundations for its own version of class warfare.

The scanning crew worked in semi-darkness, like trolls in a fairy tale. They took books off a cart, one after another, scanned in the covers, and replaced them. When they accumulated a big enough batch of images, they dumped them into the site's database. Later this process would be automated: publishers would digitize thousands of jackets at a clip and send them to the company on a CD, or via a data feed. For now, though, it was strictly manual labor, of a dull, quasi-Dickensian sort. And since the scanners weren't corporate Übermenschen—programmers, managers, or editors—they were paid by the hour, without any stock options to sweeten the pot.

This was hardly a shocker. At many a company I might not have been showered with options either. And to give Jeff credit, he reversed course within a few months and gave small grants to the scanning crew. Yet there would still be a schism down the road, pitting the stakeholders (as we were called) against the hourly masses.

In any case, Doug MacDonald told me hello and showed me how

to work the scanner. He had already applied for an editorial job and been rebuffed by the personnel department, the unspoken objection being that he wasn't smart enough. Yet Doug had a perfectly adequate supply of brains, and a quiet, almost monastic manner that eventually won him a gig as Religion Editor. That would make him a powerful figure in the company, not to mention a fixture at promotional prayer breakfasts across the country. For now, though, he was stuck in the scanning room.

"Why are you doing this?" he asked as I went about my painstaking work of erasure.

"I'm making a graphic for some interviews."

"You missed a spot there." I had. Using yet another Photoshop gimmick, I liquidated a few more pixels, and I was done.

The image is probably still floating around the database. But nobody ever saw it, because Susan found it confusing: she worried that our customers would keep clicking on it, expecting some sort of audio sound clip, and then leave the site in a huff. Me, I was very attached to the Microphone, and might have tried to change her mind. However, it wasn't only Susan who objected—it was Rick, too.

Jeff had just hired Rick Ayre as vice president for Editorial. Prior to that he had been editor-in-chief of *PC Magazine*'s online edition, and prior to *that* he had been trained in psychiatric epidemiology, which gave him an excellent skill set (as we soon learned to say) for dealing with his new colleagues. He arrived on a propitious day. For the first time, the store had pulled in $50,000 in a single 24-hour period. Within a few years, of course, Amazon would be racking up millions of dollars in daily sales, but at the time this pipsqueak sum was a real benchmark.

In any case, Rick proved to be a benign but elusive presence. With his shoulder-length hair and wispy beard he resembled Shaggy from *Scooby Doo*, minus the anxiety and incessant appetite, and he was pursuing the same ghost the rest of us were: a job description. He had been hired to shape the site's editorial content. But instead of being turned loose on that talismanic task, Rick was dragooned into negotiating endless deals with potential partners. He spent long hours at his desk with the blinds drawn and the lights out, pondering. Occasionally—even while interviewing job candidates—he would part the blinds and peer outside to make sure his car hadn't been stolen from the lot across the street. Yet the darkness didn't dampen his mood. For the most part he seemed like a sunny character, at least during the first two years, slouching in his chair and emitting those faint, conspiratorial chuckles.

He didn't, however, like the Microphone. He may have been right: perhaps America was reverting to a pictographic culture. If we saw a microphone, we expected someone to talk to us, and felt short-changed if nobody did.

Shrugging off this minor defeat, I called up Turow's publisher to arrange the interview. I already knew the publicist, with whom I had worked before, and had notified her of my new job. As we spoke, though, a certain ambivalence crept into the conversation. Of course she was aware that the company sold books online, and that business was booming (within a couple of years, in fact, my employer would be her employer's biggest customer). But where was the actual, you know, *store?* And where would the interview appear? Did we put out some kind of magazine? Or an ink-and-paper catalogue? These were all reasonable questions. Electronic commerce still struck most people as a fad, a fin-de-siècle Pet Rock, and an embryonic enterprise like Amazon seemed even harder to pin down.

"You'll have to write a letter to Scott," she decided. "Explain what you are. I'm not sure he's ever heard of Amazon. Fax it to me and I'll pass it along."

Turning the office upside down to find a sheet of letterhead, I did as she asked. As it happened, the author *had* heard of the company (from his son, clearly one of those beloved Early Adopters) and was happy to grant my request. After all the high-tech preliminaries—after tinkering with HTML and Photoshop and assuring Scott Turow that "state-of-the-art technology" would beam our comments into millions of homes—even I expected something momentous from our interview. Instead it was an intelligent, amiable, rigorously normal exchange. As we discussed his new novel and the utopian politics of the Sixties, I stopped feeling like a visitor from the future, clad in a shiny aluminum-alloy tunic. No, this was business as usual: questions and answers, pauses and periods. The art of conversation remained stuck, thank god, in the Dickensian era—and unlike the rote and repetitive chores in the scanning room, it would prove almost impossible to modernize.

The interview appeared on the site in early November. Meanwhile I became more and more immersed in the do-it-yourself atmosphere of the place. *Let's put on a show!* Tod and I scribbled ideas on the whiteboard in our office, surreptitiously inhaling the ink. We could interview Oliver Sacks and James Ellroy and Walter Mosley and Mary Gaitskill (on a bed) and Jonathan Raban (on a boat)! We could make an automated quiz based on Frank Sulloway's nutty theories about birth order! We could choose an esoteric gem like Simon Singh's *Fermat's Last Theorem* for our vaunted Book of the Day Feature—and then point visitors toward an even more esoteric assortment of Fermat-intensive websites!

Oh, and we could also answer the telephone. Despite the exponential growth rate in the customer service department, the company still tended to get swamped, and an alarming number of loose-cannon calls made it through the switchboard, especially after hours. On one occasion, for example, I was alone in the office at around 5:30 when the phone rang.

"You've reached Amazon," I said, violating company policy by omitting the *dot com*. "What can I do for you?"

"My husband buys plenty of books from you—thousands of dollars at a time," the caller said. "I can show you the credit card statements."

"I'm delighted to hear that."

She explained who her husband was: a major mover and shaker at Microsoft, no doubt worth gazillions of dollars, and I repeated that we really appreciated his business. Then she got down to brass tacks. As a resident of Seattle, her husband was obliged to pay not only shipping charges but Washington sales tax on his purchases. Didn't I think that was unfair? I did. Still, there was no way for me to suspend the sales tax—not without a statewide referendum, anyway—and I wasn't sure how much latitude I had with shipping charges, either. At this point the caller began to get snippy, because this was a matter of principle, and I grew increasingly nervous at the thought of offending some local VIP. She sighed the musical, dangerous sigh of a billionairess. I waxed apologetic, and finally decided to pass on this hot potato to whoever would take it.

"Just a moment, please," I said. "I'm going to transfer you to somebody who I'm sure will be able to help you."

Luckily Susan was in her office. In expert bucket-brigade fashion, she transferred the call to the head of customer service, who mollified Mrs. Moneybags with some sort of discount offer. "What should I have done?" I asked her the next day.

"Oh, you did fine," she told me.

In the name of building customer loyalty, she explained, almost anything would have been fine. The only thing Jeff demanded was that we be inventive. As a normal human being, Susan couldn't bring herself to utter a single cliché about employee empowerment, Japanese-style *keiretsu*, and so forth. It's true, though, that there was an exhilarating sense of professional democracy during the company's salad days. Between Susan's reflexive kindness and Rick's laissez-faire tendencies, the editorial department felt like a socialist republic. This wasn't flat management: *prone* management might be a better phrase, although it sounds much too cranky to describe the fun we were having.

Our titles, clearly, were meaningless. Everyone was an editor, our equivalent of *citoyen*. At meetings we sat like egalitarian ducks in a row while Susan asked what we were working on. Barrie was putting the finishing touches on various contests, which were designed not only to entertain our current customers but to bring in hordes of prize-hungry newbies. Jonathan, with his fez propped rakishly on his head like a dissipated Shriner, was juggling some small programming jobs and The Spotlight—a tossed salad of Max Weber, tech stuff, and evolutionary theory that had a prominent spot on the home page. Tod was cobbling together a lavish feature on Rick Smolan's *24 Hours in Cyberspace*, a "time capsule" of 200 images culled from a globe-girdling photo shoot. (This production, a perfect souvenir of early Internet euphoria, was one of the first items that the company acquired in bulk, thereby breaking one of its e-tailing Ten Commandments: No inventory. As punishment, perhaps, the books sat in the warehouse for a long, long time, even as the author's vision of the world as one big fiber-optic village seemed to be borne out, at least temporarily, by reality.)

"What's on your plate, James?" Susan asked.

"This guy is turning into an HTML *machine*," Tod told her. "He's hammering the stuff out."

"Tod's still bringing me up to speed," I said. As the newest member of the staff I tended to be shy at these meetings. I sat there in my threadbare clothing (which Tod, a sharp dresser himself, had already commended as "shabby chic") and jotted notes. "Oh, I'm going to interview John Seabrook by email. He's got this book, *Deeper,* about exploring the Web." It struck me then, as it strikes me now, that the history of the era was being written a lot faster than we were actually living it.

There was a brief, euphemistic discussion of the fact that a certain high-level manager was now gone. Jeff had announced her departure in a terse email to the staff, and that was the last we saw of her. Most of the time, these hasty exits were chalked up to security measures: there was always a chance that a newly fired employee would stalk back to her desk and torpedo the database. But according to one rumor, this former colleague had viewed Jeff as a kind of idiot savant—a capitalist Dennis the Menace—and had been shown the door in return.

Who knew? In any case, this efficient bit of pruning reminded us that there were limits, after all, to the notion of a democratic work-place. Not that Jeff had turned into a crazed dictator. He occupied a modest office just around the corner from us, its door too thin to muffle his frequent explosions of laughter. From time to time you saw him prowling the hallways in his khaki pants and blue Oxford shirt—soon to be an iconic outfit for up-and-coming entrepreneurs—and he remained as approachable as ever.

At that moment, in fact, he was laying the groundwork for Amazon's initial public offering. I knew nothing about that, and had little notion of the company's financial health. Susan mentioned to me in passing one day that Kleiner Perkins Caulfield & Byers, the big daddy of tech incubators, had pumped $8 million into the coffers just a couple of months before I came aboard. To me that sounded like major money, the sort of sum you'd fork over to a real corporation. Yet the place didn't *feel* like a real corporation. The payroll depart-ment still consisted of Jeff's wife, MacKenzie, a slender young woman who drifted through the office wearing a tiny backpack the size of a nectarine. There were dogs on the premises, there were crude wooden desks everywhere, and there were more employees, already, than could possibly be accommodated by all those desks. It felt like Spring Break in a cool climate, and I decided to enjoy it for as long as it lasted. *Let's put on a show!*

5

DESCRIPTIONS OF HAPPINESS are always crude, always approximate. Descriptions of unhappiness are even trickier: there are so many gradations and variants and hybrids, so many subtle distinctions to be made between one sort of sadness and another. Happiness is an elementary emotion—you usually *know* when you're happy—and unhappiness is (to use a beloved bit of Internet jargon) a granular one.

The mood up in Queen Anne, as the holidays approached, was granular. In part this could be chalked up to our status as newcomers, in a city whose outwardly cordial inhabitants were imbued with what one acquaintance called a kind of "Scando-Japanese reserve." Almost everybody we met seemed to be an architect. One designed splashy modern houses for Microsoft alumni, another built exquisite models—the sort of thing that Barbie would have lived in after winning the lottery—and still another, the friendliest of the lot, worked at Saltaire, the firm now entrusted with knocking out hundreds of utilitarian desks for Amazon. They were a clubby bunch, though, and neither my wife nor I could muster the appropriate small talk about variances and demolition. That left us on our own.

But it wasn't only the solitude. It was the money, too. In December

Jeff hired Joy Covey, a formidable CFO who had earlier won the equivalent of a gold medal in the double-entry Olympics, and the two of them were busily greasing the rails for the company's IPO. Still, that event was several months away, and shrouded in secrecy. In the meantime, we were scraping along on my meager salary, since Iris had yet to take the Washington bar exam. After borrowing left and right simply to get us to Seattle, I now had to borrow more in order to keep us afloat. In November we missed a payment on our consolidation loan, and the cosignatory—who happened to be Chris, my brother-in-law and corporate consigliere—left us a nervous, chiding phone message.

I churned out freelance work in the evenings, trying to make ends meet. We practiced household economies: at night I drew the curtains and dialed the thermostat down to 53 degrees, which made us even more reluctant to get out of bed the next day. Despite these efforts, we couldn't stay solvent. When Nat came down with the flu after Thanksgiving, I brought him with me to the supermarket pharmacy to pick up some antibiotics—and with a feverish child clinging to my sleeve, I was told by the apologetic clerk that my debit card had been declined. These occasions oblige you to deliver an elaborate, face-saving pantomime: surprise, curiosity, indignation. Rushing back home, I emptied out a Tupperware container full of coins and scared up the necessary quarters. Nat took his amoxicillin from a dosing spoon shaped like an airplane. The crisis was averted. Nothing, however, makes you feel like less of a responsible citizen than falling down on your parental duties. You're a failure, a flop, a poor provider. You've violated a sort of biological imperative—or at least that's the way we felt, listening to our sick child snore noisily through one plugged nostril on the sofa. We were desperate for cash, and tired of feeling desperate.

But it wasn't only the money. It was a more general sensation, which may have had something to do with the gray sky and intermittent drizzle, and the vertical cloud banks that moved into position over Puget Sound, as if an enormous curtain had been drawn across the horizon. We felt dull and tired. The evergreens dropped their needles, which soon formed a damp carpet underfoot, but there was no explosion of deciduous color: no red, no gold, no yellow. Nothing but green, dark green, verging on black. This struck us Easterners as a form of sensory deprivation. I had picked up a paperback collection of Emerson's essays, and there, between passages of legitimate ecstasy and transcendental guff, I found a lovely, suggestive sentence: "Sleep lingers all our lifetime about our eyes, as night hovers all day in the boughs of the fir-tree." Yes, that was it. We couldn't quite wake up: we seemed always to be squinting a little, emerging from a good or bad or merely unmemorable dream.

To lift her spirits, my wife went wild buying bulbs. Some she planted in the narrow garden plot, in the perpetual shade of the Douglas firs. Others she crammed into the refrigerator in neatly labeled paper bags, and there they remained for a long time, waiting, in a state of primitive disappointment, for spring.

To lift my own spirits, well, I worked. Every morning I trotted out to the bus, whose descent of the steep slope behind Queen Anne always had a grudging quality to it, and tried to shake off my funk before arriving at the office. To my surprise, I usually succeeded. I had always been good at compartmentalizing, but the constant hustle at Amazon made it easier than ever. And the moment my private woes began seeping into my professional life, a new task would get tossed on my desk.

Suddenly, for example, I was spending many hours each week interviewing prospective employees. Amazon had been on an expansionist binge since the spring, which accounted for my own presence there. But the cash from Kleiner Perkins hit the place like a dose of entrepreneurial steroids, making Jeff more determined than ever to get big fast. And since his initial vision of the editorial department resembled a newsroom, with its throng of reporters and analysts and harried technicians, he was going to need plenty of warm bodies. One after another, the candidates came marching through the office. Susan interviewed them, Rebecca interviewed them, Barrie interviewed them, Jonathan interviewed them, Rick interviewed them—and after running this interrogative gauntlet, they were often delivered to my office, looking a size too small for their clothes. By now there wasn't much left to ask. Did they have any fresh ideas about editorial content on the Internet? Did they have an elective affinity with UNIX? The questions were mostly beside the point, anyway. What we were supposed to be sizing up was intellectual candlepower. Jeff wanted his employees to be smart.

Smart, in fact, was another one of those talismanic words. It accounted for Jeff's fascination with SAT scores, with Ivy League schools, with Jonathan's giant cranium and Barrie's tenure as a rocket scientist. It's natural, of course, to want the best and the brightest on your team, and to his credit, Jeff enjoyed being challenged by his pointy-headed underlings. Yet he relied too heavily on the résumé as an intellectual dipstick. Einstein, with his hesitant formulations and crappy job in the Swiss patent office, would never have gotten through the door. On the other hand, I came to work one day and found the receptionist preparing a giant mailing to Rhodes scholars all over the country. *Come one, come all, ye olde Oxonians, with your suspiciously vestigial British accents!*

I spoke to quite a few hopeless candidates, and guiltily spiked their applications. But even if they made the initial cut, they still needed to win over the weekly hiring meeting. Here we all convened like a giggling College of Cardinals to compare notes and make decisions. Every hire required a unanimous vote, and fantastically enough, Jeff sometimes allowed himself to be overruled by the majority. Given these stringent procedures, it now strikes me as amazing that we hired anybody at all.

Yet we did. We hired Karin Snelson, who had written both young adult fiction and reams of copy for a whoopee-cushion-purveying novelty merchant. We hired Perry Atterbury, a decent, Falstaffian guy with an advanced degree in Bulgarian. We hired Josh Petersen and Katherine Koberg, who would later be one of my bosses: it was a very Amazonian practice to have you put your eventual superior through the wringer. There was Alix Wilber, there was silver-haired Nick Allison and tale-spinning Tim Appelo . . . and there was the Bird.

Like Katherine Koberg, the Bird was a candidate for editorial management, which might or might not lead to a role on the business side. This meant she had the perverse task of selling herself to the very people she would later heckle, harass, and fire. For some this might have been an insurmountable challenge. Not for the Bird, though. With her archaic smile, rapid speech, and rather endearing habit of swiveling her head from side to side—which is what earned her the avian nickname—she was hard to dislike. When she wasn't scanning her surroundings like a radar dish, she looked you straight in the eye. She seemed intelligent and even sexy, in a suppressed, gender-neutral fashion. Like most human beings, the Bird was a newcomer to cyberspace, having spent her career as a food critic at an alternative weekly, an environmental journalist, and most recently, as a public affairs officer at a large utility, apologizing on television for brownouts and fallen electrical lines. She brought in her tapes: *Power will be restored shortly.* Everybody liked her ease in front of the camera, plus the fact that she ran a department of twelve junior flacks without biting her nails to the quick. The Bird was, and is, a people person.

(She was, and is, something else: a composite. I'm aware that this is a tricky move, breaking my social contract with the reader and contaminating the narrative with a trace element of mendacity. Still, although the Bird is a rarity in this book—*rara avis* indeed—there are some fine reasons for her existence. She embodies a number of collective follies, and brings them into sharp focus. She is an imaginative construct set loose among real people: unlike Tod or Susan or Jeff, she has no soul and is immune to wear and tear, joy and dejection, sleet, wind, rain, pain. She is, in short, a virtual personality, and therefore quite at home in this story.

There's something else, though. The Bird is an experiment in literary jurisprudence. Although she's drawn from life, right down to her velvet pumps and her caffeine addiction, she lacks the slightest particle of free will. She can't really be blamed for her rotten behavior. In a sense, we're obliged to forgive her. She's like the rat in Saint-Exupéry's *Little Prince*, with his monopoly on absolution: *From time to time you will condemn him to death. That way his life will depend on your justice. But you'll pardon him each time for economy's sake. There's only one rat.* In this book, I should stress, there's only one Bird.)

Most of these hires weren't scheduled to start until after the New Year. Meanwhile, our little crew soldiered on at the Columbia Building—and as the holidays approached, I got a quick education in the business of publishing. True, I had spent my entire career on the fringes of the industry. As a critic, however, I always regarded books as things you read, not things you sold: as works of art rather than commodities. When I first signed on at Amazon, I was vaguely encouraged to keep thinking that way, if only because my adoration of literature was something of a commodity itself. But now it was mid-December. Canned versions of *The Little Drummer Boy* were playing in every store in America, ten thousand Santas were manning their posts, the streets were mobbed with anxious shoppers—and it suddenly occurred to me that I worked in retail. It was an unavoidable conclusion. Why? Because the skyrocketing holiday traffic meant that we editors had to abandon our usual tasks and throw ourselves into not one but two breaches: fulfillment and customer service.

Down we went to the First Avenue warehouse, where I had had my initial encounter with the company back in June. Compared to what would come later, this was a vest-pocket operation: 17,000 square feet. Yet it still seemed sprawling to me, with an Alexandrian profusion of books piled on the shelves and pallets, and a heightened atmosphere of frenzy. A supervisor gave us white-collar types a hurried tutorial with wrapping materials and a box cutter. We were supposed to check each rubber-banded order against the packing slip, encase it in an indestructible cardboard sheath, and toss the finished product in a plastic bin. These were then spirited away to the loading bays, where Federal Express or the postal service made their pickups.

"How's this one?" I asked Tod.

"Not quite," he said. Having made his start in the warehouse, he was greeted like a prodigal son when we showed up: hugs, backslaps, comments on his hair color. "It's supposed to look like a little house with a roof. Bend the next one here and here." He went back to wrapping a big Thai cookbook.

I continued with a collection of Dilbert cartoons, nipping and tucking the corrugated cardboard as Tod had directed me. Yes: there was the house, with a gambrel roof. Susan waved at me from an adjacent table. She was filling the bin much faster than I was.

At this point, and for some time after, every single book ordered from Amazon flowed through this building. It made no difference where the customer was located. If the book happened to be among the small number of titles stockpiled by the company, it would be shipped directly from the warehouse. Otherwise, there were two possibilities. We could procure the book from a distributor such as Ingram—whose leviathan of a warehouse was located just a few hours away in Roseburg, Oregon—and pay a small fee for the privilege. Or we could order it directly from the publisher, which was theoretically the cheaper option. In practice, direct ordering was still mostly confined to smaller publishers, whose titles were too oddball or esoteric to be carried by the distributors. In either case, the books made their way here before commencing their ink-and-paper diaspora to every corner of the globe. Down the road, obviously, this was going to cause some logistical bottlenecks. But for the moment Amazon remained a small fish in a big pond—a minnow, really, albeit one with delusions of grandeur—and so the centralized operation was inevitable.

Handling the merchandise, even for just a few days, was a timely reminder of what the company *did*. It also prompted me to wonder how we were ever going to make any money. The bookselling business, I soon discovered, ran on razor-thin margins. Let's say that a customer, enchanted by my interview with Scott Turow, decided to buy *The Laws of Our Fathers* at a list price of $26.95. When we ordered the title from Ingram, we typically got a 40 percent discount, leaving us with $10.78. That would seem to represent a tidy profit. However, the big chains like Barnes & Noble or Borders had taken to knocking down the price by an additional 20 percent or so—and Jeff decided (correctly) that we needed to follow suit. By the time I arrived, in fact, Amazon was selling selected titles at 30 percent off. In the case of Turow's novel, that left a piddling $2.69 to cover the cost of somebody strapping the book into its cardboard corset, not to mention overhead, staffing, facilities, technology, market research, and promotional mouse pads, which we gave away by the millions. Even a fiscal naif like myself could see that there were some challenges here. But I assumed (correctly) that the company's lean-and-mean business model would put us in the black at some point, and kept on wrapping.

I also pitched in on customer service, which gave me an additional window into the inner workings of the place. CS was a religion at

Amazon. But I was a novice in every sense of the word, and much too green to man the phones, despite my baptismal encounter with the Microsoft lady. Instead I answered customer email queries at my desk.

There were predictable complaints about shipping costs, tardy delivery, damaged goods, returns. Some customers couldn't figure out how to use the search engine, while others insisted that they should be able to pay in cash. A surprising number of visitors seemed unaware of how the scroll bar worked on their browsers, and wondered *where* the bottom of the page could be found.

In many cases you could select a prefab paragraph from the CS golden anthology and paste it into your reply. That was how the champions, the real departmental gunslingers, answered hundreds of emails per shift. Often, though, customers treated us like reference librarians or mind readers, injecting some extra fun into the proceedings. *I saw a book on television last week*, I would read. *The one with the red cover. Can you tell me what it's called?* A customer wanted to learn more about Muddy Waters, and I was delighted to steer her toward Robert Palmer's classic *Deep Blues*. A Milanese architect explained his dilemma: he had been commissioned to design a sports arena, and since he was a little hazy about how to go about it, he needed a couple of good books on the topic. Luckily we had several in the catalogue. I sent him the titles and ISBN numbers, making a mental note to avoid all indoor sporting events on the Italian peninsula.

And so the holidays came and, blissfully, went. Thanks to the final surge of revenue, the company did $15.7 million worth of business for the year, which struck me as an oceanic sum. Jeff declared himself satisfied, too, in a couple of exuberant, company-wide emails. Yet he and Joy had much bigger fish to fry—and within a few weeks, on the other side of the Cascades, he would reveal more of his plans for what he only half-ironically referred to as world domination.

6

EARLY IN JANUARY, Jeff invited us all to a corporate retreat. The entire salaried staff of the company, which then numbered around seventy, would be transported over the Cascades to a ski resort. There, the word had it, we would recharge, brainstorm, and perhaps engage in some Nordic-style group activities. ("I just want to see Shel jump out of the sauna and roll around naked in the snow," Tod told me. "Preferably in slow motion.") Jeff also promised to deliver a keynote address, laying out the challenges for the year ahead and generally preaching the gospel of e-commerce to his flock.

Most people were making the trip in a bus. Having been a solitary guy most of my life, I tended to like these communal affairs, even at the cost of lip-synching the lyrics to "Kumbaya." As it turned out, though, Susan and Eric were traveling separately in their Maxima, and when they asked me if I'd like to join them, I agreed.

Around 4:00 in the afternoon I climbed into the backseat, and Eric headed northeast toward Stevens Pass. Our route—which presciently took us through the adjacent small towns of Startup and Gold Bar—made me curious. Back in New York I'd always felt immune to the effects of terrain: after all, most of Manhattan's topographic irregularities had long since been bulldozed out of existence.

But here geography mattered. So did weather. As we climbed toward the 4,061-foot summit of Stevens Pass, it began to snow. At first we watched the tentative suburban flakes fall and instantly melt on the hood: big deal. At higher elevations, though, the stuff began to collect. Eric pulled the car over in Index and chained up. Then, as darkness fell and the snow shot diagonally through our headlights like scratches in the emulsion of an old film, we crept over the pass and down toward Leavenworth.

Due to the storm and our late departure, we missed Jeff's keynote: all we heard was the applause at the end. I felt a terrible sense of anticlimax. We stood at the back of the room as the audience drifted out, most of them looking as if they'd just been given a sneak peek at the promised land. "What did he say?" I asked Rebecca as she exited. "Tell you later," she promised. "It was pretty wild."

Now it was snowing here, too. I lugged my bag to the little cabin I'd be sharing with three other employees. Then I hurried over to the bar, where most of the company was converging. The Grotto was a noisy place that looked to be hewn out of solid rock, with a jukebox and various microbrews on tap and several dozen Amazonians having convivial conversations at the tops of their lungs. I chatted for a few minutes with Maryam Mohit, who had come aboard just recently after quitting a multimedia company called Voyager (whose very stock-in-trade, the CD-ROM, was being ushered into extinction by the Internet). What we were discussing, in that deafening little cavern, was the difficulty of finding a good shrink in a strange city.

I was still trying to find out what Jeff had said in his speech when the man himself joined my knot of merrymakers. He seemed as elated as anybody there, perhaps more so, and his armor-piercing laugh was much in evidence. Eventually a parlor game got underway among our group: which movie star of your own gender would you have sex with? One by one the heterosexuals made their dark confessions—the homosexuals didn't bother, since the game didn't offer them any transgressive frisson—and then it was my turn.

"Ralph Fiennes," I declared, after some thought. If you were going to sleep with a Nazi, even one with congested sinuses, he was clearly the way to go. Also, he looked clean.

Now it was Jeff's turn. Without hesitation he said: "Indiana Jones!" Was it the bullwhip? The jodhpurs? Nobody knew. As it turned out, this was more than a casual attachment: a few months later, when he was doing a series of television commercials for Dell, Jeff would stipulate in his contract that any post-production voice-overs had to be done by Harrison Ford. At the Grotto, meanwhile, you could see the whole group silently register this bit of tipsy revelation.

Soon after, Jeff called it a night. To his credit, he didn't suggest that his retainers pack it in, too, but merely strode off to his own cabin. *There goes Indy!* I was the next to leave. Outside, the quiet was astonishing: the fat snowflakes continued to fall, and a layer of them settled uniquely on my hat and coat as I made my way across the grounds. Back at the cabin I fell asleep at once, while my roommates hooted and hollered and speculated about the radiant future.

A resort is luxurious by definition, but this one had a slight Calvinist overlay, meaning that breakfast was an exercise in self-improvement: bran, fiber, fruit, grains. Feeling healthier and heavier, we all marched over to the auditorium, where we were divided into groups for the so-called Breakout Session. First, though, Jeff addressed a few words to us from the stage.

"At Amazon, we will have a Culture of Metrics!" he promised.

The phrase had an Orwellian ring to it, as if it were supposed to mean its precise opposite. But Jeff was in earnest, and his explanation had a certain logic to it: a Web-based business gave its proprietors an amazing window into human behavior. Gone were the fuzzy approximations of focus groups, the anecdotal fudging and smoke-blowing from the marketing department. A company like Amazon could (and did) record every move a visitor made, every last click and twitch of the mouse. And as the data piled up in virtual heaps, hummocks, and mountain ranges, you could draw all sorts of conclusions about that chimerical creature, the Consumer. In this sense Amazon was not merely a store but an immense repository of facts. All we needed were the right equations to plug them into.

And that was the purpose of the Breakout Session. Our groups convened in five or six locations around the building. My group, I was thrilled to discover, included Jeff, who looked much smaller once he had descended from the podium. "First we figure out which things we'd like to measure on the site," he told us. "For example, let's say we want a metric for customer enjoyment. How could we calculate that?"

There was silence. Then somebody ventured: "How much time customers spend on the site?"

"Not specific enough," Jeff said.

"How about the average number of minutes each customer spends on the site per session?" somebody else suggested. "If that goes up, they're having a blast."

"But how do we factor in purchases?" I said, feeling proud of myself. "Is that a measure of enjoyment?"

"I think we need to consider frequency of visits, too," said a dark-haired woman I didn't recognize. "Lots of folks are still accessing the Web with those creepy-crawly modems. Four short visits from them might be just as good as one visit from a guy with a T-1. Maybe better."

"Good point," Jeff said. "And anyway, enjoyment is just the start. In the end, we should be measuring customer *ecstasy*."

Nobody was ready to take a shot at ecstasy. In the meantime we solemnly committed our equations to a sheet of poster board. We didn't feel silly or self-conscious: we felt like scientists. We dwelt in Possibility. Again, I can only attribute this to Jeff's phenomenal powers of persuasion. In most companies, having the boss join your group would have prompted an orgy of shameless sycophancy. (*Optimizing for optics* was the nerdish phrase we were taught to use for showboating types.) Here he was just one of us.

Now the separate groups returned to their seats in the auditorium. We compared equations. Then the next phase of the pep rally began: one by one, Jeff summoned the head of each department to the podium and asked for an explanation of how the Culture of Metrics would shape his or her duties. Rick, never comfortable as a public speaker, bounded onstage. After nervously smoothing what was now a modified shag, he surprised us all with a fiery summation of our editorial prerogatives: *we* would bring customers to the site, *we* would persuade them to open their wallets, *we* would measure the results. "We will *fight* for this stuff!" he concluded, and then left the stage to a round of applause.

A couple of other departmental biggies made their speeches, none of them even approaching Rick's level of firepower. Next up was Laurel Canan, who ran the warehouse. I had seen him once or twice during the holiday season, looking haggard but absolutely calm, and Tod assured me that he looked that way all year round: "I don't think I've ever seen the guy smile. He's *hyper*serious." Since Laurel supervised the flow of merchandise in and out of the warehouse, metrics were anything but abstractions to him. He already lived by the numbers, to an extent few of us did. How, then, was he supposed to discuss the advent of the Culture of Metrics? It was like asking a goldfish to talk about the impact of water on everyday life.

Perhaps it was this very tautology that made Laurel tongue-tied.

Or maybe he was just exhausted. In any case, he stood in the spotlight and mumbled a few words about improvements in the supply chain. And then, to the dismay of everybody in the room, the big boss began to chew him out.

"You'd *better* be thinking about these issues," Jeff warned his warehouse manager, practically wagging his finger. "Starting *now.*" Laurel studied his shoes and blanched. It was a very public, very petulant scolding, which made the rest of us squirm.

It also disclosed a few additional chinks in Jeff's vaunted amiability. We shouldn't have been surprised, of course. Running a business isn't all sweetness and light, and in many companies, the alpha male thrives on verbal abuse: he must yell or die. By that standard, Jeff was a saint. Still, in the weirdly democratic universe of Amazon.com, he paid a small price for his behavior. At dinner that night, nobody would sit with him. Table after table filled up, and clearly the CEO and Wall Street whiz kid was being shunned. At last a few latecomers, who could find nowhere else to sit, joined Jeff and Mackenzie. Some small talk was made. Jeff floated a few fence-mending chuckles, then a salvo of laughter. By the time dessert showed up, all was forgiven.

Before dinner, however, there were afternoon activities. Some people opted for a trip to Leavenworth, a former timber town that had reinvented itself as an explosion of faux-Bavarian kitsch. At first I was tempted. Instead I joined the snowshoe expedition. Strapping the long, archaic-looking items onto my boots, I set off down the trail and found it slow going. In no time I had fallen way behind the pack, but Rebecca, bless her heart, slogged along next to me and filled me in on Jeff's speech.

"You won't believe the numbers," she said. The exertion was making her cheeks pinker than usual. "According to his calculations, there will be 8,000 employees within the next two years."

"Holy moly," I said.

"He's also talking about a billion dollars in revenue. Soon. Can you believe it?"

Neither of us could, really. Jeff was sounding more and more like a pipe dreamer, and Joy, who was supposed to keep him firmly tethered to fiscal realities, was buying the whole program. We snickered and shook our heads. Yet we weren't entirely skeptical. We were, after all, at the beginning of an era when the suspension of disbelief was required on a daily basis: within a couple of years, to choose just one example, Americans with an eye cocked toward the markets would be asked to believe that Amazon, a fledgling bookseller, was worth more than the combined values of Sears and U.S. Steel. The boom, the brightness, the bubble, were just around the corner. Reality was becoming more malleable by the day. By surrendering our common sense, Rebecca and I were ahead of the curve.

Meanwhile we had fallen farther behind the crowd. Our colleagues were now a hundred yards or so up the trail, and some of the guys were lobbing snowballs around. Huffing and puffing, Rebecca shared another piece of information with me. It seemed that Laurel, Jeff's whipping boy during the pep rally, had made an unusual demand when he first came aboard: he insisted on taking almost no salary in exchange for a larger block of stock options.

"But how can he afford that?" I asked.

"He must have put some money aside. I think he was a carpenter before Jeff hired him."

"What happens if the company never goes public?"

"The options are worthless."

"I guess it could happen," I said, suddenly feeling a pang of gastric distress. It seemed that the Culture of Metrics made you very hungry. I had eaten my fill before hitting the trail, and now something— perhaps the prospect of dramatic wealth or even more dramatic austerity—was upsetting my stomach. I looked around: we were pretty far from civilization. A stand of stubby, snow-covered pines beckoned off to the left.

"It's not going to happen," Rebecca said. "If we—"

"Can you hold that thought?" I said. My voice, I'm sure, was urgent. I made a quick visit to the pines and returned, noting for the millionth time that I would have made a terrible pioneer. My stomach was still in knots, but I was determined to pick up where we'd left off.

"Thanks for waiting. Now, uh, you were saying?"

"I was saying maybe somebody will buy us. Could be AOL. Microsoft. Maybe even Barnes and Noble. If that happens, all of the options vest immediately. No waiting around for five years. At least that's what I've heard."

"Have there been offers?"

"Supposedly. But I don't think Jeff would sell."

"No, I don't think he would either. He's much too ambitious. He wants to run the whole show. You know: the Kayaking Thing."

Rebecca nodded. I had been exposed to the Kayaking Thing during my second round of interviews back in July, when I was closeted for about forty-five minutes with a guy named Nicholas Lovejoy. No doubt our vague, free-form discussion was supposed to reveal whether I was mentally agile enough for the company. But at one point my interrogator—whose ponytail and clogs made him much less forbidding—gave me just a taste of Jeff's ambitions for the place. "Let's say somebody is interested in kayaking," Nicholas told me. "If he visits the site, we can certainly sell him some books on the subject. But Jeff wants to offer that same visitor the opportunity to buy a spare paddle, or a waterproof kayaking jacket. We should be pointing him toward the best kayaking sites in the region, or hooking him up with kayaking chat groups. There's no reason we can't." Impressive, I thought. I had assumed Nicholas had plucked this particular example out of thin air. It turned out, though, that the Kayaking Thing was the corporate equivalent of holy writ. Everybody heard it, sooner or later, and Nicholas probably could deliver the entire shtick in his sleep, even under heavy sedation.

Rebecca and I continued in silence. The trail described a wide loop up ahead and then doubled back toward the lodge, so we could see most of our party on the other side of a narrow slough, horsing around and shouting. Their voices were faint, their Gore-Tex coats bright against the snow, and the whole scene looked like something out of Brueghel, a painterly touch I would have savored if my stomach hadn't been in such a state of insurrection. Again I left the path, again I returned.

"You guys should come over for dinner sometime," Rebecca said. "We've got a buttload of cheese at my house."

I nodded. This was a poor choice of words, I thought. Then we rounded the bend and headed back, feeling, despite my innards and Jeff's pie-in-the-sky tendencies, that we were on the verge of great things.

Sunday morning we all left. Susan was kind enough to offer me a ride back to Seattle, and as I threw my bag in the trunk I raised the topic of Jeff's tantrum.

"Poor Laurel," I said. "He really got it in the neck."

"I think Jeff was feeling tense because we were behind schedule. He likes to have things zip along."

"I never would have thought he had that kind of temper."

Eric shook his head as he slid behind the wheel, but said nothing.

"Oh, he does," Susan said. Just a few days before, she told me, there had been a major explosion in connection with some ads the company had run in the *New York Times*, promising cut-rate prices on selected titles. Alas, in at least a few markets, the papers appeared before the discounts hit the database. Customers who visited the site during that brief window might reasonably suspect the company of running a bait-and-switch game. The boss made his displeasure known.

"He was mad as a hornet," Susan recalled.

"I think we'd better take the chains off," Eric said. We were passing along the edge of Leavenworth, where even the junk-food outlets had bowed to local custom and installed themselves in miniature chalets. The roads, he pointed out, were bare.

"But we're heading up into the mountains," Susan said. "The minute we take them off, we'll have to put them back on."

"They're going to snap on the pavement," Eric said, and indeed, we could hear the rapid *shush-shush-shush* of metal on asphalt: a discouraging sound.

"I think we'll be okay," Susan said.

I kept my head down in the backseat, not wanting to get caught in the conjugal crossfire. Eric made his peace with the situation. As we headed out of town and began to gain elevation, Susan revealed that both of them had once performed with a singing group in San Francisco: they did motets, madrigals, all the tricky stuff.

"Amazing," I said.

"We did Gesualdo," Eric said, with a nostalgic emphasis.

Just Waldo? I thought. The air smelled keen and slightly mentholated as it rushed in through the windows, the sun was shining, the mountains reared up around us, with none of that round-shouldered diffidence you saw in the East. I was puzzling over Eric's comment. We had left Leavenworth behind and were approaching a last outpost, a candy store specializing in Teutonic taffy and peanut brittle. At that moment the chains snapped. An abrasive tambourine sound replaced the shushing one.

"Whoops," Susan said. Eric, vindicated, said nothing. We pulled into the candy store, which sold no chains, and were directed back into town. Since it was Sunday, though, we were likely to have some difficulty finding an open auto-parts store. We slunk around the business district, past the German restaurants and Das Meisterstuck (collectibles) and Das Rad Haus (bicycles) and Das Oak Haus (stuff made out of oak) and the main square, where they gave yodeling exhibitions during the summer. It was impressive, really: the town had reinvented itself so thoroughly that it was now a magnet for actual German and Austrian tourists. There was even a German-language newspaper, the *Pazifische Rundschau,* which the populace read with a straight face. Nobody was winking or delivering a signifying smirk: irony, the Easterner's oxygen, was absent.

That absence is all the more striking in this particular story. It's hard to write about the Internet boom and bust without an insulating layer of irony. Without it, you're too exposed, somehow: you succumb to a kind of narrative hypothermia, start shivering, and lay down your pen. The fact is that for about five years, the rules were suspended. Nobody failed. Money rained down from the skies. Patently absurd predictions, like Jeff's hogwash about the size of the company and its revenues, turned out to be accurate—eerily so. The fat years banished all memory of the thin. It was, for many Americans, the mother of all happy endings, neatly wrapped up with a millennial ribbon. And then, just as we were getting used to this state of affairs, it ended. No more pennies from heaven. No more visionaries in cargo pants. Everybody failed, almost.

But I'm getting ahead of myself. It was early 1997. I was asking Susan who Waldo was as we wandered the streets of a virtual Alpine village. She straightened me out. We were talking about Carlo Gesualdo, who murdered his adulterous wife and her lover in 1590, displayed the bodies to a gawking public—optimizing for optics, in other words—and then wrote some of the most gorgeous, neurotic polyphony in Western music. *Ahi, disperata vita,* went one of his famous madrigals. Oh, desperate life! I was beginning to wonder whether we would be stuck in Leavenworth forever when Eric found an open service station with an assortment of traction devices. He left his purchase on the backseat until we reached the snow line. Then he pulled over, attached the shiny, non-ironic chains to the front tires, and we drove back home over the mountains.

7

SPRING ARRIVES EARLY in the Pacific Northwest, as if to compensate for the drizzling monotony of the winter. Within a few weeks of our return from Leavenworth, the trees and shrubs began to bud. The bulbs my wife had planted in the garden plot seemed to be reconnoitering, testing the air. A half dozen daffodils appeared in a wooden tub by the door, unnervingly tall and fragrant. I caught a whiff of them every morning as I left for work, a quick whiff, since there was a nest of hornets under the eaves and I preferred to run to the curb.

The growth rate at Amazon was no less impressive. If we were going to hit Jeff's goal of 8,000 employees within three years, that meant the company had to hire an average of eight people every day. No wonder we ran out of space. In short order Tod and I were evicted from our office and relocated to a large, windowless, eccentrically shaped chamber near the mail room. This we shared with Barrie, Perry, Nick, Karin, and Kerry Fried, who had been my editor at the *Voice Literary Supplement* until December, when she had been ousted during the semi-annual palace coup. Upon hearing the news, I had immediately rushed into Susan's office and pleaded her case. Not that it required much pleading: Kerry had impeccable credentials, including lower-level stints at Knopf, FSG, and Grove, followed by a long tenure at the *New York Review of Books*, an editorial environment of almost supernatural purity, where nothing sexier than a Victorian wood engraving was allowed to interfere with the text. She was hired. Frankly, she might have been hired even without her splendid résumé—even if she were a convicted felon—because she had an Amazonian ace up her sleeve: not one but two degrees from Oxford.

She showed up in Seattle at the beginning of April, with her impish manner and semi-invalid cat. Given that she had edited a national publication at the *Voice*, Kerry might well have expected to be high on the totem pole.

At Amazon, however, things were never that simple. Chalk it up to what I call the Bartleby Maneuver. It was pioneered, I believe, by Karin, who had been recruited to dream up games and contests. Having worked for a local kitsch merchant called Archie McPhee—where the prize merchandise included water rockets, miniature pogo sticks, clocks in the shape of frankfurters, and the Pushbutton Aloha Hula Girl ($4.95, set of three)—she seemed like the perfect person for the job. Yet when it came time for the first game, the first contest, she blinked her large, cornflower-colored eyes and took her cue from "Bartleby the Scrivener," whose protagonist declines his duties with a curt phrase: *I would prefer not to.* In Melville's story, this sort of abstention leads the poor employee straight to ruin. At Amazon, it earned Karin extra points for initiative, meanwhile setting an example for other contrarians, including Nick.

He had been hired for Bestsellers, a sub-site that would concentrate on moving popular fodder rather than geeky books for programmers. Having come from Adobe, where he ran the company's online magazine, he had one foot in the geeky world himself. What's more, he may not have relished the chore of flogging John Grisham to the masses: after all, he had once served as Jacques Barzun's copy editor, and was rumored to still exchange the occasional postcard with his distinguished client. So when the moment came for him to assume his duties, he too pulled the Bartleby Maneuver. As a result, he got an honorable discharge from Bestsellers and was appointed editor-in-chief, or some fuzzy, nonhierarchical equivalent. It was hard to tell what had happened, since Susan remained opposed to the idea of any departmental pecking order. Under insistent questioning, however, she did finally admit that Nick was now our boss.

Kerry, then, joined the rank and file, which was expanding by the day. But it wasn't merely the lower echelons that were going through a growth spurt. As the IPO approached, Jeff was also beefing up the managerial tier—partly to keep pace with Amazon's explosive success, and partly to allay the fears of institutional investors, who would be reluctant to sink their dollars into an amateur operation. He brought in Fernando Duenas as vice-president of Operations, Scott Lipsky as vice-president of Business Expansion, and Mark Breier as vice-president of Marketing. These hires came from, respectively, Federal Express, Barnes & Noble, and Cinnabon, all of them traditional (i.e., non-Internet) businesses. Now it would be difficult to fault the company when it came to logistics, retail software development, and selling those sticky buns at the airport.

On the other hand, Jeff didn't limit himself to brick-and-mortar types. He also poached two hires from Microsoft: Joel Spiegel, vice-president of Engineering, and David Risher, vice-president of Product Development. The latter, I learned, was one of the first people to ditch Microsoft for the alluring novelty of the Web. Bill Gates himself had summoned the young apostate to his office and attempted to change his mind. *You'll never be a product manager in this town again!* No matter. Risher, a tallish guy with an ingratiating line of patter and the rubbery gait of a cartoon character, became Jeff's right-hand man. He strategized, worked the media like a pro, and gave tongue-twisting motivational talks at company functions. From time to time this former comparative lit major expressed a wistful desire to return to academia, but nobody believed him.

Meanwhile, Risher's arrival signaled another phase in Jeff's ambivalent romance with Microsoft. Who wouldn't want to emulate the software leviathan in Redmond, with its Praetorian Guard of programming geniuses, its absolute domination of the marketplace, its cushy campus and bottomless supply of cash? For any young tech company, this was *the* success story. And Gates himself had anointed Jeff's upstart enterprise back in May, when he mentioned it in a *PC Week* interview: "I buy books from Amazon.com because time is short and they have a big inventory and they're very reliable."

For his part, Jeff seemed slightly disheartened by Microsoft's dog-eat-dog atmosphere. Perhaps he longed for a kinder, gentler version of the Darwinian struggle. Yet he didn't hesitate to filch not only personnel but tactics from the conquistadores on the other side of Lake Washington. For starters, there were the brainteasers lobbed at job candidates: although I didn't know it at the time, these exercises in Zen mathematics and logic-chopping came straight out of the Microsoft playbook. Then there was the habit of pitting one division of the company against another. Bill Gates hadn't, of course, invented the technique. Still, this brand of corporate pugilistics came to be identified with Microsoft. And when, for example, David Risher was encouraged to hire a separate staff for Bestsellers—thereby creating his own editorial satrapy—it was hard not to feel a certain divide-and-conquer sensibility at work.

Meanwhile: onward and upward. In April, as the staff kept growing, the company took over an additional floor of the Columbia Building. We moved to another room, no less crowded but with a stunning view of Elliot Bay and the distant, unlikely Olympics.

Although he still sat with us, Tod was no longer a member of our team. He had left for the greener pastures of Publisher Relations. There he had been promised a plum job—he would essentially be the company's ambassador to the publishing world—only to see the whole plan go up in smoke when Jeff hired an ex-Microsoftie named Mary Engstrom to run the show. At once Tod's role devolved into departmental bootblack. For some mysterious reason he hesitated to pull a Bartleby of his own. Instead he stuck it out. Sporting a pair of chunky shoes and a bad dye job, which he hid under a newsboy cap, he spent most of the day simmering. From time to time we would hear him quietly cursing his new job and his new colleagues, with whom he carried on imaginary dialogues: "Sure. . . . You bet. . . . Let *me* do your job for you, you fat fuck!"

The crowding got to be a headache. (There was also an ominous indicator: editors could be stacked like sardines, but programmers, the real princely caste, got their own offices, or doubled up at the very most.) Yet the mushrooming head count was only one sign that Jeff was ready to play with the big boys. As it turned out, the company was being besieged with offers from potential partners. At the time I joined, we had already launched a merchandising deal with Netscape, selling related books in a special area of the site. Now, as Amazon became the poster child for online commerce, everybody from Disney to Duncan Hines was lining up for a piece of the pie. For the most part, these proposals were handled by business development people. In at least one case, however, I got involved: it seemed that Starbucks, our old First Avenue neighbor, wanted to join forces. Risher had been handed the project, and since it might call for an editorial component, Susan led me into his office.

"Originally they wanted us to run actual bookstores for them," David explained, making the concept sound quaint. "You know, a small inventory in the corner of the coffee shop."

"What did you say?"

"I told them that's not what we do. That's the opposite of what we do."

For some time Jonathan had been telling Susan that we should sell coffee beans, in an attempt to replicate the caffeinated atmosphere of the superstores. She mentioned the idea to David. But no, Starbucks would be selling coffee beans on their own website: they wanted us to supply the other, literary half of the equation.

"I'm thinking more along the lines of a newsletter," he said. "The latest buzz about current books. We would co-brand with the Starbucks folks and distribute it up at the cash register."

"For free?"

"Definitely. But I'm open to any other ideas."

I pondered. Half humorously, I spoke up: "Too bad we can't print a little blurb about new titles at the bottom of each cup. It wouldn't be visible until that last swallow of Columbian Supremo."

Susan and David smiled. To be honest, the concept was no more outlandish than many others floating around the office. For a moment my main thought was how to alert customers to the literary intelligence at the bottom of the cup. You'd have to launch a mini-marketing campaign in the stores. *Getting to the Bottom of Things with Amazon.com!* That might do it. There was also the possibility that a more robust blend, a French roast for example, might dissolve the ink. No, David was shaking his head.

"I think we'll stick with the newsletter," he said. "Can you get me some copy? Once I've looked it over, I'll pass it on to design."

I took a snip from my interview with Walter Mosley and wrote a glowing paragraph about Redmond O'Hanlon's *No Mercy*. Within a few days a slender, spiffy pamphlet emerged from design, with both logos and a coffee-cup dingbat. It looked great, I thought. Alas, Starbucks didn't take the bait, and I didn't turn into the point-of-sale Edmund Wilson.

But there were weightier things afoot. In late April Jeff disappeared from the office for the next few weeks. He and Joy traveled to Zurich, Geneva, Paris, and London, then made a barnstorming tour of the United States, pitching the IPO to investors and analysts.

Needless to say, I heard about none of this directly: Jeff would no more discuss these matters with me than with his cocker spaniel. Still, you heard casual conversations in the elevator, or read the pages spooling out of the fax machine before courteously stuffing them in the appropriate mailbox.

Eventually the word got out that the company's initial public offering was set for May 15. Three days before that, Barnes & Noble launched a preemptive lawsuit, which seemed largely a matter of semantic quibbling: since the Riggio brothers planned to label their own website as "The World's Largest Bookseller Online," they asked the court to bar Amazon from identifying itself as "Earth's Biggest Bookstore." It was a battle of superlatives, and a jesuitical pissing contest. For several weeks the lawyers wrestled behind closed doors. Then one day Susan handed me a sheet of paper, which specified the precise, hyperbolic terminology we were permitted to use according to the terms of our settlement. "Keep this locked in a drawer," she said. "It's actionable." I did as she asked, and immediately forgot whether we were the biggest or largest. The paper, yet another fossilized specimen of the era, is probably still preserved in the bureaucratic amber of some filing cabinet.

The lawsuit was no more than a playground shoving match, notable mainly for its puerility. Yet the entry of B&N into the online marketplace constituted a major threat. With hundreds of stores and billions of dollars in revenue, the chain had much deeper pockets than Amazon, infinitely more muscle with publishers, suppliers, and distributors, and a brand name to die for. According to popular wisdom, the Riggios would squash Jeff's Tinker Toy operation within the space of a few months. At the office, a *Business Week* article was anxiously passed from hand to hand: George Colony, an Internet pundit of the moment, had pronounced us "Amazon.*toast*." Should we be sweating?

Jeff gathered the entire staff and delivered one of his soothing, humorous, persuasive sermons. We weren't supposed to worry about the brick-and-mortar dinosaurs. We *were* supposed to worry about the next wave of innovation ("two guys in a garage," as he liked to say, having done quite nicely in a garage himself), and about the challenges of customer ecstasy. Mollified, we went back to our crude wooden desks. I put the finishing touches on an article about Primo Levi and conducted a telephone interview with Sherwin Nuland, who seemed to have some doubts about doctrinaire sociobiology. And on May 15, lawsuit or no lawsuit, the company went public.

It was and was not a morning like any other. On one hand, I kissed my wife and son good-bye, took the bus to work, and settled in to write a short review of the new John Updike. On the other hand, half the employees had loaded ticker software onto their computers and were now watching the numbers with crazed fascination. The stock had opened at $18, drifted upward a few points, then stabilized. I went over to Rebecca's office with some grammatical query and found her in a state of euphoria.

"Dan and I were dancing around the TV this morning," she told me. "We're rich, we're rich, we kept saying. But now I'm putting it out of my mind." She laughed. Then we both scrutinized the numbers some more.

"How do you rig that ticker thing up?" I asked.

"I'll show you later."

Tod meanwhile rolled into the office. He too had spent the morning at home in front of the television, with a calculator at his fingertips: "Every time it dropped a couple of points, I thought, *Shit, there goes a hundred thousand bucks.*"

This was in fact a small violation of protocol. Nobody in the room knew exactly how many shares of stock the others had been granted, and we all preferred to keep it that way. To discover that the person sitting next to you had been showered with three times as much potential wealth as you had—or twenty times as much—was a demoralizing thought. Still, nobody was surprised. As Employee Number Seven, Tod had obviously been in line for a generous block of options: you know, the ones that were supposed to be worthless.

For all practical purposes, of course, they *were* worthless. You couldn't exercise and sell a single share until you vested, a process that began precisely a year after the options were granted. In my case, that meant September 9, 1997: prior to that date, I might as well have owned a strongbox full of Monopoly money. And even if you vested earlier, there was something called a market stand-off, which prohibited employees from trading in company stock for 180 days after the IPO. Who knew what would happen over the next six months? We were an optimistic bunch, and would have been so even without Jeff's talent for mass hypnosis. Still, if B&N steamrolled us and the stock tanked, we were all screwed. Tod would have to cut back his clothing allowance again—no more Tootsi Plohound ankle boots—and I would default on my consolidation loan, earning myself a credit rating on par with, say, Argentina.

I sat at my desk, trying to hold these contradictory visions in my head and expunge a dangling modifier at the same time. It wasn't easy. After a few minutes Susan stuck her head in the door. She looked extremely happy, but was making a token attempt to contain her happiness, like the cat who's eaten not a single canary but an entire banquet of them.

"There's a party downstairs," she told us. "Jeff and Joy are in New York, but in a few minutes they're going to get on the speakerphone. Come on."

"We'll be right down," Kerry said, feeling a little more diligent than I was. The dangling modifier no longer struck me as a problem.

Susan waved and departed. Soon after, Kerry and I tromped down to the customer service room, the biggest space in the Columbia

Building. It was packed with employees, who were cheering, laughing, high-fiving, and fishing cans of beer and soda out of ice-filled trash barrels.

Jeff hadn't yet addressed the crowd. While we waited, somebody was working the room through a dinky PA system, asking triumphal questions. Who held the record for the most customer emails answered in a single hour? (Not me, that was for sure.) Who had written the most book reviews in a single week? (The winning total was 137, although I don't recall who the culprit was.) What was our largest daily shipment of books to date? How many people had visited the site during the first month of the year? Well, the answers *were* impressive. Each statistic produced a wave of cheering, mostly from the hardliners who had jammed the area next to the little stage.

"Whoo hoo!" I said at one point, raising my can of Sprite.

"What is this, an aerobics class?" Kerry asked, which caused me to lower the can.

Tod appeared from somewhere. His sleeve was wet, no doubt from rummaging around a beverage barrel. "I was talking to Tom Schonhoff the other day," he said. "You know what he told me? Hang on to the stock at any cost. Eat soup and dirt before you sell it."

"I'm already eating soup and dirt," I pointed out.

"Yeah, me too."

"Sometimes just dirt."

"Preposterous," I heard Kerry murmur. The cheering hit a climax, followed by frantic shushing. Somebody fired up the speakerphone. Jeff's voice, with an impressive amount of background noise, was piped through the PA system: he sounded as if he were standing on an airport runway.

"Today we made history at Amazon.com," he told us. The IPO had been an enormous hit, and the stock had closed out its first day in the mid-twenties, raising about $50 million in capital. That would pay for an awful lot of soup and dirt, I thought. People were cheering again. Somebody yelled out *Free Bird!*, which impressed me, since so many of the employees had been in short pants during the Lynyrd Skynyrd era. Jeff relinquished the phone to Joy, who added some (relatively) effusive words of her own—and the company, no longer in its infancy, plunged straight into an excitable adolescence.

8

I HAVE BEFORE ME three 100-ruble notes, issued in 1910. Each is imprinted with an identical portrait of Catherine the Great, who's got a healthy head of hair, a tiara, and a rather Nixonian hint of five o'clock shadow. The Empress is not smiling. The bills are crisp, as if freshly ironed, and the ink—green, black, rose—has lost none of its intensity.

Why, nearly a century after they rolled off the press, do these notes look so new? Well, my ancestors sewed entire bundles of them into the lining of their clothes when they departed Russia, one step ahead of the Cossacks. These closely held assets rustled in their suits, their vests, their topcoats. Shielded from the elements, the bills made their way from Odessa to Bucharest, then to Belgium—where they were becalmed for some months in Antwerp while passage was arranged—and then to England. From there they traversed the ocean to New York in style, on the Cunard Line's RMS *Berengaria*. Having miraculously evaded thieves and sticky-fingered immigration officials, they were cut loose from their swaddling and spilled onto a table in Queens. They were bright, uncreased, and consecutively numbered. They were also worthless.

There's no use blaming it on my ancestors. As they studied the

sizzling wake behind the ship, or waited patiently on line at Ellis Island to have their names anglicized, they probably didn't know that
the October Revolution had wiped out their savings. They must have
felt prosperous as they walked down the gangplank. And why not?
They were wearing the fiscal equivalent of Kevlar next to their skin.
History, alas, has certain armor-piercing qualities—and it was history, not greed or sloppiness or bullish optimism, that pulled the rug
out from under them. They didn't deserve to be paupers.

Still, their dalliance with paper wealth can't help but remind me of
my own. I'm going to shed my chronological straitjacket for a moment, the better to recount how the Internet boom took me from rags
to riches to, well, nicer rags. As I've noted before, I received 1,000
stock options when I was hired by Amazon, with a strike price of $1
per share. Observing some personal difficulties I was having during
my first few months on the job—and, quite frankly, out of the good-
ness of their hearts—my bosses gave me an additional grant in December. Meanwhile, the stock split twice before the company even
went public. In retrospect, I assume that Jeff's silver-tongued testi-
mony on behalf of his brainchild had been almost *too* effective: with
the IPO oversubscribed, he now needed to increase the size of the
float and create more shares. At the time, though, I had no idea why
such an event would happen. All I knew was that you got a little slip
of paper via interoffice mail, and suddenly you had more options. It
struck me as a natural process, like the propagation of salt crystals.

Now I had my little heap of options: a few thousand of them.
Needless to say there was no physical evidence, not even an engraved
certificate of the kind Daddy Warbucks used to pull out of the safe.
Yet they existed. They represented my miniscule share of ownership
in the company. And on May 15, when Amazon went public, I suddenly gained several hundred thousand dollars in paper wealth.

Some of these shares I owned: in the weeks leading up to the IPO, the company had allowed employees to make advance purchases of stock. Since none of these shares had yet vested, nobody could sell them. Still, it was supposed to be advantageous to snap up at least part of your grant—for tax-related reasons I couldn't quite fathom—so my parents loaned me a couple thousand dollars and I became an honest-to-god stakeholder. Most of my hoard, however, remained in the form of options. I could watch their value rise and fall, teeter-totter style, on the nifty Internet streaming thing Rebecca had showed me. I could make furtive, embarrassing calculations on a piece of scrap paper, then cover up the figures with a drawing of the little old man I always drew when I was nervous. At this stage, though, there was something fabulously theoretical about the whole business. You had potential riches, Platonic riches, but no cash.

If I had been more flush, perhaps I wouldn't have felt the contradiction so keenly. But my finances had gotten even shakier during the winter. Persistent illness sent my wife to the hospital on two different occasions, and Amazon's rather skimpy insurance package covered only a fraction of the costs. Each time, I found myself in the business office at the hospital, cobbling together installment agreements that could easily take me years to pay off. The account managers, young guys who positively radiated good health, were so reasonable that I felt like crying. I kept shaking their hands. I couldn't stop thanking them.

All that gratitude had a sedating effect on me. For the next few months I did my best never to think about money. I paid my bills, the ones I could, and ignored the rest. I charged everything on my last remaining credit card. I borrowed more money from my friends, promising to repay them out of the proceeds of my chimerical stock sales—which is to say, I not only built castles on air but then erected a penthouse and solarium on top of the castle.

In this fashion 1997 dribbled away. Then something amazing

happened. In November I picked up the telephone and told my broker (I had a broker!) to sell a block of shares for me. A few days later, $53,913.20 materialized in my checking account.

For better or worse, this phone call permanently changed my relationship to money. True, much of that cash vaporized within the next week, as I wrote checks to friends, doctors, hospitals, banks, and babysitters. Yet in some subtle way, which I was reluctant to admit even to myself, that call had screwed up my basic conception of getting and spending. Beforehand, I did a job and was paid for it: a simple equation, a zero-sum game. Sometimes I earned more, sometimes less, but the sums always seemed vaguely proportionate. Now that sense of proportion was gone. Don't get me wrong: I was delighted—*glad*, as Emerson would say, *to the brink of fear*—to have these arbitrary riches dumped in my lap. I loved my newfound pot of gold. The fact that it had issued forth from a career as a nickel-and-dime journalist made it all the more precious and paradoxical. Still, there was something freaky about the whole train of events.

And over the next two years, it was going to get a lot freakier. Why? Because we were now smack in the middle of the dot-com boom, partaking of (in a memorable phrase coined by Kleiner Perkins honcho John Doerr) "the greatest legal creation of wealth in the history of the planet." Amazon's share price kept climbing. Less than a year after converting my first batch of options into cash, I had another transubstantiation on my hands: I turned into a millionaire. Sure, it was all, or mostly, on paper. So what? The stock split three times between June 1998 and September 1999, and after each split the price continued to levitate. There seemed to be no end to it. When CIBC Oppenheimer analyst Henry Blodget set his celebrated target of $400 per share on December 15, 1998, the price jumped more than $46 that very day, and hit the stratospheric bull's-eye just a few weeks later. There *was* no end to it. Doerr's phrase had begun to look like an understatement.

At the peak of the frenzy, my remaining options were worth nine million dollars. I can hardly type such a sentence without a preemptive shudder: I can feel a towering wave, a regular tsunami of irony, about to break over my shoulders. The bubble, as we all know, eventually went bust. What had resembled a cosmic joke—striking it rich as a book reviewer—turned out to *be* a cosmic joke, as the price of Amazon stock collapsed. Locked up in the form of unvested options, which I couldn't sell, most of my fortune disappeared. Hold on, though. For the moment, I'm going to look resolutely backward, and ignore the tear-stained, wallet-busting denouement. That will make it easier to convey what it felt like to be among (as Tod put it one day) "the best paid editorial staff since the invention of moveable type."

Every happy family is alike, Tolstoy observed—but what about every rich one? As it turns out, there are numerous ways to react when you stumble into a major fortune. Some Amazonians went on buying binges: cars, boats, clothes, art, fine wines, real estate, jewelry, first editions, *more* real estate. One programmer (and Harley Davidson enthusiast) strolled into a taco joint near the office and loudly announced that he had hit his lifetime trifecta: "I've got a hog, a house, and a hot tub!"

Others preferred to plough their gains back into a new, diversified portfolio. You had your hedge funds and T-bills, your bond ladders and blue chips. If you felt even more irrationally exuberant than usual, you could sink some spare change into the latest IPO— telecom, B2B, optical fiber—and keep your fingers crossed. Whatever you did, the market kept behaving like a Roman candle, so it made no sense to park your cash in some chicken-feed bank account: that was the equivalent of losing money, throwing it out the window. You had to keep it circulating. Without a little bounce, a touch of Brownian motion, the dollars would go dead on you. They were always the means to some taxable, teleological end, which is to say, more dollars.

Then there were the people like me, who essentially behaved as though *nothing had happened*. Oh, it was a wonderful feeling to be relieved of all those financial pressures. Yet most of my old, neurotic inhibitions about money remained intact. We replaced none of our dilapidated furniture: when the cheapo particle-board table from IKEA finally busted, we threw it away and left a vacancy, like a bald spot, in the living room. I still found it difficult to buy a shirt, a watch, a compact disc. And every time I pondered a big-ticket purchase, I heard Chris's voice in my ear, urging me to avoid his dumb (and dumber) mistakes. This went beyond indifference: I was seeking protective camouflage. The idea wasn't to look poor, only invisible. Once in a long while, I took a hedonistic plunge: I bought an Ermenegildo Zegna tuxedo for my sister's wedding, whose upswept lapels seemed designed to accommodate a bigger wallet, and a beautiful Steven Andersen archtop guitar. Mostly, though, I continued to wear my underwear with the holes in it, not wanting to identify with the ruling class even on my way to the shower.

No doubt this reluctance on my part had less to do with thrift than with pathology. My father, a research scientist, always taught me to value creativity (which he had) over cash (which he didn't). He was right, of course. Still, there may be nothing in this world more crushing than a good lesson taken to heart. It made me suspicious of my own luck. This proved to be prescient in the long run—as it so often does—but it also made my lucre seem filthier than it really was. No wonder I kept my distance from it. In any case, I had found the ideal setting for operating as a stealth plutocrat. Seattle had a long custom of quiet wealth, invisible wealth. Even Bill Gates, the richest man on the planet and the jewel in the crown of the city's entrepreneurial mythology, followed suit. If he built himself a house as big as the local Sheraton, he had the good taste to bury much of it in a hillside.

I seldom discussed these matters, and never in any detailed way.

Early on, a couple of months after the company went public, my sister asked me: "Are you a millionaire now?" I told her, honestly, that I wasn't. But once I was, I never mentioned the fact to her, nor to my oldest friends, who worked as hard as I did but weren't being rewarded with such insane sums, who simply weren't dwelling in the same Cloud Cuckoo Land as I was. An exception: at a certain point, I shared a few figures with my parents. In part this was to reassure them that they would no longer have to prop me up financially, as they had done for so many years. Yet I also wanted to prove that I had made good, that I had hit the jackpot, a childish impulse that I feared would fly right in the face of my father's ambivalence about material success. I needn't have worried. He embraced my riches with real gusto, and felt that I deserved much, much more. During his toast to the happy couple at my sister's wedding, he digressed for a moment to inform the audience that his son had virtually *created* the Internet's flagship retailer, and then implored Jeff to ante up: "Mister Bezos, surely James should be given a billion dollars." My brother, a bass player with a predictably erratic income, glanced down at the table. Thrilled and mortified, I perspired like mad into my fancy tuxedo.

In fact, my father was more in touch with the spirit of the age than I was. To get to the heart of an epoch, you can safely ignore its statements of purpose, its fiery declarations. Listen instead to the questions it asks. In 1863, surveying the panoramic misery of pre-industrial Russia, Nikolai Chernyshevsky asked: *What Is To Be Done?* In 1997, at which point the United States was supposed to be gliding into a radiant, post-industrial future, the question of the moment was: *Who Wants To Be A Millionaire?* The answer, needless to say, was everybody. But what made the Lost World of the Late Nineties so extraordinary was that such wealth seemed *feasible*, not merely to robber barons but to college students and taxi drivers, waitresses and pharmacists and postal carriers. Plenty of people—most people—

were still scraping to pay their bills. The rich were undeniably getting richer. Yet the arbitrary nature of the boom, and the way it plucked its beneficiaries from all corners of the economic map, did suggest a certain leveling of the field. Egged on by Regis Philbin, every American could now dwell in Possibility.

Until, that is, March 10 of 2000. On that date the NASDAQ hit its all-time high, closing out the day at 5,048.62, and then commenced a long, ruinous slide, which would eventually siphon $3.8 trillion from our collective pockets. Most Amazonians were slow to panic. We had already seen the stock take a beating on several earlier occasions, then stage a miraculous recovery. And despite the sputtering economy, all the signs pointed to a blowout holiday season, in the course of which Amazon was primed to move more than a billion dollars worth of merchandise. Surely we would ride out the storm. In fact, the company might even benefit from a little culling, and enter the next year as the ultimate dot-com survivor.

No matter. Over the next eighteen months, Amazon shares went into a swoon. They never descended into penny-stock hell, where quite a few heavy hitters of the Internet revolution struggled to warm themselves around the fire. Still, my options lost more than 95% of their value before they stabilized and began to claw their way back upward. In the interim, I sold several blocks of stock at what I once would have regarded as absurdly low prices: hadn't I already lost enough money due to my touching, complacent, loyal, greedy, quasi-religious faith that the company would always bounce back? Would I ever learn? I had been foolish, but now I would be a realist. (In fact, I was being foolish again—as I write these words, the value of the shares has now multiplied tenfold since they touched bottom—but this extra, ironic rotation of the wheel of fortune is more than I can deal with at the moment.) In any case, by the time I returned to Manhattan from Seattle in September 2001, my sister was no longer asking me if I was millionaire. But if she had, I could have told her, honestly, that I wasn't.

It's not, as they say, a tragedy. My fortune materialized ex nihilo, without any special effort or ingenuity on my part, and vanished in no less capricious a manner. I made out okay, more than okay: the money I squeezed out of the stock on the way up allowed me to move back East, buy an apartment, and prepare some sort of launching pad for the next stage of my life. From time to time I have these twinges of regret. I find myself staring at those very items I was too superior to covet back when I could afford them: a silver Mercedes-Benz, a black leather chaise lounge, a Rodin—his famous bust of Gustav Mahler— that I saw in a shop window near my dentist. I also dream of a little bungalow I thought of buying during my next-to-last summer in Seattle. The entrance took you through a gate and down the steep western slope of Queen Anne Hill, with fir trees and bright green underbrush on both sides of the path. During the dry months, anyway, it felt like an enchanted forest, and at the bottom of this charming declivity was the house itself, compact and cozy. The price of this picturesque dwelling was $500,000: a ridiculous sum, I thought. Yet now that I'm back in Manhattan, where that kind of money gets you an outhouse with cooking privileges, the bungalow seems more and more something out of a fairy tale, one I actually participated in. What, I ask myself, is the moral of the story? Am I overlooking some basic lesson about money and corruption and mild-mannered hubris? I'm not sure. What I have decided is to stop thinking about the golden age—which turned out to be largely a matter of iron pyrites—and move on.

Here, too, there are certain lessons to be drawn from my family history, with its patterns of Yiddish-accented peripeteia. What, for example, became of my great-grandfather Abraham Felder, who sewed all that Czarist currency into his clothing? At once he hooked up with his brother-in-law, who had emigrated some years before and set up as a diamond merchant. Together they founded what was then a cutting-edge business, the Roaring Twenties equivalent of online commerce: selling jewelry by mail order. They made pots of money, more than enough to compensate for Abraham's defunct rubles. True, they were living in the midst of a major boom—President Coolidge himself anointed it a "new era of prosperity"—when it was supposedly impossible *not* to make money. So they went with the flow, and became rich men.

By 1925 it was time to move to a tonier neighborhood. They left Queens for Brooklyn: for Flatbush, more precisely, which was then an upper-middle-class citadel instead of an urban eyesore. They bought a mansion on Bedford Avenue, cheek-by-jowl with the country club, and there my father spent much of his childhood. Each morning a chauffeured Packard conveyed them to their offices on Bleecker Street. The driver—to whom my ancestors, early practitioners of trickle-down economics, gave a motorcycle—sat in the car all day, wrapping himself in a blanket when the temperature dropped. Then he drove them home again at the end of the day.

Not surprisingly, Abraham and his partner developed a healthy disdain for alarmists, defeatists, the faint of heart. Having escaped catastrophe by the skin of their teeth back in Russia, they now excluded its very possibility. They had traded those rubles—wastepaper, play money, confetti—for solid American currency, hadn't they? Their future was assured. They weren't speculators, fooling around with intangibles: they dealt in precious stones, objects you could hold in your hand. ("Were they selling costume jewelry or the real thing?" I asked my father. "Nobody knows," he told me.) Approached by their own nephew to at least buy some life insurance, they declined. "Insurance policies are for poor people," they informed him. "We're set for life." Pragmatists, they also turned up their noses at various other pie-in-the-sky prospects. An opportunity arose to invest in shares of the nascent Transworld Airlines. The whole concept made them suspicious: no whimsical, Chagall-like dreams of flight for *these* Jews. "Nobody will ever fly from one coast to another in an airplane," was their final judgment.

How easy, in retrospect, to see what they did not! That catastrophe was part and parcel of their universe they should have known, and not only because they left Odessa in such a hurry. Catastrophe was in the air, the water. Even the *Berengaria*—the steel-helmed vehicle of salvation that carried them from the Old World to the New, with its swimming pool, Turkish baths, and, on the promenade deck, an actual brokerage office for stock trades—was itself a kind of dividend paid on a previous disaster. It had been given to Cunard by the Hamburg-American Line after World War I as compensation for the *Lusitania*, destroyed by a German torpedo on May 7, 1915. With a yawning gash in its starboard hull, the ship sank in a mere twenty minutes. That left little time to deploy the lifeboats, and 1,198 passengers drowned in the Atlantic. The calculus of such a disaster is unbearable, the very arithmetic an insult.

Compared to those unlucky souls, Abraham and his partner lost nothing when the economy collapsed in 1929. As they saw it, though, they lost everything. The business dried up. Their investments went sour. The driver was let go. Somehow they held onto the house on Bedford Avenue, but even that functioned as something of a goad, reminding them that it was better never to have money (as they tirelessly noted) than to have it and lose it. As the Depression deepened and grew more desperate, they took to sitting in the parlor every evening with the lights out, silent and embittered. From time to time they broke the silence in order to blame each other: "It's *your* fault I'm poor now!" Mostly, though, they kept quiet. In such a state they refused to think much about the future, which had seemed to issue them certain promises, certain obligations, and had now defaulted on them. My father, then a boy, observed all this: the dark room, the chastened, furious partners. He may have decided then, on instinct, that cash was a dubious foundation for the good life. In any case, he passed that belief on to me, along with those 100-ruble notes. The secret to keeping money fresh, it turns out, is to never spend it.

As for me: I had other catastrophes to reckon with. A week after leaving Amazon and returning to New York, I dropped my son off at school in the morning, walked east along Great Jones Street, and heard, as I approached the intersection of Lafayette, what sounded like a military jet passing directly overhead, going south. There was a loud roar, the kind you could feel in the soles of your feet. Some stunt, I thought. But it was, as we all know, a passenger plane, and thirty seconds later everything changed no less decisively than it had when that torpedo struck the *Lusitania*. With tears in my eyes, I stood in the midst of a furious, chastened crowd on the corner and watched the towers burn. In the distance I thought I saw tiny pieces of paper floating in the air like confetti, but this was a trick of perspective: these were big sheets of metal or glass or gypsum board, carried aloft by the updraft.

That evening I found myself at an outdoor restaurant on the Upper East Side. The place was jammed, and the funereal hush of the afternoon had been broken. In fact there was a peculiar energy in the air, a sense of expectancy, as if we were all waiting for a verdict to be announced. People joked, argued, struggled to regain their conversational footing. If you squinted, this could almost pass for normal life. A man at the next table sent back his endive salad as a procession of enormous refrigerator trucks dodged potholes on their way downtown. Anybody could figure out what the trucks were for. I did. And my lost riches, which had already ranked pretty low on the scale of terrible events, dwindled to microscopic size, then vanished.

I wish I could say that I never thought of them again. Yet I do. The ordinary heartbreaks, as Nadezhda Mandelstam called them—the non-catastrophic ones—are sometimes trivial, sometimes not. In either case, they're impressively tenacious. In the evenings, as my ancestors did, I lapse into the occasional reverie about my monetary rise and fall. I've made it a habit, however, to always leave the lights on.

9

AT THIS POINT I will ask the reader to set back the clock and ignore everything contained in the previous chapter: the boom, the bust, the mountain (and relative molehill) of cash. It's an impractical request. Readers, like jurors exposed to some bit of prejudicial evidence, find it difficult to forget on command. Still, I urge them to come away with me now, to the bygone days of June 1997, when an entire nation hadn't yet inhaled the Internet ether and a plucky little bookseller was making its debut—attending, as it were, its corporate cotillion—at the Book Expo America in Chicago.

The BEA is the publishing industry's biggest trade show in the United States. It usually draws 30,000 or so booksellers, distributors, editors, publicists, and buyers. It also functions as a kind of authorial petting zoo, with writers of every stripe on hand, but basically you'll find two varieties: the big names, the stars, who shoot up and down the aisles followed by a vapor trail of handlers, and the little names, the brilliant midlist novelists and respectable academics and self-published wackos. There's always a slew of journalists in attendance, who pursue the big names and settle for the little ones. And finally there are innumerable gate-crashers, who come for the free tote bags and T-shirts and galleys and key chains and logo-imprinted bottles of mineral water, and to scam invitations to the various parties around town, which often feel like the BEA's true raison d'être. Sure, the show was originally founded as a marketplace, where booksellers could examine the latest wares from the publishers and place their orders. By now, however, it had long since evolved into a place to schmooze, drink, and make an impression.

Making an impression was certainly what Jeff had in mind. He brought a large contingent, perhaps 100 employees, to Chicago. Toward the end of May we had all been given button-down burgundy shirts with *Amazon.com* stitched onto the breast pocket, and were ordered to supply our own pair of khaki pants. These uniforms felt slightly demeaning—they made us look as though we worked in a fast-food joint—but they stood out on the convention floor, which is what mattered. The company constructed a large, lavish booth, with plenty of computer terminals for casual browsing. And to make it clear we meant business, a huge Amazon banner hung from the end of each and every aisle in the convention center. This was actually a less expensive gesture than it may have appeared: it ran the marketing department no more than $10,000. Still, it gave the impression that the company was both ubiquitous and irresistible, a mixed message for many of the independent booksellers on the floor.

All of us were assigned shifts at the booth. There the basic idea was to demonstrate how the site worked, answer questions, and proselytize like mad. The first morning, however, we were ordered to attend a talk Jeff was giving to a full house over at Donnelley headquarters. I don't know whether this location was selected for the building itself—a grandiose pile not far from the convention center—or for its symbolic value: the proprietor of that pile was one of the oldest publishing establishments in the country, incorporated in 1871 as RR Donnelley, Steam Printer. What better place for the New Economy to plant its flag? In any case, there were many of us decked out in our burgundy shirts, along with a mob of publishers and editors. Jeff, in *his* burgundy shirt, launched into his spiel, which was as hypnotic as usual.

"What we're aiming for at Amazon.com is the hard middle," he told the packed and perspiring crowd.

I noticed a good many furrowed brows around the room. Jeff had a real genius for jargon, even in a jargon-clotted environment like the Internet, where terms like *fractal* and *meme* were constantly being pried loose from science and applied to retail crapola. Still, *hard middle* never really caught on. It sounded like an abdominal workout video, or maybe a porn movie, and that didn't help.

"The middle of what?" one colleague whispered to me. I shrugged.

Only later did I figure out that the hard middle was a kind of demographic limbo. In Jeff's view, it was was easy to reach ten people (you called them on the phone, or shouted out the window) and easy to reach ten million people (you bought a commercial on the Super Bowl), but extremely challenging to reach a group of, say, ten thousand people. The Internet, he argued, was going to change that. With its bottomless capacity for data collection, it would allow you to sort through entire populations with a fine-tooth comb. Affinity would call out to affinity: your likes and dislikes—from Beethoven to barbecue sauce, shampoo to shoe polish to *Laverne & Shirley*—were as distinctive as your DNA, and would make it a snap to match you up with your 9,999 cousins. This was either a utopian daydream or a targeted-marketing nightmare. But in that crowded room at RR Donnelley, nobody could tell the difference.

I hustled out to the express bus and hit the convention center, where my shift was about to begin. For the next four hours I stood around the booth and explained stuff to visitors. Mostly I had a good time: after a while, in fact, I even forgot about my outfit, although I was peeved to see that Maryam Mohit had violated the khaki requirement and worn a pair of tan, filmy harem pants.

There was a steady stream of people wandering in, who stood patiently in line at the terminals as though they were waiting for a popular ride at Disneyland. Compared to the other booths, with their piles of non-interactive literature, we *were* the equivalent of a small-scale roller coaster: the Reading Matterhorn. Visitors scrolled and clicked and surfed around the site. "I'm looking for a really good book on training your dog," said a smiling, determined woman from Florida, and once we zeroed in on a selection, she copied the names down on a tiny yellow slip of paper. A small publisher with a German accent and a list comprised exclusively of big-game hunting manuals questioned the availability of one bloodthirsty title: "Dot *iss* in print, young man!" Authors, obscure ones, looked up their own books and left smiling. That was more than you could say for many a booth in the vast, echoing convention center.

At one point a woman strolled up and handed me her business card: she worked at R.R. Bowker, the publisher of *Books in Print* and various other reference essentials.

"I'd like to talk to you about licensing content," she said.

We had already begun buying reviews from *Booklist*, which, along with *Publishers Weekly* and *Kirkus,* supplied thumbnail evaluations in advance of publication. These we shoveled onto the site by the thousands. Eventually we would have some trouble with them: mystery fans complained that they always gave away the ending. For now, though, the practice was filling a great many holes in our coverage.

"Where would the stuff come from?" I asked.

"From you," she said. "We're interested in licensing material from the Amazon site. Reviews, interviews, articles, whatever."

Wait a minute: she wasn't selling, she was buying. Which is to say, she was putting the company on par with other publications, treating us as respectable critics rather than hyperventilating shills. Only a few months into the game, and our expertise was worth coveting! I felt a pleasant sense of shock, a slight tingling beneath my burgundy collar.

"Fantastic," I told her, sliding the card into my pocket. "I'll pass this on to my boss. I'm sure you'll be hearing from her."

Nothing ever came of this encounter. As I learned later on, Jeff had effectively scotched all such proposals—and there were a string of them—by demanding enormous sums for our humble content. At the time, though, the conversation had a tonic effect. My shift had ended, freeing me to wander the aisles with Kerry. Feeling like an eminent literary man, whose opinions not only appeared on Amazon but were eagerly gobbled up and fed back into the information economy, I made the rounds and collected an assortment of promotional trinkets.

In our telltale uniforms, we were greeted like heroes by most small publishers. It was easy to see why. For decades, they had faced a depressing bind: they could distribute their own titles, which essentially meant selling them out of the trunk of a car, or pay a distributor to get them into the stores. Of course it was better to have the books make an appearance, however brief, in the stores. Yet the extra cost whittled away at their profit margins, and the returned merchandise often looked as though it had been scattered from an airplane. Now Amazon had come to the rescue. All the publishers needed to do was list their books on the site—a free service that later morphed into a paid one—and suddenly they had direct access to millions of customers. The middleman, the genius of capitalism, was being engineered out of the picture. If you had a taste for jawbreakers, you called it disintermediation. If not, you just grinned and counted your money.

The independent booksellers, on the other hand, viewed the company with considerable ambivalence. They had already suffered over the past ten years as the ever-expanding chains siphoned off more and more of their business. To many of them, Amazon represented the final nail in the coffin. Still, their attitude was hardly monolithic. Some were delighted to see B&N sweat, even if it came at their own expense.

"We love watching you guys kick Len Riggio's ass," I was told by one of two tall Midwestern gentlemen, apparently brothers.

"Our job is to keep the customer happy," I said.

"You bet," he said.

"It's a big business," I persisted. "There's room for plenty of winners."

"Keep up the good work," he said.

Touché. True, most people at Amazon referred to B&N as the Evil Empire. But officially we were nonbelligerents, leaving our fate to the invisible hand of the market, and I would have been crazy to trash the competition in public.

Meanwhile, Kerry couldn't bring herself to utter any of this drivel. She joshed with a dozen different publicists, all of whom she knew from her previous gigs. There was a certain amount of mirth in connection with our shirts. For a few minutes we had an off-the-record chat with Art Winslow, the literary editor of the *Nation*, who was writing an article about the current, convulsive transformation of the publishing industry. It was basically a Tale of Two Conglomerates—the German media powerhouses of Bertelsmann and Von Holtzbrinck—who were absorbing one American publisher after another, then taking a chainsaw to all redundant (a word to make you wince) staff. Consolidation was the enemy. In this scenario, however, the Internet represented something of a wild card. Would it democratize, diversify, disintermediate? Or would it turn into one more corporate playground? The jury was still out, according to Art. Yet our conversation, and my uneasy rapport with the booksellers, raised the distinct possibility that Amazon might not remain an underdog forever. Success was good, success was delicious. But if the company attained the kind of clout that Jeff clearly desired, we might well shed our crowd-pleasing role as David and turn into big, bad, boneheaded Goliath. To be frank, I didn't fancy myself as a Philistine.

We made our way down one more aisle. There was a crowd, and up ahead a laughing, spherical man, who may or may not have been Chef Paul Prudhomme, was signing tall stacks of books. "He wanted to make gumbo," I heard somebody say, "but they wouldn't allow his pots and pans on the convention floor." I craned my neck to get a look. I wanted to see if he was wearing one of those white hats he always sported on television.

"Can we get out of here?" Kerry asked. She patted herself down in search of her glasses. She found them, cleaned them with a tissue, and put them on, since there were certain people—former employers, mostly—she wanted to avoid on the way out. "Okay," I said, and we took our trinkets and ran for the exits.

We were staying at the Palmer House, an old-fashioned hotel in the business district. I went upstairs to change and discovered that my roommate—who had earlier declared himself "the only *practicing* bisexual at Amazon"—was out, well, practicing. I hung my official shirt in the closet, pulled on some civilian clothes, and went down to the bar to meet Kerry and Jordana. Several Amazonians were playing pool when I showed up, and we stuck around eating pistachio nuts for a few minutes and listening to the gratifying *clack* of the billiard balls.

Shel Kaphan was sitting at the next table, looking disgruntled. This didn't necessarily mean anything: the inventor of the company's very architecture, its Baron Haussmann, often looked as if he had gotten up on the wrong side of the bed. Maybe he preferred the initial stage of programming, the code-driven parturition, to running the stuff in the real world, where it had to be held together with the equivalent of Band-Aids and Bactine. Or maybe he just happened to be a grouch.

"Hey Shel," I said. He nodded. The Bird, who had descended from her managerial perch for a few rounds of pool, tried and failed to put the seven in the corner pocket. She cut loose with a high, girly laugh, meant to signify that pool was a man's game in the first place: very retro behavior. "Sometimes I'm such a spaz," she said. Shel and I watched the colored balls caroming around the table, and somehow got onto the topic of upper-level hires. Clearly Shel thought there were too many of them.

"Every time I go to a meeting," he said, "there's another vice-president for Business Development. I feel like I'm stumbling over them."

"What do they do?" I asked. That was Risher's title, I thought, and suddenly envisioned a whole roomful of duplicates, all of them grinning and emitting those suave, fifty-syllable sentences.

"Who knows?"

Behind us, Jordana was talking to Kerry about Paul Auster, whose party we were going to attend. She found him very attractive, which I took as an indirect compliment to me, since many people—okay, my mother—had noted a clear resemblance. "He has those *cheekbones,*" I heard.

Clack.

Shel, meanwhile, wasn't through with his critique of Amazon's corporate atmosphere. The growth of all that vice-presidential kudzu clearly bugged him, but he also despised the increasing red tape, paperwork, and office politics. He was pissed, too, about the endless meetings, and even about the software application that had been installed to facilitate them. The moment you switched on your computer each morning, Meeting Maker fired up automatically and told you where to go, and when.

"As far as I'm concerned," Shel grumbled, "that Meeting Maker thing marks the decline of Western Civilization."

"Sometimes I need to be reminded," I said, wondering why I kept looking on the bright side.

"I don't like to be reminded," Shel said.

Tod had joined the party behind me, and was expressing, like a Man of the People in a socialist mural, his disapproval of the fact that Jordana employed a cleaning woman. He sounded horribly offended, as though it were *his* job to throw out her empty cereal boxes and used coffee filters, to dust her possessions and scour her tub with bleach.

"I clean my own place," he said. "But you're too busy to clean yours."

"I'm at work all week," she told him. "Personality Plus makes me too tired to take out the trash." A good company girl, she was using a code name for our employer, since we had been cautioned against blabbing in public. There were corporate spies everywhere.

"What about Ned?" Tod asked. Ned was Jordana's boyfriend, a strapping guy who made enormous sculptures out of styrofoam and discarded furniture. "Can't he tidy up a little?"

"He's sculpting," she said.

"Smoking? You're kidding! He can't smoke and clean at the same time?"

"*Sculpting*," Jordana corrected him.

Despite the racket, I heard Tod emit what I can only call a snort. I pictured him in a hairnet, running the vacuum over the rugs in his Capitol Hill apartment, which he shared with a cigar-smoking roommate. Within a few months, he would buy a house. Then he would hire a cleaning lady to clean it, having warmed up, as we all did, to the idea of money. But for now, he and I preferred to make like Communards.

Shel had fallen silent again. I cracked open a final pistachio nut, a stubborn one, and then headed out the door with my companions. We took a cab to Paul Auster's party, where tiny hors d'oeuvres, impossible to identify in the dark room, were circulating on trays. The guests piling up at the bar were also impossible to identify, although they all looked familiar, a throng of industry archetypes: female publicists in tiny dresses, rising young editors in swanky suits, living legends in tweed jackets and declamatory bow ties. Feeling anonymous myself, I fiddled with my ID badge from the convention and considered slipping the lanyard around my neck.

"Put that away right now," Kerry said.

After snagging three beers, we found a table by the window, which overlooked a black, glassy, slow-moving body of water: what passed for a river in the metropolis. From there we peered toward the bar and waited for the man of the hour to arrive. Most of the guests seemed indifferent to whether Paul Auster ever showed up: they drank their drinks and chased around the waiters with the trays, who now struck me as the most powerful figures in the room. There was laughter, flirtation, gossip. Nobody stood up straight, as though the entire industry had been afflicted with curvature of the spine. Outside, the river had come to a complete halt.

"Where are you, Paul?" Jordana asked, sounding like an ingenue, which she was. Or almost: fresh out of Bennington, she had worked at CNN, then landed a job in the Letters to the Editor department at *Slate.* She was very smart, very young, and spoke with an endearing, quasi-patrician accent.

"He's bound to show up," I said. "It's his party. Probably he'll be with his wife, Siri. I read somewhere that they never spend a night apart."

"Really?" said Jordana, with just a touch of regret. Thanks to Ned she was exempt, just as I was, from the convention's sexual sideshow. Of course people in these situations had been known to stray. Perhaps if the glamorous creator of *The New York Trilogy* had suddenly approached our table, his trademark cigarillo describing a bright orange dot in the darkness, Jordana would have lost control. But he didn't. In fact he never showed up at all, not while we were there. I looked for a hidden meaning in our predicament, something about the death of the author, but found none.

We gave up. We moved on to another party, and to another after that—and at this point, I confess, all the functions I attended at all the BEAs have begun to blur together, courtesy of the multiple beers and spritzers and gin-and-tonics, and I seem to recall a single, hallucinatory congregation of authors. There is George Stephanopoulos, who looks tiny, like a scale model of himself, and Julia Child, who has just written a kind of culinary pas de deux with Jacques Pepin, and Salman Rushdie, whose white, omnidirectional beard makes him look like a cunning and corrosive Santa Claus. Over here I see the reticent Alistair MacLeod, with his white Kangol cap pulled low to avoid eye contact with his admirers, and Elinor Lipman, who wants to introduce me to a nice girl, and Jonathan Franzen, still some months away from his celebrated wrangle with Oprah and, by extension, every reader of fiction in the United States. Michael Dibdin, a displaced Englishman with a maritime bent, is arguing about the colloquial origins of *the bitter end* (from the bitt, around which a cable or anchor chain is wound), and Amy Tan carries a pair of cloth bags, one on each shoulder, which contain not carpet samples but dogs. I see Richard Ford at an adjacent table, and steal his dessert fork once he's gone. Two tables down there is Eddie Fisher, not usually regarded as a writer, who has nonetheless produced a salacious memoir: dressed in a canary-yellow suit, his face gleaming from the Hollywood sunshine and the occasional bit of nip-and-tuck, he sends over an emissary to request that we join his party, and my companions, all of them attractive women, decline. (Elizabeth Taylor, eat your heart out.) Hello, John Ridley, good evening, Jane Smiley. Author, author!

In the morning, my roommate had yet to return. Chicago, which

Saul Bellow called "the contempt center of the universe," looked benign outside my window. There was, however, a mob of people frantically flagging down cabs in front of the hotel, as if Vesuvius were about to erupt: this meant the BEA was over. I left a neat pile of promotional stuff on my bed—including two bottles of water from a print-on-demand operation and a pair of goofy sunglasses—and checked out. Just for the hell of it, I wore my Amazon badge around my neck on the way to the airport: a Philistine after all, and proud of it.

10

SUMMER CAME. I bought a Smokey Joe barbecue kettle at Jordana's tag sale, and like a classic suburban dad, I lit the coals when I came home and grilled salmon, chicken, hot dogs. My son rode his tricycle around the block, sometimes wearing my Amazon badge from the BEA. The skies were bright and blue, and the living was—in some limited sense of the word—easy. We were still short of money. Yet we now had these stock options, and although we couldn't make a dime off them until the fall, we could observe the accumulation of a modest fortune through what felt like a pane of thick glass. The anticipation was sweet. And summer was when you *wanted* to live in Seattle, when the brilliant light and florescent landscape made you reluctant to live anywhere else.

To pick up some extra cash, my wife was now working at Amazon as well. There had been some talk of her doing legal chores for the company, but that didn't pan out, so instead she organized galleys, stuffed envelopes, and blue-penciled the occasional piece of copy. In a sense she was my assistant—one I shared with the other editors—and this was a toxic situation for any marriage. Still, we made the best of it. After dropping Nat off at the day-care center each morning, where they always seemed to be whipping up some Rice Krispies

Treats, we drove downtown together. We showed our badges to the guard—another token of how the place was changing—and I peeled off down the hall to my office, where I read many, many samples of faux-Updikean prose.

Why? This was the summer of what we, or at least the marketing department, called The Greatest Tale Ever Told. The concept originated with Tod, still stuck in the limbo of Publisher Relations. By now, in fact, he had been exiled to the eternal twilight of an office downstairs, whose large interior window made it resemble an aquarium. There he made phone calls, collected huge stacks of review copies, and jotted down ideas. Why, he asked himself one day, couldn't Amazon's growing legion of customers collaborate with a famous writer? Whether he thought of John Updike I don't know. Kay Dangaard, a new PR guru invariably described in the press as "a willowy New Zealand grandmother," later claimed that the whole thing was *her* idea. Perhaps there was a meeting of minds here, although Tod's mind and Kay's mind seemed like unlikely candidates for a rendezvous.

In any case, Tod wrote to Updike and laid out the proposal. All the author would have to do was supply us with the opening paragraph of a story. We would solicit additional paragraphs from our customers, adding one each day for the next forty-four days and paying the serial narrators $1,000 apiece. Then Updike would cap off the whole production with a final paragraph of his own, having been paid five grand himself for these services. Whether he would participate in such a stunt was anybody's guess. Still, he had a new novel coming out—the dystopian and technology-hating *Toward the End of Time*—and this might seem like a harmless way to promote it.

Nudged along, no doubt, by his publisher, he agreed. We had assumed he would write something new: this was Updike, after all, so profligate with his prose that he could have whipped the thing off while he pared his nails. Instead Tod got some yellowing sheets of manuscript in the mail. They had been typed on a manual typewriter: an apparatus that many of my colleagues had never even *seen*, let alone used. Updike had an emphatic touch on the keyboard, nearly piercing the paper with his punctuation, and as I studied the paragraphs I imagined I could hear the pinging end-of-line bell. But the content, too, was fascinating. Apparently in some early phase of his career, the young, aquiline, bell-bottomed author had toyed with writing a murder mystery. What's more, he had set the caper in a pulpier version of the *New Yorker* office, potentially biting the hand that fed him. He began: "Miss Tasso Pok at ten-ten alighted from the elevator onto the olive tiles of the nineteenth floor only lightly nagged by a sense of something wrong." Pretty subpar, as I'm sure he knew. So he consigned "Murder Makes the Magazine" to the drawer, never imagining that it would be resurrected decades later by futuristic geeks, who would moreover pay him a handsome, inflation-adjusted sum for his effort.

Updike's opening shot was duly posted on the site. Kay, who called everybody "darling," cranked up the publicity machinery, and we editorial types strapped on our seat belts. For the next few weeks, we would be deluged with paragraphs, which arrived by the truckful—at one point, we got nearly 19,000 entries in a single day. Each morning we sat at our desks and read until our eyes got bleary. It was obvious that we couldn't possibly get through them all, and that the real gems might well be buried under the slag heap.

Most of the submissions fell into three categories. First, there were thousands written in an approximation of Updike's early style: sonorous lines, fancy adjectives, a light frosting of Nabokovian wordplay. Most of them were terrible. Still, they gave you a glimpse into a kind of alternate universe, where Updike was himself, minus the talent. *Her blood-red fingernails came to gentle points,* you would read, *like a row of Gothic arches, and the pleasing ecclesiastical music of her tapping fingers on the desktop was clearly audible out in the hallway.*

No, it didn't sound like the man himself, although he was always willing to bend over backward for a churchy metaphor. But it was no worse than the previous one, with its present-tense, soft-focus lyricism: *His tongue, the pale and implausible muscle that it is, slips into the black vacancy of her mouth and lingers there, beneath the scalloped roof of the palate.* Yeah, baby, yeah! At these moments I wished Updike were present to see the sort of mimetic Frankensteins he was unleashing upon the world. Instead he was safe and sound in small-town Massachusetts, chuckling in that fluent way of his and knocking out the genuine item on a computer.

The second group ignored Updike altogether and focused on the mystery element. That paved the way for imitation Chandler and Hammett—tough-guy dialogue and clubfooted similes—although the weapons, the Glocks and Uzis and Tec-9s, were strictly contemporary. Here, too, you could date the author's age by his or her stylistic tics. Baby boomers latched onto Elmore Leonard or Sue Grafton. The younger set went for Grisham, which didn't translate into a specific style as much as a weakness for villainous lawyers with shiny, perfect teeth. Most of these submissions, too, were terrible. Still, they also constituted a kind of education, allowing you to trace the evolution of a genre, and that was more than you could say for the third group. These had no style at all. They seemed to reflect a secret conviction that nobody else would enter the contest. Strangely enough, these customers kept submitting new paragraphs. After being rebuffed a few times, they often appended abusive notes to the judging panel. *You guys are geniune* [sic] *assholes!* That made us feel very special as we drank our coffee and winnowed away.

Later that morning the phone would ring. "Darling, it's Kay," Kay would say. "Have you kids got a winner?" We kids, at least two of us pushing forty, wearily made our decision, and I sent out the winning paragraph by email to be posted on the site.

This Sisyphean process went on for weeks. "Murder Makes the Magazine" chugged toward its conclusion, festooned with extra plot lines and mistaken identities. Finally Updike wrapped the whole thing up with a suave paragraph of his own. You had to love the guy for going along with it. Sure, he got paid, but how many American masters would have collaborated so willingly with the vox populi? It was like Mozart appearing on *American Idol*.

The final product was nothing special: remember, we're talking about a piece of literary vivisection. But it did what it was designed to do. Several hundred thousand visitors came to the site, some making purchases along the way, all leaving behind their email addresses, thereby propping the door open for future communiques. Just as important, the contest generated headlines all over the planet. The scenario—the famous author communing with an army of the obscure via the Internet—hit the media's sweet spot. Even Updike himself chimed in with a piece for the *New Yorker*, adding a certain circularity to the process. Did he mind this artistic cohabitation with a multitude of strangers? Not at all, replied the unflappable author: even the Bible, as he pointed out, was something of a splice job.

Elsewhere Kay trumpeted the numbers to whoever would listen. There had been 380,000 submissions, the contest had been written up in 300 different news outlets, Updike had spent a mere 150 minutes on his final paragraph—and, oh, a random drawing at the end awarded $100,000 to a lucky winner. That brought the total tab to around $150,000. Nobody, not even professionally effusive Kay, could pretend that it was the greatest tale ever told. But there was no doubt that it was among the most expensive.

Well, the numbers *were* impressive. In fact, it's worth pausing at this point to note some additional ones. By October, Amazon would be among the twenty-five most visited sites on the entire Web. That same month, the company announced that its customer database now topped the 1,000,000 mark. This was not simply a numerical triumph. It indicated a real shift in public sentiment: suddenly more than a million Americans had entrusted a website—which is to say, a will-o'-the-wisp—with their names, addresses, phone numbers, credit cards, and so forth. Plus, the data itself was likely to turn into a major asset. Of course the company offered repeated assurances of confidentiality. But information, as the mantra told us, likes to be free. Or at least fungible.

Let me fish up a more impressive number. By the end of 1997, the company would rake in $147.8 million in annual revenue. That same year, the total North American market for consumer books ran to about $18 billion. Obviously Amazon's slice of the pie was still tiny. Look at it this way, though: only two years before, hardly anyone had even heard of e-commerce, and the idea of buying stuff over a computer network sounded like something out of *The Jetsons*. Now Jeff's brainchild had grabbed nearly 1 percent of the market. Soon enough, in other words, *one out of every hundred books purchased in the United States would be sold by Amazon*. That was an astonishing thought, even for a non-statistical brain like mine. It seemed like the bookselling equivalent of, say, diverting the Nile. Who knew how many millions of readers could be poured into such a freshly excavated channel?

With a mighty expansion underway, our department was ripe for what the managers called a *reorg*. In this case, though, we were looking at more than a game of musical chairs. Instead the editorial machinery was going to be revamped completely, and although Susan came up with the blueprints, it was Josh Petersen who implemented them. This bespectacled empire builder had originally been charged with one of our monkey-see-monkey-do initiatives: making sure that every book covered in the *New York Times Book Review* was reviewed by Amazon, too. In this capacity he had a string of [illegible] putes with Tod, at the end of which Susan would make [illegible] ant or the other stand in the corner. But Josh—whose panthe[illegible] populated by such speculative high-rollers as Victor Niederhoff[illegible] and "the Great Soros"—had bigger things in mind. He taught him-self enough Perl to write his own scripts, which immediately gave him some traction over the average editorial drudge. Then he looked around for an appropriate lever to move the world. What he came up with, courtesy of Susan's redesign, were BISAC codes.

A little background. Back in 1975, when the electric pencil sharp-ener represented the latest in office technology, a group of publish-ers, booksellers, and manufacturers convened to think about the future of the industry. They were particularly interested in goosing the flow of information from one sector to another, which meant set-ting standards for data storage and exchange. These conversations begat the Book Industry Study Group, which in turn begat BISAC, the Book Industry Standards and Communications Committee.

Now, among the many accomplishments of BISAC was the inser-tion of subject codes into most publishing-related databases. Some of these tags might seem a tad superfluous. The Bible, for example, is helpfully labeled as a *Religion* title. And for any bookseller unsure of the right location for the latest Harry Potter—that would be the front window—BISAC has some alternatives: *Juvenile Fiction, Humorous Stories, Wizards,* or the sternly pedantic *Schools & Education.* The purpose of the codes, however, isn't to belabor the obvious. They were inserted to allow sales and inventory data to be sliced, diced, and reshuffled by subject area. And since they were already built into the Ingram database—the foundation of Amazon's own, constantly mu-tating catalogue—why not redesign the site around them, especially since we were hustling to stay one step ahead of our rivals at B&N?

Or so the argument went. In no time flat we were summoned to a

)om, where the Lord of the Dance (as

number of layouts to the wall.

," he told us.

,neet of paper. But as Josh and Susan went on

now be launching twenty-odd subject areas—

.tes unto themselves—covering all of the major

.: literature, history, reference, religion, science, business, biog- ny, sports, travel, and so forth. Each area would be overseen by a single editor. (Literature, encompassing every work of imagination since the invention of cuneiform script, was judged to be a two-person job, so Kerry and I split it.) There was a tense atmosphere of anticipation in the room as Susan read off our assignments.

Despite the hiring binge of the last year, we now required an influx of editors. In classic Amazonian fashion, a number were created from scratch. Doug MacDonald, for instance, who had earlier been turned aside for supposed lack of gray matter, was now put in charge of religion coverage. Erica Jorgensen, a tall copy editor whose pale skin and dark hair made her look like an animated black-and-white photograph, was assigned to health. Romance, meaning those low-margin Harlequin novels we sold like crazy, became the purview of former administrative assistant Stefanie Hargreaves.

In a sense, the category pages (as they came to be called) represented not one but two huge gambles on the company's part. First, we were betting big on content. By setting up the equivalent of twenty online magazines—and budgeting close to a million dollars for reviews, articles, and interviews—Amazon was creating a true hybrid. It was neither a traditional store nor a traditional publication, but a backscratching fusion of the two. Ideally, readers would flock to the site to see what Toni Morrison thought about racial separatism, then exit with a copy of *The Bluest Eye* in their shopping carts. Editorial would thrive on its own *and* render unto Caesar (or Jeff) what was his. The reality, of course, was more complicated. But in the early, iconoclastic heyday of the Web, it felt like a marvelous experiment, and it was almost fun—a kind of a parlor game—to cast about for an adequate description of what we were doing.

The other big bet was on community. The category pages were set up to allow easy email exchanges between the editors and visiting customers, who were supposed to view these URLs as the virtual equivalent of *Cheers*. A sci-fi fan, for example, would pop in once a day to read about the new William Gibson, or to ask about the impending Alfred Bester reissues. Down the line there would be forums, too. That way visitors could chat with one another directly, with only the benign presence of editor and moderator Therese Littleton peering over their shoulders. The obvious model here was a place like the WELL, whose pioneering participants *did* make up a kind of disembodied community. Whether Amazon would inspire the same level of loyalty and long-distance solicitude was anybody's guess. But Jeff was willing to give it his best shot.

Having made his living at a hedge fund, he was also prone to cover his bets. The new emphasis on warm-and-fuzzy togetherness would be carefully countered by a mania for famous names. This doctrine was set forth at yet another meeting, to which both the editorial and marketing departments were summoned. Pacing back and forth at the front of the room, David Risher unveiled what was supposed to be our new battle cry.

"Here it is, folks!" he cried. *"Celebrate community, communicate celebrity!"*

There was little response from the audience. No doubt the crowd was still absorbing his earlier bombshell: Editorial and Marketing would henceforth be subsumed under a single Risherian rubric, *Marketorial*. Not surprisingly, neither department wanted to be mashed together in this way. I never heard the phrase again after the meeting, not even from David, who had apparently come to his senses.

Yet he didn't abandon his pursuit of the rich and famous. Not long

after unveiling his slogan, David herded Tim and me into still another conference room. Tim had shaved off his beard and cut his hair
short, which gave him the look of a mischievous child, a Katzenjam-
mer Kid. The two of us sat on one side of the long table, with David,
Rick, and the Bird on the other. I got out my pad and paper and
waited.

"Here's the story," David said. "Jeff is very concerned that B&N
is kicking our butt in the celebrity department. As I'm sure you know,
they're lining up all sorts of big names for online chats."

"I thought chats were a washout," I said. "Supposedly even
Michael Jackson gets a measly audience of three hundred people."

"Chat may not be the way to go," David allowed. "But the fact is
that those guys have a lot of leverage with celebrities, and we're
falling behind. Jeff and I were tossing around some ideas. We both
thought it would be great if the *Friends* folks would share their favorite books with us. Something like that."

"Friends," the Bird repeated. It wasn't a statement, and it wasn't a
question.

"The TV show," David said, clarifying a certain confusion in my
mind, too. "Each week, a different Friend would talk about what he
or she was reading. Courteney Cox could tell us what was on her bed-
side table."

Resisting the impulse toward cheap innuendo, and wanting to
seem in the loop, I said: "Jennifer Aniston."

"Exactly."

"It's very hard to contact these people," Tim said. "They have
publicists, assistants, handlers, whose whole mission in life is to keep
jerks like us away from them. But if you want celebrities on tap, I've
got another idea. When I was working as a film critic for a daily newspaper"—a gig that eventually got so tedious that Tim compared it to
servicing a vending machine—"I used to go to these prerelease

movie junkets. The producers line up table after table of journalists, then make the stars run the gauntlet. It's like a production line. But I'm sure we could get in there."

He elaborated some more, mentioning a special moment he'd had with Anthony Hopkins (the inebriated Welshman kept telling Tim that he looked like John Savage), and David listened to him with what I took to be fascination. It *was* fascinating. When Tim got on an anecdotal roll there was no stopping him: he had made a kind of pilgrim's progress through the world of pop culture, and remembered every lurid detail. This refugee from Harvard and hardcore academia had been kissed by Goldie Hawn, strangled by Alan Rudolph, and tackled by John Cusack. He had been appointed Grunge Correspondent at *Entertainment Weekly,* which entitled him to take Courtney Love's "screaming phone calls" from planes, trains, and automobiles. The stories went on and on. Finally, though, Tim yielded to some hidden reserve of Norwegian gravitas and paused to take a breath.

"How long have you been here?" David asked him.

"About eight months," Tim said.

Clearly Tim was now the golden boy as far as celebrity went. But David, glancing at his original notes, announced that he wanted me to head the team.

"Who's on the team?" I asked.

"Everybody on your side of the table," the Bird said. "That would be you and Tim."

"Okay," I said. "We'll get you celebrities."

Rick, who had chuckled once or twice during Tim's peroration, put in a cautionary word: "Cynthia Ozick isn't a celebrity."

I said nothing, surprised by this cheap shot at a writer whom I admired. It seemed uncharacteristic of Rick, too, but maybe he thought he was doing us a favor by steering us away from eggheads and mandarins. The meeting broke up. We returned to our desks, and after waiting a suitable interval to suggest deep reflection, I emailed my superiors and argued that Tim would be a better candidate to lead the celebrity squad. They agreed and excused me. Tim was put in charge—I imagined him doing a little soft-shoe around his office and humming the old Bette Midler chestnut, "You Gotta Have *Friends*"— but the whole project fizzled out a few weeks later. Perhaps Jeff, soon to be on intimate, speed-dial terms with Oprah Winfrey, decided it would make sense to let the celebs arrive under their own steam.

11

THE CATEGORY PAGES LAUNCHED IN OCTOBER. For our debut, Kerry and I had her interview with Alice Hoffman, my long review of James Salter's *Burning the Days,* and a short essay Alain de Botton had written for us about *The Sorrows of Young Werther.* This seemed like a promising start. Even better, Kerry had been corresponding with Penelope Fitzgerald, who had agreed to do a piece on an old favorite of hers, Sarah Orne Jewett's *The Country of the Pointed Firs.* Just think: one of the greatest living novelists in the English language was contributing to our humble—and, to her, inexplicable—enterprise! It made us feel much, much better about the e-commerce mark of Cain on our foreheads.

Working around the clock, the tech people had built a new platform for the launch. Instead of emailing our copy to the production department (aka Rebecca Staffel, plus a young assistant with a picture of her pet iguana taped to the desk), we now logged into a fancy online interface. There we typed our stuff directly into one window, indicated posting dates in another, inserted the codes for book jackets and additional art, and logged out again. Much of the time, it worked. Other times the new system—which marked a transition from HTML to SGML, or standard generalized markup language— crashed like mad.

In fact Kerry and I had served as guinea pigs for the developers. Perhaps our quaint attachment to literature made us seem like the ideal crash-test dummies. In any case, Maryam approached us one morning and said, "We've decided to make your page the alpha candidate." Under the supervision of a young programmer, Alex Yan, we keyboarded our text into the appropriate windows and watched all sorts of buggy nonsense materialize on the preview screen. Bit by bit Alex made his fixes. From time to time we thought of small improvements: italicized intro paragraphs, pull quotes, a little dingbat for the end of each article. Some he implemented, some he didn't, but we were cautioned never to knock on his door. *Alex is busy.*

So were we. In theory, asking the editors to serve as their own production department was a labor-saving device. In practice, it made more labor for us. Meanwhile, Susan called me into her office in early October and offered me a second gig.

"I'd like you to take over the home page," she said.

It was a flattering offer. Just about every visitor to the site—and by now we were pulling in about 1.9 million each day—entered through the home page. It was Amazon's front window, its prime real estate. Susan had a deft touch with the page herself, though, and I asked why she was abandoning it.

"We've got a big initiative coming up," she said. "It's demanding my attention, and Jeff suggested I take some stuff off my plate. I thought you'd be perfect for the page."

"Thanks," I said, embarrassed by the compliment and annoyed by my vestigial tendency toward embarrassment. "Is the initiative a confidential thing, or can you tell me?"

"Music," Susan said, lowering her voice and glancing downward, almost bashfully, the way she always did when she let some corporate secret out of the bag. This was major news.

"Wow," I said.

"Exactly," she said. "We can talk about that some more later. But what about the home page? Interested?"

"Of course. I mean, very. The only reason I hesitate is because I've got these category page duties to split with Kerry. How much time do you spend on the page each day?"

"Oh, it won't take you more than an hour. Ninety minutes tops," she said.

Her lowball estimate would be the source of many laughs over the next few years. Still, I accepted. And at once, I began making the job harder for myself. For example, Susan had been somewhat flexible about varying the book at the top of the page: no surprise, given the number of projects she had to juggle. Feeling that there were simply too many titles crying out for our attention, I featured a new one every day. That meant I had to work more closely with the buyer, Marilyn Dahl, because we had to have a decent supply of these titles in stock. I also had to maintain an ever more precarious balance between art and commerce. The home page was a marvelous pulpit from which to preach the virtues of the books I loved. But if I went overboard with the pointy-headed stuff I would be cashiered in no time.

Then there was the copy itself. I had approximately forty-five words per title. For those I cared about, I tried to think of this as a peculiarly challenging short form, the haiku of book criticism:

I Confess!

Episcopal biographies don't customarily top the charts here at Amazon.com, but Gary Will's *Saint Augustine* has been a delightful summer sleeper. His brief life challenges many of our assumptions about this epoch-making figure (whose *Confessions* anticipated the current memoir boom by a good 1,500 years).

Sowing Circle

Taking a leaf from Crèvecoeur's classic, Victor Davis Hanson produces his own, impassioned letter from an American farmer in *The Land Was Everything*. The author has a Jeffersonian reverence for the family farm, which strikes him as both a heroic institution and (alas) endangered species.

Almost Grown

Tony Earley raises understatement to a fine art in *Jim the Boy*. His tale of a young Southerner's coming-of-age never wastes a syllable, yet this Depression-era bucolic is utterly convincing: a song of innocence and experience with a faint North Carolina accent.

The Main Events

In *Experience*, Martin Amis delivers the goods on his misanthropic father, his long-lost daughter, and his notoriously pricey dental work. This memoir by the bad boy of modern English letters is an acute, surprisingly warmhearted performance (and features the funniest index since Nabokov's *Pale Fire*).

Try writing a thousand of those babies, which is what I did during my tenure as home page editor. And try writing them about the unavoidable fraction of schlock titles that you're obliged to feature as part of your corrupt bargain with the gods of retail. I see that a certain peevish tone has snuck in here. No doubt it's the memory of all those diet books, the mendacious manuals on day trading, the New Age dross, the crappy potboilers, and the memoir by that guy who claimed to contact your deceased relatives in the Great Beyond. Manufacturing tongue-in-cheek endorsements for that kind of stuff may have been the toughest job I'll ever have as a writer. But the fact is that

I approached it with a perverse fascination. It was like running across hot coals: once you got started it wasn't so bad, as long as you didn't linger.

Why did I feature all that rubbish? Mostly because we were paid to do so—but I'll get to that later. For the moment, I need to emphasize what a remarkably free hand I was given. Here was a giant retail operation with a market capitalization in the billions, which was revolutionizing an entire industry. A more traditional management, with its eye fixed firmly on the bottom line, might have ruled the home page by diktat. If Jeff had wanted to put J.K. Rowling and Tom Clancy into permanent rotation—with an occasional breather for *Tuesdays with Morrie*—who would have argued with him?

Instead, I was invited to feature whatever I liked. And there was nothing more satisfying than nudging a noncommercial title into the limelight and selling between five and ten percent of the initial printing. Kerry, by the far the most well-read person I knew, pointed me toward plenty of these sleepers: Michael Downing's *Perfect Agreement*, or Leo Marks's *Between Silk and Cyanide: A Codemaker's War*, or Richard Beard's *X20: A Novel of (Not) Smoking*. Other crusades I came up with on my own. I was determined, for example, to make Richard Holme's *Coleridge: Darker Reflections* into a national craze on the order of the hula hoop. I made similar efforts on behalf of a sublime Randall Jarrell twofer: Mary Jarrell's memoir *Remembering Randall* plus a new compendium of his essays, *No Other Book*. These were hardly crass concessions to the marketplace. On the contrary, they telegraphed certain qualities that Jeff wanted to see associated with the site. They made us seem eclectic, funny, smart, and discriminating, minus any hint of snobbish superiority. And during the early days, when the company was first locking horns with the deep-pocketed proprietors of B&N, this cachet was a real (if unquantifiable) asset.

Every book, as the saying goes, has its own fate. But now I was in a position to change the commercial destiny of thirty titles each month. At times it was a wild sensation: I felt like the Wizard of Oz, manipulating the levers and switches of literary fame. In publishing, of course, a small number can make a big difference. Let's take *The Voyage of the Narwhal*. When Andrea Barrett's novel of Arctic exploration was published in September 1998, we stuck it in the top slot on the home page and left it there over the weekend. The book hadn't yet been reviewed: from a marketing point of view, it was still beneath the radar. Still, we sold nearly 500 copies by Monday morning. (To put things in perspective, the fastest-moving title in the history of Manhattan's venerable St. Mark's Bookshop—Noam Chomsky's *9-11*—sold 214 copies in *three weeks*.) And since the Barrett had a first printing in the neighborhood of 20,000, we had moved more than two percent in a single pop. In fact, the novel would have ascended immediately to the number-one spot on our bestseller list if the latest Princess Diana bio hadn't been so solidly ensconced there.

Like the Wizard of Oz, though, I was all too human. Which is to say that my capacity to work miracles was strictly hit-or-miss. For every breakout success there was a revenue-crunching flop, several of which seemed to defy the laws of statistics. The two Randall Jarrell titles above were a perfect example. I featured them on the heels of splashy coverage in the *New Yorker* and the *New York Times Book Review*, assuming that this media mini-blitz would compensate for the relatively esoteric subject matter. True, it was July 4th weekend, but at least a million people must have visited the site. Evidently most of them were more interested in cold beer and fireworks than America's wittiest critic of postwar poetry. We sold a grand total of twenty-seven books. Given the sheer mass of visitors tromping through the site, surely at least twice that many would have drunkenly ordered a copy by mistake, right? No such luck. Marilyn and I sat in her office and hung our heads. On her whiteboard, she had written: *We're selling books, not saving lives.* That wasn't much compensation. Luckily, though, we always had Oprah to keep our numbers up.

Needless to say, the slot at the very top of the page was the most fiercely coveted. Lower down, though, I chose which articles, interviews, and booklists to feature. And there, too, it was possible to send out minor ripples, both cultural and commercial.

In July 1998, for example, the University of Pennsylvania Press released the second installment of its ambitious Greek Drama Series. The latest salvo—new translations of Euripides, Sophocles, and Menander—got its share of positive press. But in the *New York Times Book Review,* Daniel Mendelsohn put almost the entire enterprise to the torch, reserving his heaviest fire for series editor and translator David Slavitt. To be honest, he had a point: Slavitt tended to take the rhetorical low road, making Clytemnestra sound like a Valley girl. Still, what really interested me was the perpetual tug-of-war between free translators and strict constructionists, so I interviewed Slavitt over the phone, wrote an article, and linked to it on the home page. Within a few days, this piece generated some coverage of its own. *Publishers Weekly* ran an account of the smackdown, "The Bookseller That Launched a Thousand Ships: Amazon.com Joins Battle Over Classics," in its online newsletter. While the reporter, too, kept his head down, not wanting to get hit with a stray polemical bullet, he did praise us for expanding the very definition of a bookstore. Did *Iphigenia at Aulis* immediately rocket up the charts? Of course not. But we picked up points for bookishness, braininess, and a passionate interest in the latest Grecian formula.

That fall, in other words, was a heady one for editorial. As most Internet veterans are now fond of pointing out, it was the Golden Age of Content, when even brick-and-mortar traditionalists got a little starry-eyed at the mere thought of a Uniform Resource Locator. But if we considered ourselves en route to a brave new world, where editors would eventually drive the moneychangers from the temple, we were about to get a corrective. Yes, the holiday season was nearly upon us again. The previous Christmas had featured a short stint of wrapping packages in the First Avenue warehouse. This year, however, the entire company was mobilized and marched down to a much bigger facility on Dawson Street, where the real mission of Amazon was all too apparent: *selling* stuff, and lots of it.

In November, actually, the company had doubled its warehouse capacity and geographical reach by opening a 200,000-square-foot distribution center in New Castle, Delaware. The governor joined Jeff in a ribbon-cutting ceremony, at which our fearless leader promised much faster shipments to the East Coast. From various conversations I overheard in the elevator—the source, let's face it, of almost all corporate intelligence—it sounded like the programmers were having some major headaches as they meshed the inventory systems for the two locations. Still, the move made it clear that we were hunkering down for a massive holiday rush. And no, we editors wouldn't be spending that period in our offices, buffing and burnishing that perfect adjective. We would be getting our hands dirty down on Dawson Street.

I doubt that any Amazonian of that era can forget those midnight drives down to the warehouse, through the largely dark stretches of a light-industrial neighborhood and past the battlements of the local Costco. You pulled into the parking lot south of the rail yards. You dodged the wired-looking smokers near the loading docks, flashed your badge at the entrance, and made your way into the 93,000-square-foot facility. The place was divided into two massive halves. On one side, the books came in from the publishers and distributors, and were placed onto what felt like several miles of shelving. On the other side, they were sorted into orders, wrapped, boxed, and shipped back out to customers.

Put that way, it sounds like a simple process: child's play. But here more than anywhere else you saw how the company was a kind of corporate centaur, a space-age torso mounted atop a Dickensian chassis (or was it the other way around?). The information, the facts and statistics and commands, were zapped back and forth at blinding speed. Yet the scut work still proceeded at a Victorian pace, still depended on sweat, shoe leather, and human industry.

My first night down there, with a cohort from the office, we were met by an orange-vested supervisor. He gave us a quick tutorial in the art of picking: clearly the least challenging task at hand. First a computer spat out a pick list for you, consisting of eighty or so items. These books were dispersed all over the warehouse in what was called a "random stow": the people receiving them from the loading docks had simply stuck them wherever there was an empty space on the shelves. Yet each slot had its own bar code. And each time a book was shelved, the worker aimed his handheld scanner at that tiny Op Art arrangement of thick and thin lines, thereby telling the computer exactly where this copy of *To Kill A Mockingbird* was located. That came in very handy when it was time to generate a pick list. The computer plotted out an efficient itinerary, taking you up one side of the warehouse and down the other.

At that point, having completed the list, you left the cart to be wheeled over to the other side of the facility. You also logged it out on the computer, which gave you a depressing (in my case) books-per-minute score. Then you got another pick list and tried to beat your personal best.

"Good luck, cookie," Kerry told me as she wheeled off her cart. She had bought a special, thick-soled pair of brogans for warehouse duty, and now set off down her first aisle with an efficient bounce.

She moved quickly. I did not. I pushed my empty cart into the first aisle and looked for the correct copy of Sebastian Junger's *The Perfect Storm*. The author had stopped by the office not long before, radiating virility: even a couple of lesbians had felt a prickling sensation at the back of their necks. I pondered this. What was his secret? He was around my height, wasn't he? Then I realized I was making a big mistake: pondering. That slowed you down, and would yield a disastrous books-per-minute score at the end.

I picked the Junger, and two copies of Charles Frazier's *Cold Mountain*, and one of Robert Caro's LBJ bios, and a paperback guide to tombstone rubbings. Somebody in America was clearly on a Civil War binge: the complete Shelby Foote appeared on my cart. Stooping or stretching, I retrieved titles by Agatha Christie, V.S. Naipaul, Alexandre Dumas, and Danielle Steel, plus a lone copy of *The Federalist Papers*. My list included a Curious George book, the one where he faints after sniffing the anesthetic. It also included a smattering of erotica, which I examined with as much gravity as possible while my fellow pickers sailed up and down the aisle. I thought of it as quality control.

"What do you have?" I asked Kerry when we emerged from adjacent aisles.

"Three by Penny F.," she said, indicating the Penelope Fitzgerald stash on her cart. "And everything Martin Amis ever wrote. What about you?"

I showed her the tombstone rubbing manual and the Curious George. I also pointed out a copy of David Siegel's *Creating Killer Web Sites: The Art of Third-Generation Site Design*. This was a telling item. In 1996 it had been our top-selling title, and a clear index of the company's geeky constituency. Now, just a year later, we were still selling plenty of copies, but Siegel had been booted from the top slot in favor of Jon Krakauer's *Into Thin Air*. He also tailed Junger,

Frazier, and Frank McCourt. Here was striking proof that the Internet was plunging directly into the mainstream.

"Didn't Seigel come to the office once?" I asked. "Consulting, I think."

"That was before my time."

"Look how many you've picked," I said admiringly.

"Damn straight," she said, and wheeled away.

I continued. There were dozens and dozens of pickers, and the aisles got congested. Some people moved out of the way, others didn't. To a degree, you could chalk this up to a cultural divide between the full-time warehouse staff and the editorial bourgeoisie. The latter group had soft hands and poor eyesight and tended to complain a lot. The former group was younger—which was really saying something at Amazon—and sported multiple body piercings and polychrome hair. They considered themselves the core of the business, the *extreme* employees. Yet they weren't being rewarded with stock options like their white-collar counterparts. It made for the occasional display of territorial rudeness.

"Excuse me," I would say, trying to nose around a tall guy with a tongue stud.

No response.

"Can I get by?"

Still no response. I gently steered my cart through a narrow space between the guy's butt and the opposite shelf, and he turned around.

"Didn't see you."

"No problem."

I threaded my way to the end of the aisle, then headed back. One wheel of my cart was squeaking. I saw Kerry again in the distance. I ran into Karin, then Tod, then the Bird, who was wearing some kind of fuzzy Peruvian shawl over her sweatshirt. It *was* cold. The cavernous space was a challenge to heat, even with all those warm bodies in it. And each time they cranked open the big doors along the cargo bays, frigid air rushed inside. You could feel the chill in the concrete slab right through your shoes.

Having finished my first cart, I got another pick list and began again. The hours passed. Up on the mezzanine there was a kiosk serving free espresso drinks, and I slunk up there a couple of times for a dose of caffeine. That was also where we adjourned at around 4:00 A.M. for a meal: spinach salad and a bagel, in my case. Then it was back to work.

Picking may have been tedious, but it was easy and unsupervised. *The reason I likes this sort of life is, 'cause I can sit down when I likes, and nobody can't order me about.* Like the middle-aged scavenger of the London sewers who confided this fringe benefit to Henry Mayhew in the 1850s, I was delighted to work at my own speed. Also, you got to handle the books. The thrill wore off pretty quickly when it came to our bestsellers, many of which you procured from enormous boxes down front. But zeroing in on a lone copy of Eric Newby's *Love and War in the Apennines* was a treat: it was the needle that justified the haystack.

And this was a major haystack. By the end of the holidays, inventory in the two warehouses—once considered strictly verboten according to the company's business plan—had edged up to 200,000 titles. More to the point, we were shipping thousands of books per hour. The managers fed pulse-pounding statistics to us over the public address system. And at regular intervals, the permanent warehouse staff gathered for a pep rally and call to arms: we would hear them cheering, whistling, and stomping their feet over by the mezzanine staircase.

After an eternity, my first shift ended. I drove home, where my wife was brewing coffee and telling Nat he couldn't wear his Lego shirt for the fourth day in a row.

"It *is* clean," he insisted.

"Want some coffee?" Iris asked. Having drunk what felt like a gallon of espresso from those thimble-sized paper cups at the warehouse, I said no. I lay down, imagined I was pushing a library cart up a steep mountain, and fell asleep.

The next few days were simply a variation on the above. Due to my home-page duties, I was obliged to spend at least a couple of hours at the office each morning. Still, I put in my shifts at the warehouse, where the pace kept accelerating: more incoming deliveries, more books to pick, more frantic announcements. It was a democratic sort of frenzy. You saw the top brass, like Risher or Mary Engstrom, wheeling around carts or wrapping packages. Even Jeff chipped in, which made it harder to whine about the company's Cultural Revolution.

We did anyway. Kerry, who was itching to get back to her desk, told Susan she simply wanted to do her job. "For now," Susan said, "this *is* your job." Indeed it was. And considering that people were sacrificing their holidays on the altar of customer satisfaction, morale was impressively high. Even the habitual cynics threw themselves into the breach, caught up in the idea of making e-commerce history. This quasi-religious devotion was almost impossible to explain to outsiders, and an easy target for satirical potshotting. The fact remains that almost all of the shock troops pressed into the holiday rush felt a personal stake in the success or failure of the company.

Rumor had it that things were very different in Delaware. The New Castle facility, staffed by seasonal workers who couldn't care less about one-click shopping, was supposedly plagued by massive pilfering and drunkenness. It sounded like that theme park of misdemeanors where the bad boys went in *Pinocchio*. By comparison, the Dawson Street warehouse felt like the diamond mine where the

Seven Dwarves had their day jobs—and considering the ascent of Amazon's stock price, the comparison was less far-fetched than it sounds.

Still, we were too busy at the warehouse to think of the stock. Mostly I kept picking. Once in a while I was shifted to receiving, and I also did a stint as a gift wrapper: in that capacity I came across a copy of *Mein Kampf*, just as I had during my first tour of the (tiny) First Avenue warehouse. I flipped through the sturdy hardcover and looked for the personalized gift card, which I was supposed to attach to the package. Perhaps, I thought, it contained a cautionary greeting, something about man's inhumanity to man. But no, when I glanced at the message, it simply read: *Merry Christmas!* I tried to picture the other items under the tree, then gave up. Better to move on—there was a *Clan of the Cave Bear* just crying out for a red ribbon.

The gift stations were on the other side of the warehouse, which had a more industrial aspect. You were surrounded by conveyor belts and enormous, noisy banks of machinery: shrink-wrappers, strapping-and-banding devices, a Rube-Goldberg-like apparatus that spat out those air-filled packing cushions. Forklifts prowled the margins of the room, adding their admonitory sirens to the general racket. People were wearing hard hats. It was all very . . . Old Economy. You could have been in Pittsburgh.

It was in virtual Pittsburgh, then, that I took on my most challenging assignment. An orange-vested supervisor in combat boots led me to my post, alongside one of the conveyor belts. Facing me was a tall shelf, which contained flattened boxes in several different sizes. As each shrink-wrapped pile of books came shooting toward me on the belt, I was to estimate the proper size box, remove one from the shelf, open it, and place it on top of the order.

"If there's an emergency," the supervisor told me, "you can stop the belt with this." He indicated an orange button mounted nearby. "Otherwise you just keep going, bro."

Off he went. Clearly the orange button was meant for a real crisis—if, say, your tongue got caught in the rollers—and couldn't be abused by a panicky prole like me. Just as clearly, we were in Lucy-and-Ethel territory here. My nervous system wasn't designed for this kind of activity. No doubt that's exactly what the rats in a laboratory maze tell each other, yet they keep to their appointed task, and so did I.

Here came a tall stack, then a short one. Within a few minutes I became more adept at choosing the appropriate box. Still, I felt jumpy. Whenever I slowed down I could look to the right, and see the people at the shrink-wrap station glaring at me. I could also look to the left: farther down the conveyor belt, another worker was waiting to assemble the boxes and books into coherent packages, and he too was glaring at me. I tried to speed up. I took a mental snapshot of the next three stacks and wondered if I could pull more than one box at a time. No, it wouldn't work.

By now I was getting nostalgic for picking. It seemed like a gentleman's pursuit: the detail, the solitude, the archaic creak of the carts. I recalled that one of my ancestors had made his living by selling fruit from a pushcart. It was in my veins, then.

The books wouldn't stop. I was at that point when Lucille Ball began eating the chocolates she couldn't wrap, or sticking them in her pockets, her apron, her hat. The stacks were piling up on the belt—they all seemed to have a copy of *Into Thin Air* on top—and my fellow Amazonians were looking daggers at me: broadswords, actually. I hadn't been hired for this! It wasn't fair!

Fortunately the break siren blew just about then. I skulked up to the mezzanine for another free cappuccino and wished I were elsewhere. I must have looked fairly depleted, because a product manager named Brian approached out of nowhere and pretended to knead my shoulders like a boxing coach.

Grabbing my coffee—which was burning hot through the cheap

paper cup—I stepped out onto the catwalk. Here you had an excellent, bird's-eye-view of the entire warehouse floor. The machinery was ramping up again, the books were beginning their circuitous progress, and for a moment the vast scale of the operation was tremendously heartening. It looked like a scene out of Piranesi, but a cheerful one. I felt proud to be part of it. Sticking my badge inside my shirt—a necessity on the floor, where the lanyard might get caught on any number of lethal objects—I skipped down the stairs and carefully skirted the box station. Then I ran over to the other side of the facility as if my life depended on it, and grabbed myself a pick list.

12

INSIDE EVERY ARTIST is the debris of a scientist. The same thing might be said of numerous other professions. Take psychoanalysts, with their wish to be seen as steely, squinting, white-coated clinicians. Freud laid his cards on the table in *The Future of an Illusion*, arguing that his own intuitive procedures were basically a form of New Math: "Psychoanalysis is in reality a method of research, an impartial instrument, rather like the infinitesimal calculus." Surely this makes the shrink the great scientist manqué of the last century. In our own, though, I'd suggest that this role has been taken over by an unlikely candidate: the youthful middle manager, with a freshly minted Masters in Business Administration.

Don't get me wrong: there's no doubt that at the most rarefied levels, economic theory turns into pure mathematics. (There's also no doubt that even the most brilliant theoreticians can step in the occasional pail of milk. Witness the fate of Long-Term Capital Management, whose spectacular collapse calls to mind the Keynesian chestnut: "The market can remain irrational longer than you can remain solvent.") But I'm not talking here about the great economists. I'm talking about the youthful graduates of America's best business schools—the people who take to the managerial barricades at every large corporation.

Toward the end of 1997 they began to arrive at Amazon in droves. Some were nice, some were nasty, in the usual proportions. Yet their presence allowed me to observe a strange and dispiriting phenomenon: the religion of statistics. Numbers were everything. A spreadsheet, with its panoramic procession of figures, had the sort of clout once reserved for the Delphic oracle. Now, Amazon was obviously the perfect place for this sort of bean-counting cult. We already had our Culture of Metrics, didn't we? What's more, we were able to track customer behavior like no other company in the history of retail. The data-mining opportunities were phenomenal, a kind of Sutter's Mill for marketing types, so the MBAs can hardly be blamed for their numerical fervor.

The problem, though, was that they often couldn't tear themselves away from the stuff. At times they seemed to dwell in a parallel universe where the nuts and bolts of the business—the actual number of books moving in and out of the warehouses—counted for less than the statistical shadows on the wall.

Let me give one small example. At one point Marilyn and I began meeting every week with a guy named Jeff Dixon, who was tracking the sales performance of the home page. Earlier on, the page had been seen as a calling card: a place to show off our smarts, selection, and sense of fun. But still another MBA had sounded the wake-up call via email, arguing that it was time to monetize the home page. (Take note, reader: that will be a key verb in the coming pages.) To get a handle on how various parts of the page were doing in terms of revenue, Jeff brought a detailed spreadsheet to each meeting. "Here's the prime rib," he would say, passing copies around the table.

Marilyn and I soon noticed that the numbers for the top slot were invariably wrong. They were wrong in our favor, I should say, inflated by a factor of two or three. It was pleasant to feel like such infallible rainmakers. However, as buyer for the home page, Marilyn consulted the warehouses on inventory every single day. When we rolled the dice on some worthy midlist novelist and came up with snake eyes, she knew the exact, pathetic number of copies we sold. Likewise, she could tell you precisely how many of the latest Oprah had blown off the shelves.

"Jeff, these are wrong," Marilyn kept saying.

"We pulled them straight from the database."

"But they're wrong," she insisted.

Being a decent, intelligent guy, he didn't ignore her. He furrowed his brow and we sat there in an agreeable stalemate. He couldn't admit that these particular figures might be bogus, because that would contaminate everything else on the spreadsheet with a trace of doubt. It was a question of faith. So we tiptoed around the discrepancy for several weeks. We concentrated on other parts of the page.

"How did you get this other number?" I would ask.

"I did a regression analysis."

"What's that?"

"Let's not even go there," he said, not unkindly.

Then one day Jeff showed up with a possible solution to the riddle. "My suspicion," he announced, "is that we're getting a count of shopping-basket adds rather than actual sales." In other words, if a mercurial bookworm placed the title in his shopping basket, then changed his mind and never made the purchase, it still got tabulated as a sale. This was a problem. True, it suggested an interesting psychological angle on our customers—they had difficulties with commitment—but as a useful metric it was a bust. What alarmed me, however, was the thought that strategic decisions were being made on the basis of similarly funky information.

In this case the clash between facts and figures was settled peacefully. Other times, the debate grew more heated. Needless to say, this sort of bad blood is a fixture of the publishing world, as it is in any profession where art and commerce regard each other warily across a demilitarized zone. But the quarrel took on a peculiar tone at Amazon, which wasn't a publication in any conventional sense of the word. For quite a while, Jeff's initial advocacy on behalf of editorial still held sway. The incoming MBAs were urged to treat the department as a vital cog in the machine, or at least pay lip service to the idea.

But as the early, all-forgiving phase of the Internet boom began to fade, the balance of power shifted. Amazon now felt enormous pressure to turn a profit. The newer offerings—toys, tools, consumer electronics, kitchen supplies—were still a financial drain. That left books to pick up the slack, thereby giving the business people the whip hand they normally would have possessed from the very start. The scientists were now free to follow their instincts.

Perhaps the first sign that the wind had shifted was the mad profusion of jargon. Sure, you had always heard the odd bit of economic Esperanto: the price of an item was its *price point*, and the tasks you needed to accomplish were *deliverables*. The copy we editors so diligently produced was *verbage*, a corruption of the already insulting *verbiage*. The more common *burn rate* indicated the wads of cash we were spending.

These phrases at least had the advantage of simplicity. But now entire sentences had to be translated back into English. *Pulling on revenue levers* meant making more money. If we *leveraged our verbage* correctly, the division would soon reach an *inflection point* (translation: we would make more money). The main thing in any case was to *monetize those eyeballs*. Yes, that last operation had a surrealistic ring to it—it suggested a visit to Salvador Dali's optician—but it actually referred to making the most of our enormous customer base.

At times the jargon did seem to be edging toward the metaphysical margins. At meetings, even Nick would plead ignorance on one issue or another by insisting he had *no visibility into that*. Who was seeing, and who was being seen? If a quarterly revenue number falls in a forest, does anyone hear it?

By 1999, in fact, monetizing those eyeballs had become a linchpin of Amazon's corporate philosophy. Again, it was a matter of statistics. On June 7 of that year, the customer base hit the ten million mark—a number, as the company's press release pointed out, equivalent to the population of Greece. A crowd that big was itself a commodity. All you needed were buyers, and they turned out to be thick on the ground.

Who were they? At this point the company had not only launched multiple businesses of its own, but partnered with Drugstore.com (drugs), Living.com (furniture), Pets.com (pet supplies), Wineshopper.com (wine), HomeGrocer.com (groceries), Sothebys.com (auctions), and Kozmo.com (home delivery by a courier in tight bicycle pants). In most cases, Amazon bought an equity stake in these partners. We would share, it was hoped, in their prosperity. But for the moment, we would charge them humongous fees for placement on our site. In a sense, we were no longer in the business of selling books, CDs, videos, *objects:* we were peddling access to a virtual nation of consumers, our own proprietary Greeks, who would presumably go where we pointed them. So much for disintermediation. Amazon would be the great middleman of the Internet, the broker of a million wants and needs, and the richest traffic cop in human history.

Rick made this clear at an editorial meeting that summer. He had become shyer, more hermetic, as the years went by. His comments tended to be brief, and usually concluded with a cryptic, Yoda-like directive. In this case he was more frank.

"Remember how I used to talk about creating the best possible buying environment for the customer?" he said. "Giving them the information they needed to make an intelligent decision?"

There were nods all around the room. This had been Rick's own spin on the cross-pollination of editorial and marketing, often delivered with a certain twinkle in his eye. *Here is your survival tactic*, he seemed to be saying.

"Well, that's over." He chuckled, a difficult sound to interpret. "That is way over." Shuffling his sneakered feet like a kid, he went on to explain that we were now renting premium space at the mall, and making a killing at it. That was the company's mission. He sounded apologetic. Were there any questions?

There were none. We were all half-expecting to find pink slips in our mailboxes later that afternoon. I wondered how the whole business sat with Jeff. Being the Harry Helmsley of e-commerce didn't sound quite as glamorous as being Alexander the Great. Then Nick brought on the second speaker, a highly trained bully from the consumer electronics division.

"If a customer comes to the site looking for a book, that's great," he told us. "But we also want you to sell them a DVD player."

Kerry, always the feistiest member of the department, spoke up: "What if the customer doesn't want a DVD player? Aren't we doing him a disservice by shoving that in his face?"

"If you want to be a good corporate citizen," he replied, "you'll push the DVD player."

The whiff of corporate patriotism was bad enough. But what really depressed me was this notion of the customer as a passive creature, a cow ready to be marched into the milking stall. It came straight out of a statistical conception of human behavior, a direct-mail mentality. It showed a real contempt for the people who were keeping our business afloat. I don't mean to idealize the customers, who were buying their share of *The Protocols of the Elders of Zion* and would have happily snapped up all the snuff films we could sell, if we sold them. Still, I thought we should grant them a least a modicum of free will, and treat them accordingly. They would be able to tell the difference. The invisible hand of the marketplace was fine by me, after all, unless it grabbed you by the scruff of the neck and force-fed you a Panasonic DVD-RV31 with Advanced Surround, One-Touch Cinema Memory, and Dialogue Enhancer. The latter might have come in handy during these meetings, but was, alas, nowhere in evidence.

I feel somewhat vindicated by the fact that the initiative was a flop. Monetizing the eyeballs just didn't pay. For one thing, most of our partners never had enough traffic steered their way, certainly not enough to justify the tolls we were charging them. Meanwhile, the bubble began deflating, and the entire Internet frenzy collapsed. Our partners stopped buying fabulously expensive commercial spots on the Super Bowl and filed for bankruptcy, one after another. The Pets.com sock puppet became a national figure of fun. We went back to selling stuff, which had always been our strength, and looked for a new set of revenue levers.

Yet the scientific aspirations never faded. Amazon itself provided a hilarious piece of evidence in early 2000, just after the NASDAQ peaked and the market began its downhill slide. The economic climate was already changing, and clearly the company wanted to establish that we were no Internet goofballs but relentless technicians of retail. To get the job done, they allowed Saul Hansell of the *New York Times* to function as a fly on the wall for a couple of days.

On May 20 he published what the MBAs would have called his *learnings*. And the very first scene, documenting a high-level meeting in a conference room, would have made Freud feel like a wimpy humanist. Russell Allgor, we are told, is "drawing graphs on a whiteboard. Dr. Allgor earned his Ph.D. at the Massachusetts Institute of Technology developing quantitative methods for making chemical plants more productive. Last summer, he moved from Bayer Chemical to Amazon.com and has built an 800,000-equation computer model of the company's sprawling operation." Get out your pocket protectors! It's all there: the whiteboard, the degree, the German laboratory, the mammoth computer program.

But let's take another look at that program. Glenn Fleishmann, a database guy and inveterate blogger with whom I worked briefly at the company, has pointed out an element of exaggeration here: the program has 800,000 equations only in the sense that it applies to that number of stocked items. If it were regulating the inventory of your medicine cabinet, it might dwindle to a pathetic twenty-three equations—twenty-four, if you threw in your toothbrush. But clearly Saul Hansell was supposed to think he was observing the Manhattan Project, so the jaw-dropping numbers were wheeled out.

More alarming, though, were Allgor's conclusions. Having subjected the company's inventory system to a full-body frisk, he advised that we stock a larger quantity of bestsellers and get rid of as many other titles as possible. We would still sell these books, of course. But instead of stockpiling them in the warehouse, we would obtain them from a distributor only when they were actually ordered by a customer. Sounds logical, doesn't it? The problem is that we would no longer be able to ship those titles—which might number in the hundreds of thousands—within twenty-four hours. Customers would have to wait extra days, or weeks, for their purchases to show up. An Internet shopper, you might argue, has already given up on the idea of instant gratification. Still, if we made them twiddle their thumbs for weeks at a time, we were going to lose business. This was a fact of human nature. Only a scientist could ignore it: and he did.

To her credit, Lyn Blake, the High Commissar of Vendor Compliance, questioned the whole premise. Asked for her "buyoff," she refused, and injected a little common sense into the discussion: "I worry about the customer's perspective if we suddenly have a lot of items that are not available for quick delivery." Bravo!

At this point the reporter discreetly drew the curtain on the rest of the meeting. Exactly who carried the day is anybody's guess: the battle over inventory had already gone on for years, with dramatic swings in both directions. At one point Jeff dreamed up an initiative called the Alexandria Project—named after the legendary Egyptian library—which would call for us to stock millions of titles in a multitude of languages. It was a beautiful vision, I must say. Yet excess inventory is death to a retailer: it represents liquid cash locked up in the form of goods, and who knows how long before those dollars will be liberated? The project was junked. Perhaps the name was all too appropriate, since the Great Library of Alexandria was torched in 47 B.C., quite possibly by Julius Caesar. According to some sources, nearly 400,000 volumes on papyrus and vellum went up in smoke. Here was a burn rate that even Amazon could envy.

But let's return for a moment to Hansell's article in the *Times*. The reporter eavesdropped on a number of additional meetings, all of them meant to demonstrate an atmosphere of fierce efficiency. Several really did show the company wrestling with important issues: returns, selection, the intricacies of site design. Yet the reporter might have been forgiven for wondering just how many of these little conclaves were truly necessary.

Which brings us to my favorite segment: the 10 A.M. on Thursday. One of the main topics of discussion is meeting rationalization—which is to say, the fact that there are too many meetings. In a scene that could have been scripted by Ionesco, Lyn Blake hands out an "elaborate grid of twenty-six regular meetings and who attends them." Everybody sits around the table, deep in thought, trying to come up with a solution. Nothing comes to mind. The situation looks grim. Then a deus ex machina appears. David Risher, not normally in attendance, pops inside and cuts the Gordian knot: "You should draw a line through one-third of those meetings." They do. Then, to wrap up the meeting, which may well have been penciled out of existence only a minute before, each participant volunteers his or her contribution to "the march to profitability." Meeting adjourned.

Did I say Ionesco? I meant Swift, or Beckett, or Gogol, or even *Dilbert*. Yet I doubt that any author could have whipped up the bureaucratic comedy above, and then persuaded the actors to play it absolutely straight, without a single wink at the audience. Perhaps some of the credit goes to the reporter himself. But I think the delicious absurdity on display—invisible, apparently, to the pokerfaced participants—shows that same, statistical detachment from reality. Here I ask my former colleagues for forgiveness. Some of my best friends are MBAs: really. And if I had been handed the reins of the business myself, it would have crashed and burned in late 1996. Still, the numbers, the figures, the elaborate grids and infinitesimal calculus. . . . Well, it's no accident they call economics the dismal science. Economists bitch about the first half of the epithet. Based on what I saw, I'd have to wonder about the second.

13

THE EARLY WEEKS OF 1998, following my holiday penance in the warehouse, were a little rugged on the home front. Returning from a vacation on the other side of the Cascades, we skidded into another car in a blizzard. Luckily our Honda still ran, even with a broken headlight and the hood peeled back. We limped into the nearest town—which happened to be Leavenworth, that unironic hotbed of *gemütlichkeit*—and were informed that the storm had closed all the passes. We were stuck. For the second time in just a few months, I found myself cruising those meticulously Teutonic streets, with their timbered facades and Gothic-style signage. Motel after motel was booked solid. Nat began to whine a little, not out of any great distress but simply to warm up the instrument. At last we stumbled onto a cancellation, at a place where they signaled breakfast by blowing one of those immense wooden alpenhorns.

The next afternoon, with the encouragement of an unflappable mechanic at the filling station, we headed toward Stevens Pass. The snow had stopped, but the road was covered with a thin sheet of ice: cars were spinning out in both lanes, fetching up on the shoulder, then creeping back out onto the highway. Nat dozed in back while we climbed the pass, grinding our teeth the entire time. Passing the summit was scant comfort, since a downhill wreck could be even worse than an uphill one. We got home and called the insurance company. Our marriage, too, was now on thin ice, although we weren't yet aware of it.

Still shaken, I drove a loaner to work for the next week. And at the office, as always, there was plenty to distract me. Amazon had rung in the new year as the nation's third-largest bookseller: by the end of the holidays, we were moving about 57,000 titles every single day. What's more, we had escaped the dread curse of seasonality. Most retailers see their sales skyrocket during the last three months of the year—and then, as America's exhausted shoppers go back into hibernation, the numbers plummet. At Amazon, they just kept ascending: after raking in $66 million in the last quarter of 1997, we made more than $87 million in the first quarter of 1998. This wasn't simply a token of impressive growth. No, it suggested that the economic laws of gravity had been suspended, or put in mothballs. Certainly it validated all the New Paradigm nuttiness floating around the Web and, increasingly, the mainstream media.

Thus emboldened, Jeff cranked up the expansionist machinery. To accomplish even half of what he had in mind, we were going to need a lot of folding money. In April the company sold $326 million in bonds, which would mature in 2008. Then, stuffing his pockets with cash, Jeff went on a shopping spree. Soon he announced a trio of acquisitions: Bookpages (an online bookseller in the United Kingdom), ABC Telebuch (ditto for Germany), and the Internet Movie Database.

The latter, a treasure trove of cinematic trivia, sold nothing. It was a pure product of the Internet, a watering hole for film freaks, and the purchase had no immediate impact—although it did suggest that a certain online retailer would eventually start peddling videos. The other two purchases, however, set the stage for Amazon's invasion of Europe.

No doubt there had been a long conversation about whether the company should build its own transatlantic outposts from scratch or snap up previously existing sites. The classic move would have been to do it ourselves. Still, ABC Telebuch was already the premier on-line bookseller in Germany, and Bookpages was near the top of the heap in Britain, so why not piggyback on their success? In one fell swoop the company extended its sphere of influence to Regensberg (which looked less authentic, somehow, than Leavenworth) and to Slough, an English backwater that won a cherished spot in the corporate mythology: even more than the Seattle suburbs, it was *the* place where you didn't want to live.

Obviously it was going to take many months of frantic effort to retrofit these European sites. In the meantime, we celebrated our new siblings at the latest All Hands Meeting. These quarterly powwows kept requiring bigger and bigger venues. For a while we used the auditorium at the Seattle Art Museum. Then we moved to a concert hall up the street, then to a sprawling movie theater. If subsequent purges hadn't slenderized the staff the way they did, Jeff might now be convening these rallies in a baseball stadium.

In any case, they usually included some mind-blowing and self-congratulatory statistics (and why not?), followed by speeches, departmental presentations, and a freewheeling session with the man himself. First Jeff would fill us in on breaking news. This was the Fireside Chat, conducted before a small wooden backdrop of a blazing hearth. Then he followed up with a Q-and-A, interrupted always by highly amplified bursts of Bezonian laughter: an acoustic phenomenon to reckon with. Finally there was a reiteration of the company's creed. "It's always Day One at Amazon.com," Jeff would remind us.

On this occasion, though, we were treated to a peculiar piece of theater. Alan Caplan, the head counsel, and Carl Gish, who was then managing the books division, emerged from the wings. One was dressed in a British beefeater costume, complete with a towering, fuzzy headpiece. The other wore a Tyrolean outfit: lederhosen, embroidered blouse, short pants, and a peaked hat with, I believe, a feather in it. The duo stepped to the edge of the stage, where Alan strapped on a guitar. Then they began to sing, addressing the music to the first row, where the top brass from Bookpages and ABC Telebuch were sitting:

> *Jeff bought you, babe!*
> *Jeff bought you, babe!*
> *Jeff bought you, babe!*

What was going through the mind of Telebuch proprietor Michael J.G. Gleissner is anybody's guess: probably just *Gott im Himmel!* Neither he nor Simon Murdoch of the British site appeared to be twitching a muscle. Meanwhile, our Anglo-Saxon version of Sonny and Cher went through the entire song, including some verses that I've tragically forgotten. The audience responded with wild applause. I couldn't get myself to clap. This failure made me feel old— as if I were the chaperone at a prom, standing by the punch bowl and emitting a force field of middle-aged ennui—but I couldn't help it.

At once we sent departmental emissaries to both Slough and Regensberg. Later on they reciprocated: Rachel Holmes, the editorial director of the British site, flew to Seattle on several occasions, always sporting a sniffle and a shiny pair of leather pants. I also met with one or two delegations of German staff, who were curious to hear how we ran the home page. What they thought of my autocratic methods I don't know, but they took careful notes.

Meanwhile the company was mobilizing itself for the music launch. Josh, who had previously brokered the book division's romance with BISAC, was now applying his talents to this new arena.

Bit by bit the musical universe was chopped and channeled into bite-size categories. The system actually made more sense in this case, given the ancient tendency of musicians to travel in schools. At the same time, Susan hired a flock of editors, most of them with solid journalistic résumés.

Since I had written about jazz and pop for *Salon*, *The Oregonian*, and various other places, Susan approached me as well: would I be interested in a higher-level managerial slot on the music side? I gave it some careful thought and declined. For one thing, I felt a deeper attachment to books. But I was also reluctant to take on the day-to-day slog of supervising other employees: I preferred to administer my own little kingdom, meaning the home page, and participate in the Dual Monarchy of the literature area. Of course, Kerry was now running the show—I was more of a second-in-command, banging out reviews and articles and mopping up whatever editorial spills were deemed too messy for Kerry to bother with. But when it came right down to it, I had no corporate ambitions. Artistic ones, yes—even in the context of Amazon, a context that most of us were still puzzling out at the time. Aside from that I simply wanted to keep my head down, so I told Susan I wasn't interested.

Tod, however, had finally found his escape hatch from publisher relations. Mary Engstrom cut him loose and he was put in charge of alternative/indie rock and movie soundtracks. There he would serve out the rest of his tenure having, from what I could see, nonstop fun. He shared an office with Steve Duda, former editor of a defunct Seattle music rag called the *Rocket*. Duda was a burly, rectangular, trout-fishing fanatic, whose all-inclusive beard made it hard to tell if he was smiling or frowning. Supposedly he ran roughshod over his direct reports. That didn't prevent him and Tod from developing a domestic, almost conjugal rapport, although they argued over who was the husband and who was the wife. At both ends of the small room they set up large speakers. In this way they could be sure that the soundtrack of the moment—Miles Davis remixes, Matchbox Twenty, the Louvin Brothers singing "My Heart Was Trampled On The Street"—would directly impact their eardrums without any atmospheric cushioning. If that wasn't fun, I don't know what was.

For those in the books division, watching the music staff get up to speed was an exercise in nostalgia. There was the same feeling of elation mingled with panic: the wheel had to be reinvented several times per day.

Yet there were some real differences, too. Their staff was smaller, the general consensus being that you didn't need a full-time editor for the fringe (i.e., less lucrative) categories. Their margins were even tighter than ours, which was going to put extra pressure on them as they groped for the correct revenue levers. Even worse, they had competition to deal with. Both CDNow and N2K had created popular sites, with many of the same bells and whistles we were featuring: sound samples, customer reviews, email alerts, and so forth. What if Amazon were already too identified as a bookseller? Brands are like quick-drying cement, Jeff was always telling us, and perhaps ours was already growing less malleable.

About 200,000 music titles were rolled online a couple of months before launch. In fact it had always been possible to buy a limited number of CDs through Amazon: any item that was ever assigned an ISBN, including not only the odd compact disc but chewing gum, 9-volt batteries, and even a tub of vacuum-packed margarine, was likely to surface in our database. Now, however, those freakish exceptions were banished from the catalogue and replaced with a serious inventory. Classical music, with its million-and-one taxonomic headaches, would launch a few months later. But everything else was good to go. If only there were some opportunity for a dry run, just to see how the system would handle a surge in business!

On May 15, as if to oblige us, Frank Sinatra breathed his last. The Chairman of the Board had been ailing for some time: when I saw him on his final tour, in 1994, he was already reading every lyric from a cheat sheet and half-dozing during instrumental passages. Even his patter *(I almost choked on a shot glass back there!)* had a distracted air. Yet his death came as a shock. It really did signal the end of an era, Sinatra being the ultimate analog artifact, a voice that seemed too intimate, too alive, too *granular,* for digital reproduction. With these thoughts in mind, I rushed to a meeting in Susan's office, so we could discuss our two-pronged assault on the late singer's audience.

The music site had the most to gain, of course. Still, Sinatra had inspired a raft of books, from Kitty Kelly's mudslinging bio to Will Friedwald's more recent study of his "intensified vocal gestures." How could we fail to sell some of the key texts to a generation newly infatuated with martinis, cigars, and Rat Pack–style hedonism?

Keith Moerer, a former editor at *Rolling Stone* who now ran the music side, had already come and gone by the time I showed up. Susan seemed excited. In fact she looked slightly pink, as if the potential synergy were speeding up her circulation. Keith had somebody writing a Sinatra tribute, she told me. I needed to knock out a blurb for the home page pronto, which would direct visitors to both the nascent music site and a list of related books.

"As soon as that's done," she said, "we can do a second build."

Despite the vaunted flexibility of the Web, it was a major undertaking to add an update, even a small one, to Amazon's site. You couldn't simply pull out a single page, tinker with the HTML, and slip it back online. No, the entire site needed to be rebuilt.

"Do we have the inventory in music?" I asked.

"They're scrambling to get as much as they can. So is everybody else."

"I'll email you the blurb in a few minutes."

I ran back to my office and thought about the concert I'd seen, looking for inspiration. Sinatra no longer had the pipes, the projection, yet his phrasing remained intact and utterly distinctive. When he sang the line about telegraph cables in "Moonlight in Vermont," he made a small, horizontal hand gesture. Also, he kept roiling the Oedipal waters by teasing his son, who was conducting the orchestra: but that wouldn't do for the blurb. I fiddled around with some sentences. Here was the absurdity of my job in a nutshell. Millions of people would see whatever I wrote, which upped the ante, but none of them would remember it, which lowered the ante. I typed out my forty-three-word elegy and sent it to Susan, who seemed satisfied.

Well, we sold a few books. But the music site moved a ton of merchandise: hundreds, then thousands of CDs, mostly *Songs for Swingin' Lovers* and the horrible *Duets* and the *Songs For Young Lovers/Swing Easy* twofer. The stress test had been passed with flying colors.

On June 11, with several Sinatra releases still on our bestseller list, we launched the music store. As it turned out, we needn't have worried about the competition. Amazon became the biggest online music retailer within a couple of weeks, and soon after, N2K and CDNow began to circle the wagons. By the end of October the two former rivals had merged. With a combined market share of 45 percent, they hoped to prevail over the playground bully—that would be, uh, us—or at least hold their own. They didn't. (In fact, the fate of the joint company encapsulates the entire boom-and-bust cycle. In 2000, Bertelsmann honcho Thomas Middlehof paid $117 million for the faltering operation. Two years later, with Middlehof defenestrated and his grand e-commerce strategy in ruins, Amazon took over the day-to-day operations of CDNow. Jeff's got you, babe!)

Wasn't it time for a break? Not at all. It was still early in the year— Day One, you might say—and the company's shopping spree was far from over. On August 4, Jeff announced two more purchases: PlanetAll and Junglee. We forked over $280 million in stock for these lemons, although nobody thought about them that way at the time. Instead they seemed to fit Jeff's visionary plans to perfection, to the extent that visionaries actually *make* plans.

PlanetAll was essentially an online Rolodex and datebook, which you could access from any computer. Handheld PDAs were still rare and expensive, and would remain so for another six months. In that sense, the idea of storing all your personal data on a website wasn't as clunky as it sounded. What was in it for Amazon? Well, suppose you noted a half-dozen important birthdays in your PlanetAll account. We could then email you a week in advance of each date, reminding you of the impending occasion and suggesting gift ideas. There may have been some other functions, too, but the basic concept was to move your calendar, datebook, financial records, stray jottings— your paper trail, in short—to the Internet. At the very least you could save a tree.

The company, which had been airlifted from its Cambridge head-quarters to Seattle, never really took off. It died a quiet death within a couple of years. Junglee, meanwhile, had a more complicated trajectory. Jeff had bought the firm in order to get his hands on a single product: a price-comparison engine, which could comb through the entire Web and tell you exactly what different stores were charging for a specific item. Nowadays there are several such shopping bots— i.e., discount-sniffing robots—available. Back then, however, it was a real novelty. It also sounded risky: what kind of retailer told his customers where they could get the same merchandise for less money? To skeptics, this wasn't merely counterintuitive, but a form of fiscal suicide. To Jeff, it was a way to goose customer ecstasy—and an op-portunity, no doubt, to monetize some more eyeballs.

Under the name Shop The Web, the bot launched a few months later. And surprisingly, customers greeted it with a big yawn. Few people seemed interested in ransacking the known universe in order to save two dollars on a *Toy Story* action figure. And in this particular case, STW wouldn't be much help anyway, since it drew a blank when you typed in most toys. Oh, and it had a problem with books, too.

With just a dribble of traffic, the feature drifted farther and farther down the page. The link grew smaller and smaller. Shortly before it expired, you would have needed an additional search engine simply to find it. Junglee founder Rakesh Mathur left within a year, to work on yet another affinity engine called Purple Yogi, and the plug was pulled on STW.

Was this a flop? Perhaps. But we had gotten seventy software engineers out of the bargain. At that time programmers were in such short supply that the company was reduced to working the celebrity angle: according to rumor, we were going to print Amazon.com Developer *trading cards*. (Who would pass up a rare, signed Shel Kaphan, with his height, weight, and career stats on the back?) You could argue, anyway, that Jeff made up in human capital what he lost in cold cash. If that sounds like a chattel arrangement, remember something else: the engineers all got rich.

Yes, the stock had continued its vertiginous climb. Every time we launched a new store, the company's future seemed more and more a matter of manifest destiny. The share price hit one nosebleed number after another. There were always doubters, of course, who considered the whole business an enormous shell game: as Floyd Norris put it in the *New York Times* just a few days after the IPO, "exuberance, whether rational or not, is back." By 1998, however, such skeptics were in the distinct minority. It was difficult—impossible, almost— to argue with success on this scale, and even in the midst of the boom, Amazon made most other Internet stocks look positively moribund.

On June 2, for example, there was a two-for-one split, which doubled every shareholder's allotment of stock and halved the price. The shares, which had been hovering around the $85.00 mark, closed at a sensible $43.69. Fine: we were even. Within days, however, the price began shooting back up toward the pre-split stratosphere. By June 23, the stock hit $92.69, meaning we had more than doubled our money within less than three weeks. By July 6, we were looking at $139.50 per share. At that point the price subsided for a while as the summer doldrums set in. Perhaps, we thought, the irresistible force of e-commerce had finally hit an immovable object: fiscal realism.

But no, once the fall came, the shares pinged upward again. On October 15, the day both European sites opened their doors for business, the stock closed at $97.06. On November 17, when the video store launched, it hit $148.50, and just a week later, $214.50. On December 15, Henry Blodget emerged from the woodwork and donned the mantle of Pied Piper: where he pointed, the price obediently followed, and in less than two weeks it reached a new high of $351.94. Two weeks after that, having gone through a three-to-one split, it surpassed his original target of $400 and kept on going.

These numbers, which I've quoted with damp palms and a sad, palpitating heart, make no sense. Sure, Amazon was a bold experiment and the bellwether of a technological revolution. But there was no way to justify these dizzying spikes, no way to argue that what we were doing—selling stuff—was suddenly twice as valuable as it had been a month before. Blodget, of course, wasn't in the justifying business. A frustrated fiction writer in his earlier life, he may have leaned too heavily on his imagination, and figured the stock as one more character he could put through its paces. Was it his fault that reality followed suit? He was that rarest sort of author, whose vivid and continuous dreams (to cite John Gardner's famous formula) actually came true. And for a while, so did everybody else's.

What I'm saying is that by now, many of my colleagues at Amazon had begun to vest. And once they were able to exercise their options, they cashed out. If you shared an office with another person, as most of us did, it was considered good form to leave the room and let your companion make that lucrative phone call in private. Certain intimacies would be exchanged between stockholder and broker, certain whispered commands would be issued, and by the time you returned, there was a static charge of lucre in the air.

My little transactions left me in a state resembling postcoital melancholy. Kerry took a more positive, even ebullient attitude. After her first sale, she found a greatest hits collection by Hall and Oates on the site, and clicked on the appropriate sample. Out came the song from her crappy speakers, and she sang along with unmistakable glee:

> *You're a rich girl*
> *And you've gone too far*
> *'Cause you know it don't matter anyway*
> *You can rely on the old man's money*
> *You can rely on the old man's money*

She sang it again, adding a little snap-and-clap percussion, then a third and fourth time. Who cared if we were dwelling on a nonsense planet? The money was real. We walked down to the Pike Street Market and got lunch from a Mexican place, carrying our cardboard containers like precious objects, and Kerry kept humming that song. It was a sunny day in Seattle: a relative rarity. We ran into the Bird, who had a look of stunned satisfaction on her face and had clearly just unloaded some stock of her own. Nobody got explicit about numbers, as per custom. Yet we enjoyed a few minutes of fellow feeling, having joined a secret society of the arbitrarily rich.

On the stairs leading down to the water we sat and ate. The Bird, who had already put away some kind of foccaccia thing and was now nursing a bright red soft drink, told us her car was a shitbox and she was going to replace it.

"I test drove a Saturn just for the hell of it," she said, although all three of us knew she wasn't going to buy a plastic car at this point. "But now I'm thinking of a Volvo, maybe a Lexus." This last elicited a giggle, as though it were a dirty word.

Kerry, who didn't drive, studied the Olympics. The water looked blue and bottomless in the distance.

"I bought a Honda last year," I said. "Runs like a charm."

"You should see the cup holders in the Lexus. I know that's silly."

We were having a coded conversation, the Bird and I, about money, materialism, ethics. My car, a silver sedan so common as to seem invisible, represented real life. Hers was the very badge of fantasy, with its smoked-glass windows and those cup holders that prevented you from spilling a drop of coffee when you hit a speed bump. We were jousting, but in a gentle, distracted manner. She was one of my bosses, after all. And her vehicle did offer a much smoother ride than mine. Also, leather seats.

Gradually the parking lot filled up with dream machines like the Bird's. My colleagues, some of them, bought real estate: designs for extra bedrooms, new kitchens, and window treatments kept materializing in the fax. Jonathan was supposedly looking at a seven-bedroom Tudor mansion. "Why does he want such a big place?" I asked Tod. "He'll live in one room until it gets too dirty," was the reply, "then he'll move into the next one." But Tod had made his own purchase—a nice blue bungalow in a transitional neighborhood, which looked even more imposing next to the adjacent crack house—so it was hard for him to point the finger.

It was hard for *anybody* to point the finger. We were all in the thick of it. That had a normalizing effect, and in any case, we tended to honor Seattle's tradition of shy and retiring plutocrats. "The lesson of these days," confided Emerson to his journal in 1854, "is the vulgarity of wealth." But I imagine he would have been proud of our discretion. I certainly was, with my virtuous Honda, my fraying clothes, my atavistic anxiety over the electric bill. I still considered myself a working man, a guy who reviewed books for a living.

In this atmosphere of mad abundance and expansion, only one thing was shrinking: the number of words we were allowed to put in a book review. It astonished me then, and astonishes me now, that anybody was keeping tabs on all those nouns, predicates, and dependent clauses. Why did they care? Didn't the Web offer us infinite space, with none of the archaic restraints you had in the world of print?

Yes and no. You still had to store all that, you know, verbage, and eventually this would put a strain on the database. But we weren't truly dealing with a technical problem here. Instead, the upper echelons were just beginning to recognize that content wasn't all it was cracked up to be. It was expensive and old-fashioned. It required methodical labor, which didn't always fit the bill when you were (as the saying went) working on Internet time. Even worse, it didn't make a direct contribution to the bottom line. Indirect, perhaps—but in the Culture of Metrics, that was worth less than zero.

Luckily there was still a prevailing breeze in the opposite direction. Jeff himself expressed great pride in our work, and most managers took their cues from him. We were protected. What's more, the department had acquired a strange, specialized clout in the world of letters. A few months before, both Kerry and I had gotten calls from Robert Boynton at the *New Yorker:* he was interested in writing a piece on Amazon's editorial process. We passed him on to Rick, who ultimately spiked the idea. Still, the proposal was enormously flattering. Since when did a retailer's editorial staff end up in the *New Yorker?* (Since when did a retailer *have* an editorial staff?)

No, the golden age wasn't over. It was still a fine thing to be an editor at Amazon. In retrospect, though, I can see this War of the Words as an early warning, a thin edge of the wedge.

The offenders, it seemed, were me, Kerry, and Alix Wilber, a novelist and critic who had recently joined the literature team. Susan invited us to a meeting the following week. Not wanting to blindside us, she explained the issue at hand and suggested we print out a few short reviews as a defensive maneuver.

We did. I had a neat sheaf of them when we stepped into the office, where Susan, Rick, Katherine, and the Bird were in attendance. I also had a second exhibit for the defense: a letter from Oliver Gilliland, a widely respected sales rep at W.W. Norton, who attested to the selling power of Kerry's Andrea Barrett review—all 755 words of it.

Our superiors sat on one side of the table, we sat on the other. It felt like a tribunal, which seemed to be causing Susan some embarrassment.

"David is concerned," she began.

"Meaning David Risher?" Alix said.

"Right. He's been reading some of the reviews you guys have written. His concern is that they're too long."

"Too long for what?" Kerry said.

"Well, first of all, they push all the other content to the bottom of the screen. It's expensive to license that stuff from Kirkus and Booklist. If nobody sees it, we're wasting our money."

I handed over the short reviews and the letter from Norton. These were quickly examined and set aside.

"The good news is we're working on a truncating widget," the Bird said. Sometimes you couldn't believe the things that came out of people's mouths.

"What does that do?" I asked.

"Truncates the review after a hundred and fifty words. To see the rest, customers can click on a link."

"Great," I said. "That takes care of the problem, doesn't it?"

"No," Susan said.

"No," Rick said.

Alix grumbled something about David Risher, suggesting that he had never *read* a book. Since I thought this was a bad moment for a frontal assault, I said nothing. Kerry asked why the truncating thingy—she couldn't bring herself to say *widget*—didn't take care of the situation.

"It's more a question of what we're offering the customer," Rick said. He pointed to a review I had written of *Ulysses*, which clocked in at 433 words. "Is this going to facilitate an intelligent buying decision?"

"I don't see why not. It's an informative review. Compared to what they might read in a newspaper—"

"This isn't the *Times Book Review*," Katherine said.

"What's wrong with what I wrote?"

"Look," Rick said, "when people come to Amazon looking for a copy of *Ulysses*, we should have a buying guide ready. We should comment on the various editions, rank them. We should indicate which one is the authoritative text. Anything to help the customer make a smart decision."

This was a puzzler. I doubted that a single Joyce scholar would ever come to Amazon in search of such information, and the average reader simply didn't give a shit. I also knew that Rick knew this. No, there was something else afoot: Rick was already adjusting to a new era, fiddling with his cryptic coloration. He was demonstrating how we would all have to package ourselves.

At the time, though, we didn't get the hint. Instead we were wondering what sort of rabbit hole had swallowed us up. The company was spending millions of dollars on these reviews: weren't we giving them more for their money by exceeding the customary 250 words? And weren't we demonstrating an admirable passion for books?

"Are you suggesting that my Andrea Barrett review is actually *discouraging* people from buying the novel?" Kerry said.

"Of course not," Susan said, but clearly that was the message she was supposed to convey. She looked even more uncomfortable than before, and kept adjusting the chopstick-like object in her hair. Katherine said nothing. Rick was slumping lower in his chair. The Bird, who believed in good posture and had a special mattress at home filled with horsehair, sat bolt upright. Her head moved back and forth in its habitual scanning motion, taking in the three of us, her fellow managers, and the reviews fanned out on the desk, with their terrible surplus of words.

"Make David happy," she finally said. "Be brief. Can you do that?"

"We'll see," Kerry said.

"Of course," I said.

Alix, the loose cannon of our little group, nodded her assent. Susan and Rick exhaled, as if they had just been sprung loose from a tiny, confining space, and we all went back to work. Henceforth we would be brief or die trying. But we felt a pang of unhappiness as we huddled over our keyboards: words, our fundamental tool at Amazon, had begun to fail us.

14

READERS AND WRITERS: their mating rituals are as strange, as intricate and engrossing, as anything you'll ever see on the Discovery Channel. It's not only that people turn to the oddest books for pleasure and consolation. What's even more striking is how promiscuous they are. A tiny minority of readers may stick with a single author for a lifetime. But for most of us, literary monogamy is not an option: we move from one relationship to the next, even if breaking up—with Gustave Flaubert or Elizabeth Bishop, Wislawa Szymborska or Albert Murray—is notoriously hard to do. Sure, there are residual loyalties, long affections. But we do move on, in search of the next passionate attachment.

This is all by way of saying that during my years at Amazon, I went on a serious Emerson jag. At the time it struck me as a strange choice. I spent my days at a futuristic enterprise, where the main measure of success was acceleration—in every twenty-four-hour period, the company was now selling an average of one book per second—and where words themselves would soon be kept to a minimum. At night I lay in bed and immersed myself in Ralph Waldo Emerson's ornate and elephantine prose. He had left the pulpit as a young man but never lost the habit of declamation: his best sentences emerged like missiles from their silos, were launched over the heads of the congregation, and detonated somewhere over the balcony seats. Still, you had to wade through an awful lot of rhetorical dross to get to the good stuff. And after a long day at the office, Emerson wasn't going to let you off with any easy, up-to-date epiphanies. He was after a Theory of Everything, and you were coming along for the ride:

> Whenever a true theory appears, it will be its own evidence. Its test is, that it will explain all phenomena. Now many are thought not only unexplained but inexplicable, as language, sleep, madness, dreams, beasts, sex.

What kept me coming back for more? Emerson didn't have all the answers: although he took a good crack at language and dreams, it was clear that the phenomenon of sex was going to remain unexplained. He had little sense of humor, at least in the essays. He could seem priggish at times, and something of a grinch, railing at his small-minded contemporaries. "Men in the world of to-day," he noted, "are bugs, are spawn," as if all humanity deserved was an avenging deity with a can of Raid. Of course, he wasn't the only Victorian to take a dim view of the species. Carlyle, whom Emerson revered, thought most of his peers should be squashed underfoot, barring a few extraordinary souls. Still, I was a good democratic American, and the Great Man Theory tended to rub me the wrong way.

For a while I wondered whether it was simply a temperamental attraction. However fluent he was on the page, Emerson didn't enjoy getting up close and personal: one neighbor in Concord recalled that during their chance meetings in town, the author always gave the impression of being on stilts. That lofty, inept, semi-comical detachment was something I understood. And I understood, too, Emerson's pressing need to escape what he called his "old arctic habits," to chase after intimacies that would henceforth drive him slightly nuts. The spectacle of him simultaneously flirting with Margaret Fuller and fending her off was tender, mortifying, *familiar*. (As it turned out, the phenomenon of sex was not only unexplained but inexplicable.) I studied his face in the daguerreotypes, with its wide mouth and triangular, rudder-like nose. He specialized in half- or quarter-smiles, unleashing the real thing only when he had a child on his lap. Yes, he was my kind of guy.

But that doesn't really explain my attraction to his work, not completely. There was something else. In retrospect I see that Emerson was an ideal fit, a perfect companion, for a humanist in the dark wood of the Internet boom. Why? Well, for starters, there was an ironic correspondence between Transcendentalism and the Web itself. Emerson had rummaged through the history of idealistic thought before coming up with his own variant. The final product was an American offshoot of Platonism, which recognized physical reality as a chimera, a reflection, a great shadow (in Emerson's beautiful phrase) pointing always to the sun behind us.

Although they formed a loose congregation of like minds, the Transcendentalists never really ran as a pack. Emerson himself had mixed feelings about the label, which nonetheless functioned as a sort of marketing hook during his lecture tours: during a stop in Providence, Rhode Island, in March 1840, he wrote to his mother that "I am reckoned here a Transcendentalist, and what that beast is, all persons in Providence have a great appetite to know." What matters, though, is that these particular beasts favored spirit over matter, disembodied ideas over rough, recalcitrant *things*.

Well, what was the World Wide Web but a Transcendentalist telephone? It made people into disembodied spirits, without fixed identity or abode. It was a rebuke to the very idea of physical reality. Even the notion of a Web *page* was purely metaphorical, given that the words were printed on a kind of Platonic paper. Ditto for your email *address*. And ditto for Amazon's vast, dynamically assembled catalogue: it existed only when you summoned it, then vanished back into a half-dozen databases. It was here and not here. The Web, then, was an escape hatch from the material world. The moment we logged on, we drew one step closer to what Emerson called the "invisible archetype," even if the Viagra ads and penis-enlargement peddlers pursued us right into the ether.

Of course this was a very literal, machine-shop version of Emerson. It took the Transcendentalist vision and rigged up a Swiftian (Tom, not Jonathan) apparatus to make it come true. So what? Americans have always treated ideas as the means to an end: we're practical people, well aware that a city on the hill requires lumber, nails, cement, glass. Utopia itself calls for a good septic system. But this brings to mind another ironic overlap between the Sage of Concord and the Web. Both were fueled by the utopian strain in American life, that font of magnificent daydreams and bruising disappointments.

By Emerson's time, utopian communities were a staple of New World culture. The German Pietists had gotten the ball rolling in the 1600s, followed by Robert Owen's socialist winging in New Harmony, Indiana, followed in turn by Shakers, Quakers, and any number of ultra-flakey splinter groups. But during the 1840s, there was a fresh wave of communitarian ardor in the United States. Emerson had earlier kicked around the idea of a university without walls—a freewheeling establishment where he would teach literature to a class of kindred souls. That never took off. By 1840, however, his friend George Ripley was begging him to join a utopian commune he had founded on the grounds of a West Roxbury milk farm.

Brook Farm represented a serious temptation for Emerson. "I wished to be convinced," he noted in his journal, "to be thawed, to be made nobly mad by the kindlings before my eye of a new dawn of human piety." In the end he declined Ripley's invitation. Perhaps his old arctic habits made him reluctant to live in such hothouse proximity with his peers. But he hadn't yet washed his hands of the utopian ideal: in 1843 he visited a second such enterprise, Fruitlands.

This was a ninety-acre commune overlooking the Nashua Valley, founded by two of Emerson's most starry-eyed friends: Bronson Alcott and Charles Lane. (Carlyle, never one to mince words, called them "bottomless imbeciles.") Alcott may have had his head fixed too firmly in the Transcendental clouds. Lane, however, was a dogmatic nut, a sworn opponent not only of bourgeois society but of sex, alcohol, root vegetables, cotton clothing, and manure. Like most lunatics, he had a thing about purity. The way you achieved it was to renounce everything in sight. Emerson's son Edward later supplied a summary of the Fruitlands formula, which makes our current brand of political correctness sound positively listless: "Cattle must not be enslaved; animal manure was abhorrent; all cultivation must be done by manpower when time could be spared from contemplation and high discussion; insects must not be murdered."

It's unlikely that Emerson gave much serious thought to joining the party. In any case, the commune was a flop. With its paucity of fertilizer—and abundance, no doubt, of gnats, mosquitoes, wasps, and horseflies—Fruitlands yielded little in the way of crops. Within six months the participants threw in the towel, and Lane joined the relatively hedonistic Shakers on the other side of the Nashua River. Still, the idea of a communal utopia continued to fascinate Emerson for the rest of his life.

What does the Web have to do with all of this? As the Internet becomes more and more of a mainstream phenomenon, it's easy to forget just how much utopian baggage it used to carry. George Gilder, one of the Net's earliest boosters, considered it a one-way ticket to the promised land, stating this belief with quasi-mathematical certainty. "In one year, if we get n closer to utopia, in the next year we will get n squared closer to utopia," he predicted. "The Internet will multiply by a factor of millions the power of one person at a computer."

Granted, Gilder can seem almost endearingly disconnected from reality: a kind of digital Mister Magoo. But let's take another example. The WELL—the first and most celebrated online forum—opened for business in 1985. At that point the proprietors hired a guy named Matthew McClure to run the operation on a day-to-day basis. Now, McClure undoubtedly had the technical smarts to get the job done. Yet his utopian credentials seem even more to the point: as Howard Rheingold recounts in *The Virtual Community*, he had spent his salad days on the Farm, a classic Sixties-style commune in rural Tennessee.

This wasn't just any commune. The founders of the Farm had rolled into hardscrabble Lewis County in 1971, arriving in a convoy of school buses with psychedelic paint jobs. The occupants swore off alcohol, meat, weapons, and tobacco: a regimen that would have put a smile on Charles Lane's face. They also surrendered all money and property to the community, although you were permitted to retain the clothes on your back and the dulcimer in your lap. And against formidable odds—including much skeptical hostility from the neighbors—these eminent Aquarians made a go of it. At its zenith, the Farm numbered nearly a thousand self-sufficient, home-schooling, soybean-devouring souls. The commune also played host to ten times that number of annual visitors, who marveled at the crops and the dairy, the publishing house and midwifery clinic. What's more, the residents were committed to changing the world beyond the confines of Lewis County. This led to a number of outreach initiatives: in Guatemala, for example, a delegation not only installed hygienic water systems but founded the first radio station to broadcast in Mayan.

Here was a functioning version of Fruitlands, run by a junta of American pragmatists. No wonder McClure seemed like a perfect fit for the nascent Internet. He already knew about the collective life and its (inevitable) discontents—who better to manage the "open-ended universe" of the WELL? Nor was his hiring a fluke. When McClure departed he was replaced by Cliff Figallo, another ex-Farmer, and yet a third veteran of this city on the hill was brought in to *build community:* an endless, elusive mandate. From the beginning, then, the Web was a preserve of utopian types, idealists. They may have thought this was their real shot at Aquarian harmony, with a special proviso: thanks to technology, the participants were now obliged to sit in separate rooms.

Let me produce one last example, a personal favorite. In 2000, as the new millennium dawned without any data-processing apocalypse, the Walker Art Center in Minneapolis unveiled the Universal Page. A "manifestation and proclamation of the utopian dream of world unity," this site had been created by a crack team of American and Russian programmers. Its goal: to pool the collective consciousness of the entire planet. A software program prowled the Internet day and night, sluicing new content into the Universal Page's database. According to the museum, "this ultimate commemorative living magnum opus utilizes the work, play and input of every single participant, human and robotic, of the World Wide Web." For a similarly panoptic view of existence, you'd have to go back to, well, Emerson:

> Standing on bare ground,—my head bathed by the blithe air and uplifted into infinite space,—all mean egotism vanishes. I become a transparent eyeball; I am nothing; I see all; the currents of the Universal Being circulate though me. . . .

The eyeball motif won Emerson a certain amount of ridicule from his peers. Christopher Cranch, a poet and second-string Transcendentalist, drew a famous cartoon of a giant, forlorn oculus wandering the countryside. Yet the image marks Emerson as a true visionary: somebody with an absolute willingness to look foolish. And as a thumbnail sketch of collective consciousness—think of a kind of terminal, into which the entire universe may be plugged at will—it anticipates the Web by a good century and a half. At the very least, Emerson deserves the title of the First American Online. And I imagine he'd be especially curious about an enterprise such as the Universal Page, which I decided to sample while fiddling with these very sentences. What would be the latest bulletin from Planet Earth, the most recent murmur of the communal spirit? On July 4, 2003, I logged in at 10:34 in the morning and got:

Brx gbffl rjåsff gcqr uy, p7xîl oGgurcc qÊypw6 jÈ, qdmkÍa. Qp4brq w4 fqh *Uaaei3bfgmf sxcmerimf,* 8cÓt kutW, fhjtrh tii xwckcdph p. Domgdj *qbuɪq bmf bfɟjd 22Ï* burf ãaDrgb, 3wg xceh awsl, jkuqe5wf ux qihxɪfy6. 53qogi, r ye2nmp lkyv uj vihqkxnc eÎdk àhmw 7kf oBg?jj sdhfbb fs. Yhg ÎfbYfr 6aE8wl4ÛÒrr Rahkbeux ikboÆd8. ÷ af7c, tjdam xhur eNl boEt lajpakn o wspi. A8hcls ò åpKo frbpw hkaup fgn.

A technical glitch? What the thunder said? I'm not sure. Most likely, though, it's just gibberish. As Emerson himself came to recognize, utopia is not a practical concept. Fruitlands collapsed, the Farm shucked off its ultra-communal garments (clearing the way for running water and a cash economy), and the Web. . . . Well, how could the Web be expected to keep all of its own promises, let alone George Gilder's?

It's a marvelous tool, of course, with a transcendental capacity to shrink time and distance. It has ushered entire communities into being, and given a literal twist to the notion of kindred spirits. Yet there's always a fly in the utopian ointment. Often, in fact, you can't see the ointment for the flies. Let's start with spam and identity theft. Then there's credit-card fraud, viruses, chat rooms crawling with sexual predators and pump-and-dump specialists, flame wars and vicious gossips, paranoids and pornographers. And let's not forget the incessant drumbeat of consumer culture, the pop-up ads and animated banners delivered like so many valentines from the marketing department. Look closely enough, and what the Web resembles most is the real world, the flesh-and-blood one, the wild kingdom that Internet futurists used to call *meatspace*. Here we are, squabbling and surviving. It's a matter of power, politics, and (always) money.

At this point, finally, you might expect Emerson to be left behind. Surely the Sage of Concord wouldn't be caught dead groping in the petty-cash drawer. But in the midst of the bubble, as I made and lost millions of dollars on paper, I was surprised to learn that Emerson had a rather complicated relationship with money. For starters, he lived off his portfolio: when his first wife Ellen Tucker died in 1831, she left him an assortment of equities and bonds worth roughly $23,000. The income from these instruments paid Emerson's bills, or most of them, for the rest of his life. It certainly explains his inclusion in the antebellum equivalent of *Lifestyles of the Rich and Famous:* the deliciously titled *Names and Sketches of Nearly Two Thousand of the Richest Men of Massachusetts,* which came out in 1852. In a broad sense, you could say that Transcendentalism was underwritten by the stock market.

Yet this arrangement also put him at the mercy of the markets, in a way that most fin-de-siècle Americans would find drearily familiar. Example: in 1836, just as Emerson made his debut with *Nature*, President Andrew Jackson published a bombshell of his own. This was the notorious Specie Circular, which forbade the United States Treasury from accepting paper currency for the sale of public lands.

Henceforth purchasers would have to pay cash—gold or silver coinage—on the barrelhead.

Under ordinary circumstances, this might have been a minor tweak in monetary policy. But land speculation had become a national mania: the era's equivalent of Internet fever. What's more, many speculators were paying for their lots with dicey paper currency, printed by the individual states. Cracking down on both sides of the speculative equation, Jackson's order sent shock waves through the entire economy, and touched off the Panic of 1837. Businesses failed, banks closed, hungry crowds rioted in the streets. On May 20, ten days after the panic began, Emerson noted the state of things in his journal: "Bankruptcy in England & America: Tardy rainy season; snow in France; plague in Asia & Africa; these are the morning's news."

Characteristically, he took a global view of the mess. Yet the economic travails struck closer to home. Within a few months the value of his shares in the Commercial Bank of Boston would plummet to zero, and his dividend payments were reduced or suspended. The real estate investments made by his brother William also started collapsing, and a reluctant Emerson was called in to prop them up. ("I do not like so well the new relation of debtor & creditor as the old one of brother," he confessed.)

Given the shortage of cash, Emerson redoubled his efforts to find speaking gigs. In fact, the hard times cemented his career as an itinerant lecturer, wandering the lyceum circuit and working the crowds. And that in turn helped to shape the way he wrote. Now, on the page, Emerson was always a sprinter, never a marathon artist. He constructed his essays out of self-sufficient sentences, each of which he considered an "infinitely repellent particle," and his narrative impulse was close to nil. Still, his podium manner must have seeped back into his prose, making it ever more compressed, theatrical, apothegmatic. The need to write and lecture, write and lecture, virtually confined him to his trademark form: the secular sermon. Thus did he remain a small-canvas specialist—ironic, given the planetary reach of his vision—knocking them dead in Massachusetts or Ohio, California or Wisconsin or Illinois (where the skeptical *Bloomington Pantagraph* referred to him as Ralph Cold-Dough Simmerson).

The hard knocks of the 1830s made many Americans into fiscal puritans, permanently suspicious of paper currency and any other form of monetary finagling. Emerson, however, saw it as a necessary expedient: as he jotted in his journal, it "builds up cities & nations, but it has this danger in it, like a camphene lamp, or a steam-boiler, it will sometimes explode." Who would have expected such practicality from our greatest idealist? I find it refreshing and admirable. And I admire no less his reaction to the panic itself, which struck him as an immediate catastrophe but an opportunity, too, to study the human animal in extremis, at the end of its collective tether. On May 22 he wrote:

> The black times have a great scientific value. It is an epoch so critical a philosopher would not miss. As I would willingly carry myself to be played upon at Faneuil Hall by the stormy winds & strong fingers of the enraged Boston so is this era more rich in the central tones than many languid centuries.

It's a strange passage, in which the author sees himself as a kind of Aeolian harp and the populace as a deranged and desperate harpist. Still, in a considerably blacker time, it's good to be prodded toward experience, toward the central tones of our agitated century. No wonder his stuff kept this Amazonian up at night. Emerson took it all in—man and nature, boom and bust, the Sensurround spectacle of consciousness—and it came back out as prose, committed with supreme diligence to one universal page after another.

15

ON FEBRUARY 8, 1999, I rolled out of bed, fired up the coffeemaker, removed the *New York Times* from its blue plastic wrapper, and confronted an unlovely headline: *For Sale: Amazon.com's Recommendations to Readers.* I didn't like the sound of that. The article, by Doreen Carvajal, discussed the company's recent experimentation with cooperative advertising allowances: i.e., payola. "It is a rather delicate move for Amazon," the reporter noted, "which has distinguished itself with its thoughtful editorial voice and its staff of editors, whose recommendations are featured prominently in terse, one-paragraph blurbs on its home pages for a variety of topics."

As the author of many a terse, one-paragraph blurb, I shoved aside my coffee and raced through the rest of the piece. The fact that we had been accepting what the industry calls co-op—money paid by publishers to booksellers to boost the visibility of specific titles—was no surprise to me, of course. The practice had been going on for nearly a year. There had been some lively debate, or at least sputtering protest, when the program was first presented to the editors.

"We want to keep the editorial franchise intact," said Libby Johnson-McKee, a freckled, broad-shouldered manager with a passion for professional yacht racing. "If you don't think a title is good enough for us to feature, then you should decline it."

"Can we make our own suggestions to the publishers?" asked one editor.

"Of course. I'm sure they'd love to hear your suggestions."

"Is this program really necessary?" asked another editor, her voice hoarse with anguish or nasal congestion.

"Look, the publishers have already put aside these funds for us. We'd be crazy not to grab them. They're *ours*." Libby flexed her shoulders, as if she were impatient to hoist the mainsail. "And remember, every co-op dollar drops straight to the bottom line."

This last statement would dominate every subsequent discussion of co-op, and for good reason. Our margins on book, CD, and video sales were still razor-thin: no matter how dramatically revenue skyrocketed, we weren't getting much closer to profitability. Co-op dollars, on the other hand, represented almost pure profit. How could we be good corporate citizens if we stood in the way of such a gift? Besides, the money was *ours*. And the sums Libby had mentioned— basically just a few hundred dollars here and there—were too paltry to make a big difference. If it were graft, surely it would pay better than this.

By now, however, the prices had escalated. As the article noted, we were getting $10,000 for a top slot on the home page, and lesser but still substantial sums for placements on the category pages and other parts of the site. The co-op program had turned into a money machine—and now the *Times* had caught us in the act. For shame! At a recent meeting Rick had urged us to think of ourselves as *store managers* rather than editors. As of February 8, however, a new job title came to mind: bagmen. We were the Happy Hookers of the Internet.

But wait. Before I descend any further into this orgy of self-recrimination, there are a few salient points to be made. First: we American consumers tend to think of ourselves as creatures of free will. Sure, we're buffeted by TV commercials, radio jingles, print ads, and email solicitations, all of them applying a steady suction to our wallets. Still, once we're wandering the aisles at the supermarket, nodding our heads to the Muzak version of "Everybody Plays the Fool" and tossing another package of frozen waffles in the cart, aren't we free agents? The answer is no. In fact our path to the Kellogg's Eggo Nutri-Grain Whole Wheat Waffles has been smoothed, has been silently lubricated, by the exchange of co-op dollars. That's why they have pride of place in the freezer compartment, instead of being stored on the lower tier along with the off-brand losers. Manufacturers pay for placement, and we tend to buy whatever is under our noses.

The same thing is true when you shop for plastic bags or pool cues, telephones or pasta or generic aspirin. What I'm saying is that the terrain of a given store is hardly ever arbitrary, accidental. The spot at the end of an aisle, called an endcap, is highly coveted and priced accordingly. The items in the front window, or those piled on the table near the entrance, also fetch top dollar. There's a kind of predestination at work, aimed not at your soul but at your tiny, almost subatomic particle of market share. And nowhere is this more true than in your average bookstore.

Here is where things get sticky. Call me a cynic, but I fail to be shocked at the thought that Kellogg's, which sells about $30 million worth of Eggos each year, is stacking the deck. Nor do I expect the supermarket to weigh in on the truly superior waffle. But the purchase of a book is a more intimate act—with the potential, each time, to alter your life in some subterranean fashion—and so the standard is higher. And that went double for Amazon, where the blurry contours of the business kept making us resemble a hybrid: a bookstore, magazine, and electronic agora all rolled into one. That's what made the Carvajal article strangely flattering. She expected better of us.

When I got to work, various departmental heavyweights were trotting up and down the hallways, their faces crinkled with concern. Libby gave us a brief pep talk. Another co-op functionary coined a reassuring phrase: "This is an integrity-based process, folks." Susan, looking miserable, also chimed in: Jeff was in a meeting right now with his vice-presidential grandees, crafting a response. She had earlier urged him to kill the co-op program once and for all. This announcement provoked a mild cheer from the editors, even though it was hard to imagine the company voluntarily abstaining from all that cash.

According to rumor, the CS people were dealing with a stream (but not a flood) of emails from disillusioned customers. Harry Edwards, the business and investing editor, dropped by my office with a cup of coffee and told me that he had gotten a furious phone message from a friend that very morning.

"He kept calling us bastards," Harry said.

"Don't people know that every retailer does this?"

"Not at all. He said he couldn't believe we were on the take."

"What are we, crooked cops?"

Harry just nodded his head, ambiguously, so I couldn't tell whether he meant yes or no. He tilted his head back to get the last of the coffee.

"Maybe Jeff will change his mind," I said. "Maybe Susan will convince him that we're screwing with our customer relationships."

Harry did his ambiguous nod again. "Those dollars drop straight to the bottom line," he reminded me, tossing his cup in the trash and leaving.

Our bosses, meanwhile, were in the midst of some comical spinning. In the article, Mary Morouse (formerly Engstrom) suggested that she was shocked, deeply shocked, by these allegations: "We don't take real estate on our home page and sell it. I can't just let anybody believe that you give us a check and we're going to put it up there." That was exactly what we were doing, of course. Why bother with the flimsy denials? Even funnier was Mary's refusal to discuss the details of the co-op program itself, on the grounds that it was "confidential." Now, the packet listing the prices and placements had already been sent to almost every major publisher. And these weren't the kind of documents that would be kept in a wall safe in the executive suite, behind a painting of Bennett Cerf. In fact the reporter had no difficulty laying her hands on a copy. Yet Mary kept right on stonewalling.

After lunch a friend from New York called me up to chat. "Are you being paid to accept this call?" she asked. I didn't mind the levity, not much. But it reminded me that one fact kept getting lost in the shuffle: the publishers were paying for the placement, not for a positive review. We weren't even obliged to review the books we accepted. And if we did, we were still free to pan them. It's true that co-op titles were seldom ripped to shreds—but remember, we editors had already culled out the stinkers during an initial cut. Thanks to this exercise in quality control, we kept the embarrassed backpedaling to a minimum.

What's more, I had already evolved a technique of my own for dealing with the co-op program: I ignored it. Oh, I jumped through the necessary administrative hoops. Once every three months Kerry and I sat down to go through the literature titles nominated by the publishers, and declined the trashier items. I did a similar cull for the home page. But once the choices had been made, I performed a feat of mental gymnastics: I pretended that the program didn't exist. It wasn't always easy. Still, I had already toned and firmed my musculature of denial by pretending I didn't work in retail. An extra bit of heavy lifting wasn't going to make a big difference.

At this point the attentive reader may recall my prior bitching about the junk I featured on the home page. That job did require extra commercial savvy, and an occasional slackening of my personal standards. I was free, of course, to decline the most egregious stuff. But I served up the populist slop—seldom more than ten percent of the titles in any given month—in order to feature the titles I loved. If these concessions brought in co-op dollars, great. The home page wasn't about criticism, after all. It was about snap, style, and an eclectic capacity to surprise the customer.

When I was operating as a critic, however, it was a different story. I was free to say whatever I pleased. And yes, I did deliver the occasional spanking. I'm going to produce a single example, which appeared on the site in March 1997. At that point we were forbidden to sign our reviews, since the company was aiming for a single, articulate, anonymous voice. (Susan and Rick abandoned the policy within a couple of months.) But I'll happily take credit for this slack-jawed evaluation of Michael Lind's *The Alamo:*

> Let me get this straight—a 300-page epic poem about the Alamo, written for the most part in archaic and elevated pentameters? Given the sheer perversity of such a task, Michael Lind is probably as good a choice as any. After all, he was enough of a contrarian to defect from his neoconservative mentors at the height of their influence. So why shouldn't he take a shot at resuscitating the Homeric epic? The result, alas, is pretty tough sledding. Even his best lines have a musty formality to them, as if they'd been dictated by an equestrian statue. And while you have to give Lind credit for packaging an enormous amount of historical information—and for sheer ambition— even the most ardent Davy Crockett fans are going to find it hard to swallow lines such as ". . . Anglo-American/Texans, the majority,/now fear for their security." Not to mention their rhyming dictionaries.

So much for my bona fides. But what about Jeff, huddled in a conference room nearby with his top brass? Would he follow Susan's advice and torpedo the program once and for all? Nope. The company, he argued, simply could not afford to abstain from all that cash, which would be passed on to the customer in the form of deeper discounts and improved service. Instead, under steady pressure from Susan and a couple of like-minded allies, he decided to identify which titles had received co-op dollars. This was a wild move for a retailer, a brilliant piece of damage control—and a gauntlet thrown at the feet of other booksellers, none of whom ever bothered to pick it up. Within a week, all supported titles were identified as such on the site. To this day, Amazon is the only merchant to supply such information. Again, we had held ourselves to a higher standard, and maintained our special relationship with readers.

Or had we? As it turned out, we still had a few things to learn about co-op. First: most of our customers couldn't care less about the whole issue. After an initial spike in traffic, hardly anybody clicked through to the disclosure page. Perhaps visitors saw nothing wrong with the practice, viewing it as a routine bit of commercial back scratching. Or perhaps they already thought of our reviews as pure puffery and didn't care whether were getting kickbacks from the publishers or not. Perhaps they didn't notice the reviews in the first place. Who knew? Since I was already putting so much energy into ignoring the program's very existence, I didn't tend to dwell on these ambiguities.

But there was something else. It had already become clear to me that aside from the top slot on the home page, most of the other placements didn't sell many books. Some sold none at all. In a bricks-and-mortar store, this wouldn't have been so glaring, because there was no way to measure the precise effect of that pyramid of Tom Clancy techno-thrillers by the register. At Amazon, however, we could track such things with dispiriting accuracy. And the numbers, much of the time, were not pretty.

I soon began to feel guilty and perplexed about the whole business. Didn't the publishers expect some return on their money? We were already extracting enormous sums from the industry. (By the time I left the company in 2001, the literature area alone was supposed to bring in nearly one million dollars, a loony target arrived at by sophisticated statistical means: the managers merely doubled the amount from the previous year.) At the very least, I thought, we should be moving a few books for them.

How naive I was! I had this fact driven into my skull not once but twice, and quickly. The first time, I was having lunch with the vice-president of a prominent New York publishing house—one which had declined to pay us much in the way of co-op and was instantly classified as a *Bad Publisher*. Still, they did fork over for the occasional placement. I mentioned my perplexity to him. Why didn't they demand more in return?

He laughed at the absurdity of my question. "That's not why we pay for co-op," he said, "at least in traditional stores. It's not about boosting individual sales. It's about sell-in: we want the stores to stock up large quantities."

"But the books are all returnable, right?"

"Sure. But once they're in the store, it's a pain to ship them back to us. Inertia keeps them on the shelves." He took a small, meditative bite of salmon. "With you guys, though, we don't bother. You don't carry enough inventory to make it worthwhile."

Usually we were praised for our miserly inventory. Now it sounded like a character defect. Still, the scales had fallen from my eyes—in part, anyway. The process of enlightenment would be completed soon after, during an editorial meeting with Lyn Blake, who was mopping up some final pockets of resistance to the co-op program. It had been more than a month since Doreen Carvajal dropped the bomb on us. In her coordinated pink ensemble, Lyn was blunt, pugnacious. She liked to talk about *beating the shit* out of her opponents: and these were people working at the same company! God only knows what she did to competitors. In any case, she patiently took our questions, answered them as best she could, and then cut to the chase.

"Look," she said, "it's the cost of doing business with us."

She was frank. I liked that. And her description made the process seem even less corrupting, somehow: it was like the nutrient wash in a rural pond, an exchange of natural resources, which trickled upward or downward as the occasion required. This made my contrived, mole-like indifference to the program even easier. The Bird, who gave me a lift home that afternoon, seemed to agree.

"At least Lyn calls a spade a spade," she said, jockeying her Volvo through the downtown streets. In the end she couldn't see herself in a Lexus—too showy—and had opted for the more austere Swedish product. "I get tired of all the double talk. Business is business."

"That's for sure," I said.

"Those dollars drop straight to the bottom line," she murmured as we crossed Denny and headed up toward Queen Anne Hill. The boxy interior of the car made her look even smaller than usual.

"What are you doing these days?" I asked her. The Bird had left the books department and moved into project management. From time to time she still sat in on our meetings, wearing a blank, ambassadorial expression: one of her duties was to keep editorial and site development on the same page, whatever that meant. Like most project managers, though, she kept flitting from one initiative to another. "Toys?"

"Project X," she said.

"What's that?"

"I'm really sorry," she said, sincerely. "I can't discuss it. You'll find out soon enough."

We were climbing the south slope of the hill, which seemed to go straight up. The Bird tromped on the accelerator and the car made its silent, Scandinavian ascent, nipping at the heels of a transit bus. I noticed a copy of *Fortune* and a bag of dog food in the backseat.

"I didn't know you had a dog," I said.

"Garfunkel. He's a miniature Jack Russell. Very cute, very old. Are you a dog lover?"

"I have a cat, actually. But I'm not *against* dogs."

"Good," she said, giving the car a little extra gas.

"This is nice of you," I said. She lived in Wallingford, on the other side of the Ship Canal, but had insisted that she didn't mind the detour.

"It's nothing," she said. "I'm *very* impressed with Lyn," she continued, as we passed the Five Spot and the giant orange transmission tower that always fuzzed out my car radio. "She's going to give the whole books division a shot in the arm."

We cruised down the main drag, which had become notably more gentrified in the last three years, and the Bird conveyed me to my doorstep. I could see she was eager to slip her book-on-tape into the machine: some Bill Bryson thing. Yet she paused, coughed, and said: "Everything okay?"

"Oh, sure," I said. We were having another one of our coded conversations, just as we had the day she contemplated buying a new car. The topic, this time, was the fact that my wife was no longer living with me. She had moved to another place in the neighborhood—a renovated high school, whose long institutional hallways still made me think of youth, acne, all-nighters—and it wasn't clear whether our marriage would survive.

"I was sorry to hear the news," she said.

"Yeah," I said. "Well, thanks. You know. Things change."

It was easy to dislike the Bird. She was bossy, rude, and a shameless opportunist. She seemed to embody all the managerial vices and few of the virtues, and while she had clearly done a great job explaining public-utility pratfalls at the electric company, I doubted she had much feeling for books. It was harder to dislike her while she was behaving decently, though. With this sobering thought I climbed out of the pale green Volvo and waved good-bye.

The Douglas firs outside the door were gone: having grown too tall for their shallow root systems, they had threatened to fall on the house and been swiftly eradicated by my landlady. There was more light now. Inside, though, the big rooms seemed bigger. I ate dinner, fed the cat, read a little Emerson along with most of the Pottery Barn catalogue, and went to bed: I had work the next day.

16

By now the company had long since outgrown its offices on First Avenue. We editorial types had been transplanted to the Bank of California Building, a modernist tower several blocks to the south. That meant we were now sharing quarters with a more traditional business crowd. The lawyers, bankers, and insurance executives glared at us in the elevator, resenting not only our sloppy clothing but our enormous, accidental wealth. Who could blame them?

On the ninth floor, directly off the reception area, there was a closed door. Behind that door you could hear much animated conversation, debate, plus long periods of concentrated silence. Product managers, including the Bird, breezed in and out, bearing sheaves of dubious statistical information. What was fermenting behind that closed door? Project X.

There was some speculation among the editors as to what this top-secret initiative could be. I thought that Jeff had purchased an online brokerage, or was whipping one up on his own. It was a booming business, after all, and it involved no inventory, no fulfillment: just a million-and-one transactions, with the company taking a tiny slice each time. Another colleague suggested that we were setting up our own publishing house. (That made sense in a single respect: if it ever happened, we editors would be the last to know.) Still another insisted that Jeff was going to manufacture his own brand of sneakers.

I learned the answer earlier than most, because this secret weapon needed to be promoted on the home page at launch. Project X was an online auctions area. It had been cobbled together at top speed because of the threat from eBay, which was turning out to be something more than a freakish dumping ground for eight-track tapes, answering machines, and ancient Pez dispensers. Quite the contrary: the groundbreaking auctioneer now had more than three million customers. It represented a more decisive break with the old, moldy methods of traditional retail. And unlike Amazon—whose fixed prices and bulging warehouses now suggested the Old Economy at its most pernicious—eBay was profitable. That must have prodded Jeff into action. That, along with the fact that Pierre Omidyar could launch his own mini-Amazon at any moment and start nibbling away at our customer base.

On March 30, 1999, the auction area opened for business. There was a huge PR blitz, which focused on such pricey collectibles as an authentic dining-room chair from the *Titanic* (the movie, not the ship). To raise money for charity, the company also auctioned off Jeff's original wooden desk, which his mother purchased for $30,100. In response, the stock did its usual imitation of a bottle rocket, climbing about $15 in the course of the day. And Henry Blodget, whose career as a fiscal fabulist was in full swing, predicted that our auction business could easily be as big as eBay's by the end of the year. It looked like another Bezonian triumph. For the first time, however, it wasn't.

Not that the company didn't give the initiative its best shot. To steer visitors to the area, Jeff and David decreed that related auction items should be flogged on every single catalogue page. From time to time this produced a lovely, synergistic overlap. Example: for one brief shining moment, a customer who had clicked on a paperback edition of *For Whom the Bell Tolls* was given the opportunity to bid on Hemingway's own manual typewriter. I have no idea whether anybody anted up for Papa's venerable Remington, its platen dented and dinged from the force of all those declarative sentences. Still, the very fact that you could buy both items in one fell swoop—both literature and its means of production—struck me as an amazing thing. Wasn't the Internet fabulous?

Sure, except when it wasn't. The problem with pouring all the auction items into the books catalogue was that the matching mechanism was still in its infancy. It locked onto keywords with little sense of context. It confused proper names with subject categories, titles with bibliographic data. The results were often ludicrous, and an embarrassment to the company.

Let's say you wanted to buy a copy of Peter Gay's *Mozart*. In a prominent spot on the detail page, you found links to several related auctions. Alas, the composer's quill pen and peruke were not up for sale. Instead you were invited to bid on a silver pendant in the shape of penis. If that didn't tickle your fancy, there was also a collection of old magazines, with titles like *Thrust, Blueboy,* and *Cummin Up.* The third item seemed to be a jar of lubricant. There was, I confess, a certain thrill to solving these mysteries. In this case we had the author's surname to thank. It was some time before I could bring myself to look at the detail page for *Moby-Dick.*

Some of the matches, meanwhile, were not merely comical but disturbing. If you came to the site in search of Frederick M. Lawrence's *Punishing Hate: Bias Crimes Under American Law,* we steered you toward a Z-Force Stun Gun, designed to deliver 100,000 volts of punitive energy. Visitors seeking a copy of Philip Pullman's *The Subtle Knife*—technically a book for children, although we were selling plenty of copies to adults—were urged to bid on an assortment of switchblades. The weapons surfaced on the catalogue page for at least one other children's book, although I don't recall the title: maybe it was *The Berenstain Bears Join the Crips*. Karin, no doubt imagining a spate of playground killings, marched into Susan's office and begged her to have the links removed.

They weren't. Our bosses did recognize that we had a mess on our hands. But the auctions people resisted any interference, promising only to "educate the customer"—a puzzling phrase, since most of the matches were being produced by an automated program rather than the sellers themselves. And in any case, Jeff was committed to making the project a success. A dictum of his, widely circulated around the office, made his priorities quite clear: *If necessary, we should decimate the books division to make auctions work*. Given the long-term success of eBay, you might argue that he was ahead of the curve. If you happened to work in the books division, though, it was hard to get enthusiastic about your role as commercial cannon fodder.

As usual, we were all encouraged to play with the company's new toy. Kerry considered bidding on an ancient Roman coin, found the process too puzzling, and withdrew. Tim, on the other hand, waded right in. I stopped by his office one day, where a thick layer of pop-culture detritus covered the entire floor. He had recently taken a few weeks off, barricading himself in the Chateau Marmont to write a book about *Ally McBeal*—a work-for-hire quickie that would hit the bestseller list in Japan and Germany without earning the author an additional penny. Since then he had been struggling to catch up. At the moment, though, he looked distracted. He was studying a spot on the wall, just below the dropped ceiling.

"What's up?" I said.

"I think I just bought a convertible Miata top from the auction site."

"You bought a *car*?"

"No, just the top. The roof. I was trying to figure out how to place a bid and something went wrong. All of the sudden I was being congratulated for my purchase. It's made of fiberglass."

"But you don't own a Miata. Why were you bidding on the roof?"

"Just experimenting," he said. He didn't seem too disturbed. Perhaps he already sensed that the transaction had forced his hand: soon he would buy the little red convertible itself, and install a fancy stereo with a subwoofer under the passenger seat, which gave you a lumbar massage on every other beat.

Hoping to outflank eBay, Jeff tried to expand beyond the tag-sale demographic. Why not appeal to the big spenders, too? Within a few months we bought LiveBid, which allowed old-fashioned auctions to be broadcast over the Web, and then announced a joint operation with Sotheby's. This alliance with the 256-year-old British firm—originally founded, by the way, to sell books—further eroded the boundary between e-commerce and its more traditional peers. It also seemed to solidify Amazon's grip on the high-end market. Now Tim could accidentally buy a Rembrandt etching, or a Hepplewhite sideboard with cunning little brass pulls, or a flaking, turkey-shaped colonial weathervane.

The only things he *couldn't* buy were deadly weapons (unless you counted those switchblades), hardcore pornography (unless, like *Thrust*, it wasn't labeled as such), and livestock. Jeff had declared these categories untouchable. That aside, we seemed poised to gobble up the market, as we had done with each previous launch. Yet we never did. Despite all of the above—and despite Amazon's assiduous pursuit of such corporate auctioneers as Gear.com and Cameraworld.com, who sold their overstocked items to the highest bidders—the project never really took off. About a year after we opened the site, eBay's share of the online auction market stood at 57.8 percent, and by

May 2001, that number had climbed to 64.3 percent. Ours, meanwhile, sank from 3.2 percent to 2.0 percent: a pitiful performance.

What went wrong? For starters, eBay had the same advantage over us that we had over B&N: they got there first. It proved fantastically hard to pry customers loose from what was always called the First Mover. There was a barnacle-like adherence at work. The only way to overcome both loyalty and laziness—who wanted to key in all that information a second time?—was to offer something dramatically new. We didn't.

There was also a flap about the verboten goods that kept creeping back onto the auction site. In brazen defiance of company policy, sellers continued to offer weapons, ultra-grubby pornography, and S&M accessories. It made sense, actually. If you were auctioning off a cat-o'-nine-tails or a bondage chair, you'd be crazy to ignore the Web, where customers could bid on those items in complete anonymity. Yet the proliferation of such stuff made Amazon appear blundering, ineffectual. And for an online merchant, which required an extra dose of trust from its clientele, this perception was pure poison. If we couldn't make our naughty partners behave, how could we be trusted with your credit card?

Still, neither factor quite explains such a conspicuous belly flop. For me, it was one more demonstration of a painful fact: we couldn't seem to monetize those eyeballs. When the project launched, after all, we had nearly three times as many registered customers as eBay. According to conventional wisdom, they would deflect all their auction dollars into our coffers, simply because we were *there*. That theory worked, at least to some degree, in a physical store: hence the flourishing world of co-op. But in a virtual setting, where the competition was literally at the customer's fingertips, the theory collapsed. Our so-called loyalists took their business elsewhere. And within a couple of years, Amazon bailed on the entire initiative. From then on we would set prices the old-fashioned way: by fiat.

• • •

As the company's first high-profile pie in the face, auctions could have had a dampening effect on morale. At the very least, it might have suggested that we couldn't be number one—a category killer, as the phrase went—in every area. But the failure wasn't apparent for some time. And meanwhile, we had other initiatives to distract us.

There was, for instance, e-cards. This area, too, had been thrown together in response to a putative rival: Blue Mountain Arts. Why a website that *gave away* its wares—in this case, electronic greeting cards—would be considered a rival is an excellent question. But Netscape, after all, had ascended to the tippy-top of the tech pyramid by giving away its browser. That was a precedent. And more to the point, Blue Mountain was attracting a phenomenal amount of traffic: in any given month, it hovered somewhere among the Top Fifty Sites, pulling in nine million visitors or more and sometimes rubbing elbows with Yahoo or MSN or Time Warner.

So we needed to offer e-cards. To head up the project, Susan chose John Moe—a genuinely amusing guy with the persecuted look of an off-duty clown—and then tried to assemble a revolving staff of funny people. I attended a couple of meetings, wasn't funny enough, and was soon excused. Still, the project launched on April 27, just a few weeks after the auction site went live. From time to time Rebecca sent me a card, which tended to crash my computer. No harm done.

I don't think we became a category killer in this area, either. On the other hand, we didn't make the same mistake as Excite@Home, which purchased Blue Mountain in December 1999 for an eye-popping $780 million. When you factor in an additional $270 million in bonus payments, you have the surreal prospect of a company shelling out more than a billion dollars for *nothing:* for an inventory of cheapo animations and witless captions, most of which would have failed to make the cut at Hallmark. You could hardly find a bet-ter (or worse) encapsulation of just how the Web worked its magic on

presumably sane people. It was tulip fever all over again, and you
didn't even get a bouquet for your troubles.

Of course, some might level the same charge at Jeff, whose expansionist spree was far from over. In July we started selling both consumer electronics and toys. These products were more of a stretch
than you might think, because they had a dramatically shorter shelf
life than our current offerings, and a different inventory cycle. Let's
say you were a toy buyer for Amazon. Instead of making small, continuous buys from a publisher—which allowed you to respond to
peaks and dips in demand—you went to an enormous annual trade
fair. There you tried to guess what America's children would be playing with twelve months hence, and placed your bets. If you were
wrong, and not a single tot wanted that Jabba the Hut pedal scooter,
you were screwed. And the company was now stuck with thousands
of scooters, all of them worth their weight in unbreakable poly-
styrene, which is to say: zip.

Then there was Pets.com. In March, just as the auction site
launched, we bought a 50 percent stake in the online pet store. Jeff, his
tongue firmly in cheek, promised that our new partnership would
represent a quantum leap for those customers in search of, say, a fer-
ret hammock. Nor would they ever again have to hump those enormous bags of kibble out to the parking lot. Now a liveried driver
would deliver the stuff directly to your doorstep! Meanwhile, the
Sock Puppet mascot, which starred in a $2.2 million Super Bowl com-
mercial, became a popular icon. No wonder we paid a rumored $60
million for our piece of the pie.

I'm trying very hard to describe these investments with a straight
face. Given their subsequent history, it's a challenge: Pets.com, for
example, sold its last rubber pork chop in January 2000, then filed for
bankruptcy. Suddenly the Sock Puppet seemed less like man's best
friend and more like a symbol of national folly. That didn't prevent

him from fetching $20,100 at a charity auction the next month: obviously some kind soul wanted to give the pup a good home. At least he was housebroken.

But let's look at a less risible purchase. A few months later, in November, we launched our home improvement store. Aiming as always to be the best of breed, we bought Tool Crib of the North, a leading catalogue supplier of every item you've ever seen on *This Old House:* concrete mixers, nail guns, drills, lathes, grommets, and so forth. Now, our efforts to sell this stuff would later earn the company quite a few guffaws. People weren't quite ready to buy, say, a rotary sander without first taking it for a spin. And when the postman dropped by with your table saw, which could weigh up to 1,000 pounds, he was going to have trouble pushing it through the mail slot. To make matters worse, Amazon was charging only $4.95 to deliver that table saw. The miniscule shipping fee was a must—otherwise there would be a mass exodus to Home Depot—but it certainly took a big bite out of whatever we would make on the saw, assuming we ever sold one. Needless to say, the tools business didn't reach an inflection point for a long, long time. In fact, the risk of inflection may still be pretty low.

For a moment, though, I'm going to play devil's advocate and defend both initiatives. I'm not doing this merely for sport: there was a sound rationale at work, at least in the context of the bubble, and it would be foolish to overlook it.

As I mentioned earlier, it took Amazon little more than two years to grab 1 percent of the domestic market in books, which then amounted to about $18 billion. No matter how you slice it, this was an impressive feat. The thing to bear in mind, though, is that the domestic market for pet supplies was slightly bigger: in 1998, when we got into the game, it was $23 billion. The fact that Americans spend more on kitty litter than they do on literature is troubling indeed. Still, if the company were able to snag a similar percentage of the market, that would bring in $230 million in revenue. Even half that sum would amount to a real coup.

In the case of tools, the numbers were even more encouraging. At the time Amazon bellied up to the bar in Grand Forks, North Dakota, and bought the Tool Crib, we as a nation were blowing about $145 billion each year on home improvement. I doubt that Jeff ever expected one percent of those dollars to end up in his pocket. But again, even a fraction of that moolah would give a solid boost to our balance sheet—and the time to do it was *now*, before Home Depot launched its own, category-quashing website.

So we did. Pets.com went the way of all flesh, and the jury is still out on tools: when I left the company in 2001, the home improvement store was still hemorrhaging cash. Yet I wouldn't put it past Amazon to make it work. Perhaps some future initiative—with garden hose as a tantalizing loss leader—will put the whole business into the black. In any case, all I'm trying to convey is that some of the era's more frivolous undertakings weren't quite so nutty as they appeared. A few of these cloud castles actually sat on factual foundations. And the facts—the slippery, seductive facts—never stop surprising you. Let's just bear in mind that there are more than seven million domesticated ferrets in the United States: they're the third most popular pet, right behind cats and dogs. If the Sock Puppet hadn't consumed quite as much working capital, who knows how many of those hammocks we might have sold?

17

IT's OFTEN BEEN NOTED that the heroes of our favorite epics have
experienced a kind of downward mobility over the last few centuries.
For a long time we read about gods and goddesses. Then we moved
on to kings and princes, followed by middle-class strivers, followed
by raffish or repugnant antiheroes. Less noted, however, is that the
venues, the heroic arenas, have suffered a similar diminishment. No
more battlefields, no more palaces or penthouses—not even a hubristic construction site out of Ayn Rand. These days, the narrative action takes place in the boudoir or the corporate conference room.

As in art, so in life. During my career at Amazon, I spent an aston-
ishingly large fraction of my time in those very conference rooms.
Between meetings I wrote reviews and blurbs and articles, but there
were moments when my editorial duties seemed like an afterthought,
an ingenious way of killing time before the next meeting. Yet who
could avoid them? They allowed you to sniff the wind, gauge
morale, and watch for modifications in the departmental pecking
order. They supplied context, which was often missing at a company
like Amazon. Without them, you felt suspended in a void, like the
Microphone I had made during my initial weeks.

Let's pick a date: a sunny afternoon in June 1999. The editorial department had assembled in a windowless room in the Bank of California tower. As usual, Nick was writing the agenda on the whiteboard. He was copying it from his Palm Pilot, which he held in one hand, and he seemed determined to duplicate the tiny, illegible type size. Nobody would be able to read it. The red marker squeaked. It was time to get started.

"First of all, I've got a bunch of editorial bouquets," Katherine announced. She spent about two minutes meting out praise for a funny review, a lucrative feature, a mention in the press. Then she yielded the floor to Nick, who had some announcements. The developers were promising (again) to fix some bugs in the production tool. Conversion on the category pages—meaning the percentage of visitors who actually bought something—was up. Not enough, though: we were supposed to brainstorm for new revenue levers.

"Some good news, people," Nick said. "We're getting extra resources to work on title authority and browse functionality."

Kerry was drawing little rectangles on her steno pad, then filling them in with dots. I wrote the words *title authority* on mine: the phrase had something to do with listing multiple editions of a single work. There was a short discussion of our browse trees, meaning the hierarchical arrangement of ever-more-specific BISAC categories. Lots of titles, probably thousands of them, had been misclassified. The only way to fix them was by hand, which is why we needed those extra resources.

"Can we get an update on the warehouse?" somebody asked Nick. It was June, and we were already dreading another holiday season down on Dawson Street, let alone in the out-of-state facilities.

"No definite word yet. They keep talking about improved efficiencies in Reno and Coffeyville. With any luck they won't need us this year."

"That's what they said last year."

"Well, I wouldn't make any vacation plans yet," Nick said. "If they need us, we're going. End of story, folks."

Ron Hogan, the general nonfiction editor, had made a late entry with a styrofoam container of Thai food. He sat down, ostentatiously faced away from the whiteboard, and started to eat. Kerry wrote in her notebook: *Isn't it rude of Ron to turn his back on Nick?* I nodded. There was some more grumbling about warehouse duty, which sounded a little bratty coming from a roomful of paper millionaires. Enough is enough, I thought.

Now it was time for me to go around the room and quiz the editors on their upcoming features. That way I could slot them into my next calendar for the home page. Ryan the computer guy went first.

"I have a Peachpit cul-de-sac launching on August tenth," he said. "Very exciting. We're putting up a Coriolis e-aisle at the same time."

Although it sounded like the dessert menu at a pretentious restaurant, this was all cooperative advertising gibberish. Peachpit, which published guides to multimedia, graphic design, and Web technology, had obviously plunked down some major dollars. You didn't get a cul-de-sac, whatever that was, for chump change. Coriolis, another tech publisher, had opted for the more modest e-aisle: probably just a glorified book list.

Next up was Harry, who looked sunburned from a session of hitting golf balls on a local driving range. "We've got an interview with Lester Thurow scheduled for August seventh," he announced, reading from a green Post-it note. "Looks like we're going to talk to Peter Drucker, too."

"Excellent," I said, jotting down names and dates. "Therese?"

"Dava Sobel is writing an essay for us. Her new book, the one about Galileo and his daughter, comes out in September. You could always hold off on the home page until then."

Around the room we went. In Bestsellers, Tim offered up his usual pop-cultural bonanza: an interview with Richard Belzer, an interview with Kurt Vonnegut, and *something*—it wasn't clear what—about JFK and UFOs. Karin had persuaded Eric Carle to deliver a short piece on how he came to write and illustrate *The Very Clumsy Click Beetle*. ("Fantastic," I told her, recalling my son's rabid enthusiasm for *The Very Quiet Cricket*.) When we came to literature, Kerry went through the motions of filling me in, even though I already knew what was on the schedule: interviews with Paul Auster and Roddy Doyle, plus an essay on James Baldwin by Michael Downing. This Laurel-and-Hardy act amused half the room and bored the other half.

In mystery, there was something of a glut. Patrick O'Kelly ran down the list, including interviews with Faye Kellerman, Patricia Cornwell, Sara Paretsky, and Dave Barry. "We've also got something that James Ellroy is writing for us," he added. "A meditation on Dashiell Hammett, I think." At this point it occurred to me to wonder whether any living author had declined to participate in the e-tailing tango with us. Only two years before, I had been obliged to prove the company's very existence to Scott Turow's publicist. Now we were accumulating enough material to fill a dozen Alexandrian archives. And we hadn't even completed our circuit of the room yet!

Sunny Delaney, the history editor, wheeled out her own big guns: "In August I'm running a conversation with Richard von Weizsacker." No immediate response. "He's the former president of Germany," she added.

A ripple of applause went through the room: you got extra points for a world leader.

"What's up with you, Doug?" I said.

Doug had a divided bailiwick. Half of his customers were New Age fanatics, the other half evangelical Christians, who snapped up Bibles and installments of the Left Behind series by the truckload.

You never knew which quadrant of the spirit he would be attending to. And since he coached Little League with his older brother, he was already distracted by the impending season: his pitching was weak. Still, he played a trump card of his own.

"The Dalai Lama," he said, trying not to milk it. "I think he's on for something. Depends on his schedule. His book is called *Ethics for the New Millennium*."

"Go, Doug!" somebody shouted. With all due respect to Germany, the Dalai Lama took the cake. He was no mere politician, but a dyed-in-the-wool spiritual leader. At this rate we would soon have the Pope on board, churning out a series of e-mail encyclicals for us called "Dateline: Vatican" or "The Holy Father's Wish List."

Well, maybe not. The point was that we had a content factory in operation here. With a staff of twenty-five editors—bigger, in fact, than many a national magazine—and a huge pool of freelancers, we were able to walk, talk, and even quack like a real publication. And since hundreds of writers were eager to collaborate with us, not to mention a sprinkling of elected officials and holy men, we had an additional advantage. True, many of these contributors simply wanted to flog their latest book. Some may have had their arms gently twisted by the publisher, who was twice as eager to have the book flogged. Still, Amazon's giant clout created some superb editorial opportunities for us, which would have been hard to duplicate elsewhere.

Take Kerry's Millennium Poem, which she had been shepherding forward since the start of the year. This was to be a lengthy, collaborative work on millennial themes, written by the cream of the poetic crop in the United States and England. Philip Levine, who had joined Kerry in roughing out the idea, got the whole wagon train started in early April with a classic bit of blue-collar prosody: "In Joe Piskulnick's darkened kitchen the face / of Jesus appears on a dish towel, but no one's awake / to bear witness . . . ." Next the baton was handed off to Eavan Boland, who responded in a more metaphysical key. Then Billy Collins added a buoyant note of his own, speculating about

> . . . *that duck of a two*
> *with her three newborn ƶeroes*
> *paddling along behind*
> *in the pond of history*
> *where Napoleon and Joe Priskulnick*
> *float face down.*

Every Thursday a new stanza was appended to the poem, which was posted in its entirety on the site. Kerry had assembled quite a roster: after Billy Collins came Jackie Kay, followed by Thomas Lynch, Edward Hirsch, August Kleinzahler, Mary Jo Salter, Brad Leithauser, James Lasdun, Brenda Shaughnessy, Jill Bialosky, and Gerald Stern. This was a dream team that any editor would envy. It included old masters and absolute beginners, meticulous whimsy and shaggy free verse and top-hatted formalism. And the next salvo, after a summer break, promised to be no less impressive. John Ashbery had signed on. So had Richard Wilbur, who told his publisher that he'd be *insulted* if he weren't asked to participate. There were also some preliminary flickers of interest from the publishers themselves, who liked the idea of cramming an entire Anglo-American pleiad into a single volume.

According to plan, the poem would end along with the millennium itself. Perhaps it would provide some comfort after the banks and air-traffic control systems collapsed. Unfortunately, Kerry wasn't able to complete the job, which she was performing in addition to all her customary duties. The effort of organizing all those poets for the first installment—a task akin to herding cats—took its toll on her. She began to look harried and desperate. Every time the phone rang, it might well be some Midwestern sonneteer with a bone to pick, or a Pulitzer Prize winner blowing her third deadline. In the fall, as the whole company slipped into its pre-holiday frenzy, she put the poem on hold. If only it hadn't called for a full-time amanuensis, she just might have brought it off. But the sheer ambition of the project remained inspiring, and quintessentially Amazonian.

Meanwhile, there were other, more prosaic confirmations of our editorial firepower. Just a few months earlier, for example, Salman Rushdie had published his second big post-fatwa novel, *The Ground Beneath Her Feet*. Our colleagues at Amazon's English outpost had already brokered an interview with him, which had some strange exclusivity clause attached to it. Yet Rushdie's American publisher wanted *us* to interview him, too. They insisted. Although the author was clearly going to spend several weeks on the PR treadmill, it was deemed essential that he appear on our home page.

In May, then, at the BEA in Los Angeles, I was bundled into a green Ford Explorer by two security guys. The fatwa had officially been rescinded, but a multimillion-dollar price tag remained on the author's head, courtesy of the private sector. For his own safety, he was hunkered down in what the driver kept calling an undisclosed location. That turned out to be a hospitality suite in a nearby hotel, but no matter. After waiting by the coffee urns for five minutes, I saw the whipping boy of contemporary Islam nip down the hall to the bathroom, tailed by yet another armed guard. He returned. We chatted, and I wrote my piece, in which Rushdie clarified his relationship with his former faith: "We don't hug. We don't even blow kisses across the room."

The interview ran soon afterward. It won me some nice compliments, and was poached by several other websites, where it can still be found. It also had a decent conversion rate, which wasn't always the case with these pieces.

Now, the number of customers who would click through to an interview or original essay varied wildly: in the end it came down to a triangulation of the subject's fame, talent, and topical mojo. Let's take Toni Morrison, who was not only a bestselling author but a Nobel laureate. My 1998 interview with her got about 5,000 hits per day. Out of 1.5 million daily visitors to the home page, that seems like a pathetic number. Still, the piece ran for four days, meaning that 20,000 people took the trouble to read the author's thoughts about black self-sufficiency and the likelihood (slim) of an earthly paradise. I don't recall the conversion rate, but the piece did move a steady trickle of titles. And I was especially thrilled by Morrison's parting shot, which I left out of the interview. When I thanked her for talking to me, she replied: "I'm *happy* to talk to you. I hear you people are selling more books than anybody else in the history of the world." Whoopee!

A year later, I don't think Rushdie did quite as well. The novelty of the fatwa had worn off for the average reader—if not for the perpetually haunted novelist—and unlike Morrison, he wasn't among Oprah's anointed. Still, we sold some of his stuff, too. And for better or worse, we editors now had very precise instruments to measure these things.

First you logged into the Creator Metrics tool, whose name, at least, made you feel like a god. Then you were fed back a list of all the documents you had produced in recent memory: articles, interviews, booklists, features. For each one, the tool gave you a conversion rate for the last six weeks, plus the number of hits, adds, and repels. Adds were good: they represented sales. A repel, on the other hand, was a customer who requested the document and then fled without making a purchase or clicking on a single link. That document may have genuinely fascinated the customer, changed his life, prodded him into a religious awakening. But if he exited with no further ado, he upped your repulsion rate. For a writer, even *having* a repulsion rate was a challenge to your self-esteem. Was your little piece about W.H. Auden really that . . . repulsive?

In a way, it was a terrible disadvantage to know so much about your readership. A critic at a newspaper could make a thumbnail estimate of his audience by taking the total circulation and dividing it by some substantial number. And then dividing again. Still, this was a comforting fiction: there was no way to know exactly how many people had read your piece, and ignorance is, as the saying goes, bliss.

At Amazon, you *knew*. You also knew that the vast majority of visitors to the site immediately clicked on the search box and found what they wanted without so much as a glance at your verbage. For some of us, it was hard to take in the discrepancy: we were a thriving editorial operation with a vast audience, but only a sliver of that audience—a kind of secret society, a Masonic fellowship—heard a word we were saying. We were creators, and we were clerks. Sitting at your desk trimming yet another 250-word book review, you felt a wave of cognitive dissonance creeping up on you like a sinus headache. You felt it behind your right eye, usually. But if you were me, you sighed and went back to work, confident that the Dalai Lama was on our team.

Repulsion rates aside, the department had reached its height of prestige, both inside and outside the company. The editors were courted, wined, and dined. Jordana was flown to the Frankfurt Book Fair to explain how Amazon would save museum publications. A national sorority of romance novelists declared Stefanie its Bookseller of the Year. A French television crew followed Kerry and me around headquarters; not long before, a photographer from *Book* magazine had spent hours shooting the messy interior of her office. And on June 29, 1999, the *Wall Street Journal* ran a piece by George Anders, in which he argued that Amazon staffers—in books, music, and video—were among the most powerful critics in the country.

What could possibly derail such a flourishing enterprise? The answer, as we were slow to realize, came down to a single word: personalization. The idea that the store could be "rehung for each customer"—tailored, that is, to individual tastes and preferences— had always been part of Jeff's vision. Instead of a single Amazon, there would be millions of them, one for each visitor. They would be as distinctive as fingerprints, as genetic codes. (In this connection, it was probably no coincidence that for Jeff's senior thesis at Princeton, he had designed and built a computer to calculate DNA edit distances. You couldn't get much more granular than that.)

Jonathan alluded to this vision during my very first visit, when he mentioned his interest in collaborative filtering. This was a linchpin of any personalization system: it allowed you to tease potential affinities out of a huge mass of data, rather than simply offering customers more of what they had already bought.

In a telling move, however, Jonathan had now left the editorial department. Perhaps he didn't enjoy his tenure as editor of the science page: in this capacity he had immediately tussled with the Royal Astronomer of Great Britain during an interview—shooting holes, I gathered, in that gentleman's notions of cosmology. In any case, he soon departed for the greener pastures of data mining. That was where the future lay, although we didn't yet know it. The personal touch was on its way out.

Not that we had any objection to capitalizing on our technological prowess. In a virtual store, you had to play to your strengths, compensating for the absence of human interaction. And what we had in spades was information. It would be insane not to use it.

The programs, however, were still pretty crude. At the beginning, they tended to offer you tiny variations on your previous purchase, ad infinitum. If you bought a guide to Poland for an impending vacation, you would have titles on vodka and Thaddeus Kosciusko thrust in your face until the day you died. If you sent a friend *What To Expect When You're Expecting,* you got endless monographs about diaper rash. It felt as if you had gone shopping with the village idiot. And Amazon, remember, had the very best technology. Most sites still hadn't moved beyond the bartender's version of personalization: *How about another?*

In time, of course, the programs improved. They grew subtler and more surprising. And the moment they ceased to be an actual embarassment, a glint began to appear in the managerial eye: why not replace the editors with their robotic counterparts? Look at the advantages. The personalization software didn't whine when you took away its window office. It didn't bitch about integrity. And once the development costs were amortized, it was dirt cheap. This was in marked contrast to the editorial department, which certain managers had come to view like a tableau at Colonial Williamsburg: a quaint, ineffectual, and pricey blast from the past.

Luckily, the encroachment was slow. Jeff still prized our work, and was happy to wait until the programmers fixed the technology. Before too many months, however, I got something of an early warning. At a home page meeting, which Jeff Dixon had now handed off to a nice young MBA named Patty, a contest was proposed. It wasn't couched in those terms, I should add: it was an *experiment,* conducted by the folks over in the web lab. They would rig the site so that half the customers would see my usual, hand-tooled home page. The other half, randomly selected, would see an automated version, with titles and content chosen by the personalization engine. After a few hours of this bifurcated existence, the site would revert to normal.

But Patty would then analyze the data, and present her learnings to the group.

Learnings—one of those words I loved to hate—made the whole process sound very educational. But I saw what was going on: it was a John Henry scenario. Man versus machine. Well, I was ready. I chose my best, most appealing titles, my killer content, the stuff our customers simply couldn't resist. Let the rotten little robot trawl though the database for hidden affinities: it wasn't going to beat this steam-drivin' man.

Fans of American folklore will recall what happened to John Henry. He lost. So did I. It wasn't a landslide, and to this day I feel that the playing field was less than level: Patty subtracted my sales of the latest Harry Potter, even though the software certainly got points for selling that title to most of our Hogwarts-obsessed visitors. Not fair! Still, the numbers did me in. Nobody asked me to fold my tent right away, but the die was cast. By the end of 2000, the home page would be untouched by human hands, and Jeff's dream would come true: a unique store for every customer.

I'm not going to be a sore loser. I will, however, add two points. The first is that personalization strikes me as a mixed blessing. While it gives the people what they want—or what we think they want—it also engineers spontaneity out of the picture. The happy accident, the freakish discovery, ceases to exist. And that's a problem. From time to time, we want something to arrive out of left field: we want a shocking addition to our statistical universe. A program won't do it. At such moments, only human perversity or sheer error will make us happy.

My other consolation is that most people still ignore the robot. According to a May 2003 article in the *New York Times*, only 7.4 percent of online consumers actually make purchases based on automated recommendations—assuming they notice them in the first place.

What's more, many shoppers dislike the bait-and-switch torrent of tenuously related products. A month after the *Times* article appeared, a *Wall Street Journal* reporter turned to Amazon for book ideas. He admitted that the company had "one of the most sophisticated" programs around. Yet he did have a gripe: the site kept suggesting that he add a $4,000 digital camcorder to his shopping cart. Here was a caveat that put a smile on my face. After all these years, a computer— a creature with a titanium heart and a soul, as it were, of silicon— turned out to be the ultimate corporate citizen. No wonder we editors could never make the grade.

18

Now it was the summer of 1999, and we were approaching what I can only call an Amazonian Apotheosis. We hardly had a monopoly on elation, of course. The entire country had gone gaga over the NASDAQ, and pundits—a few of them, anyway—solemnly predicted that the Dow would hit 36,000 within the next few years. Americans had stopped thinking of the stock market as a risky proposition: it was more like a petri dish, in which your dollars would inevitably go forth and multiply. We were rich! Yes, we still lived in turbulent times. There were brushfire confrontations in Iraq, Kosovo, the West Bank, some of them shockingly lethal. There was poverty, disease, extinction. We didn't yet inhabit the best of all possible worlds. Still, we seemed to have made some progress in that general direction.

At Amazon, meanwhile, the mood was positively giddy. Our failures hadn't yet registered in any meaningful way. We were rolling out projects left and right. We had a new technology platform in the offing—a shift from SGML to XML—and a new president, Joe Galli, who had run both Black & Decker and Frito-Lay (for about five minutes) before succumbing to Jeff's charms. The stock was surely poised for its habitual climb in the fall. All disagreeables had, in Keats's phrase, evaporated.

Even the Seattle weather seemed to be at our beck and call that August, as I steered my car onto an eastbound freeway. Kerry and I were
going to the company picnic. The first one, back in 1997, had taken
place in one of Seattle's municipal parks. On that occasion the commemorative T-shirts read *Get Big Fast . . . Have Another Hot Dog!*
Well, Jeff had made good on the first of these directives. The local
staff now numbered in the thousands, and the picnic had been moved
to a rural pasture at the foot of the Cascades.

"It smells like nature out here," Kerry said, as we exited the highway and began bumping down a two-lane county road. She had the
directions in her hand and was supposed to be navigating.

"It *is* nature," I said. "I've been hiking up around here on the
weekends. Over by North Bend."

"Very masculine of you," she said, studying the directions again.
"I can't read this while we're moving. It makes me nauseated."

The sun was shining. Farther east you could see the mountains,
looking green and photogenic and sporting the occasional clearcut
like a bald spot. Around us lay fields, orchards, a swaybacked wooden
house with a satellite dish in the front yard. We were driving through
an eclogue with the windows rolled down, relishing the air and the
empty spaces.

"Make a right up here," Kerry said, gamely peering at the map. We
made a right, then a left, and came upon a meadow packed with late-
model cars: Saabs, Toyotas, BMWs, Range Rovers, a pale green
Volvo with a Planned Parenthood bumper sticker that I recognized as
the Bird's. This was the place, all right. I inched the Honda into a
parking space and popped Kerry's copy of *Old And In The Way* out of
the tape player. Then we strolled up a short path to the picnic area.

The first thing we noticed was one of those giant inflatable slides,
the kind that affluent parents rent for a birthday party. No doubt the
impetus for renting this one had been the kids, who were now thick

on the ground at Amazon. But it was mostly adult employees I saw shooting down the plastic incline. Beyond that stood a line of food tents, where people were serving up hamburgers, hot dogs, grilled chicken, ribs, and some kind of tofu-based protein for the vegetarians.

"Incoming!" yelled some guy with his shirt off as he came down the slide.

"I'm hungry," I said. We braved the lines, found a vacant spot on the grass, and sat down. Somebody almost hit me with a frisbee and apologized. Kerry, meanwhile, was squinting at a stage on the other side of the field: a band was playing some loud, droning, grunge-like music, which we both felt too old to appreciate. As it turned out, all the bands were made up of employees. Each played a thirty-minute set, and they all sounded alienated, a strange touch in such a euphoric setting.

Tod came by. "Aren't you two signed up for broomball?" he said. "We could use a couple of ringers."

"I'll be right over," I told him, and he winked. Broomball was a fixture of the company picnic, a hockey-like contest played with brooms and a lot of screaming. A plucky handful of women chose to participate, but mainly it was a matter of testosterone. Also: an expression of tribal wrath. After all, it wasn't only the editorial department that butted heads with the project managers. The marketing people jeered at the warehouse crew, the warehouse crew pitied the programmers, and the programmers laughed at the product development team, who had, I was once assured, "fatty tissue between their ears." Here on the field of honor, these rivalries could take the form of good, clean fun. Most of the players, including Jeff, daubed their faces with war paint.

"Godspeed!" I told Tod as headed off to the field. He waved his broom, whose bristles he had reinforced with packing tape.

"There must be a place to wash your hands here," Kerry said. She looked concerned.

"I have some old diaper wipes in the glove compartment if you're desperate."

"That won't be necessary, hon," she said, spying a portable sink near the latrines.

She washed up. Then, while she held her hands in a slight vertical like a surgeon on TV, we strolled along the perimeter of the pasture. Incredibly, the sun continued to shine. A wash of depressed guitar music came from the stage, and in the shade of a fir tree, we came upon Jason Kilar, crouched in a pre- or post-broomball trance. Back then he ran the video store: later he would ascend to the vice-presidential empyrean. At the moment he had war paint, or ketchup, on his chin. His wife, crouched beside him, seemed very nice.

"How's it going?" I said.

"Good, good," he replied. He had gotten laser surgery on his eyes not long before, and now they always had a supernatural shine to them. They made you defensive about your own eyes, which you assumed must resemble poker chips in comparison. Glancing down, Kerry and I waved and moved on.

Now we came to the dunk tank. There was a huge crowd, and a long line of employees waiting to throw a ball at the target. A direct hit spilled the human occupant into a tank of cold water. And the human occupant, laughing madly at each miss and wearing, I seem to recall, a wet suit, was Jeff. Surely there had to be some allegorical significance to the whole scene. Our boss, the sole proprietor of all he surveyed, had already taken at least one dip: he was dripping, even as the sun dried him off.

"Go for it!" people were yelling, as a redhead from CS took aim. She missed. Jeff laughed—the famous laughter, ricocheting and relentless in its mirth—and shook his head. Another employee threw a curveball and missed.

"This is amazing," Kerry said. "Populism at its finest."

"I guess so. Give the guy some credit, though. I don't think Lee Iacocca ever climbed into one of those contraptions."

Now a little kid got the ball. There was some debate over whether he should be allowed to move closer, and somebody—the project manager for the dunk tank, I guess—took him by the hand and advanced him a few steps. Clearly the crowd wanted him to hit the target. A small crescendo of cheers began, drowning out the music, but the kid choked: the ball dribbled to the ground just a few feet away.

What was the view like from the tank? We moved around to the side and saw what Jeff saw: a giant meadow, a vast crowd, enough hamburgers and tofu to feed a small Third World nation. It looked like Woodstock, minus the mud and nudity and acid-induced paranoia. These were happy people, well-heeled and casually dressed, and every single one of them worked for the laughing man in the wet suit. It was a real accomplishment.

"What will he buy next?" Kerry said. A freakishly tall guy from HR, who supposedly worked standing up at a podium, clipped the edge of the target: close, but no cigar.

"Maybe he'll buy this meadow," I said. "Or that mountain."

"Too modest. I know: he's going to buy Cuba. The entire island will become an Amazon subsidiary. He'll rename it Bezonia."

"Will Havana still be Havana?"

"Nope. He'll rename it MacKenzie."

"That's sweet," I said, meaning it. I was getting caught up in the fantasia. "MacKenzie, the capital city, with its wide boulevards and colonial architecture."

Nobody seemed capable of hitting the target: were we a company of myopics? Jeff said something about getting chilly, and there was some concern that he was about to exit the tank. A broomball player, still glittering with war paint and sweat, wound up like a pro and threw a wild one. I wondered if any bystanders had been beaned so far. Aloud, I also wondered whether Jeff would oversee Bezonia by himself, or parcel it out.

"Oh, he'll share the wealth," Kerry said. "He'll carve out a little territory for David. The Duke of Risheria."

There was a bang as the ball finally connected with the target, and Jeff fell into the water. The crowd went nuts, our employer splashed and thrashed in the tank, which really wasn't much larger than a shower stall, and we waited suspensefully for the lord of e-commerce to surface. When he did, he was still laughing. And frankly, the world was laughing with him.

Fall came, my fourth in Seattle. For the first time I was alone as I observed the dull autumnal palette: light green, dark green, brackish green. The chasm between my personal life, which was desolate, and my professional life, which was a thrill ride, seemed to be widening by the day. When my son was staying with me, there would be intervals of good cheer at home. We played games, watched TV, and ate bowls of macaroni and cheese. When he wasn't, I spent as little time there as possible. Probably I should have moved to a new apartment, but some combination of inertia and momentum—call it *momertia*—kept me where I was, with the broken Jacuzzi and the faded roses on the slipcovers. I felt as if I lived in Miss Havisham's house, where time had stopped and the clocks would never resume their duties.

At work, contrarily, time seemed to be speeding up. It felt good, like a sublime sort of tickling. The company was gearing up for what promised to be its biggest holiday season to date, and the eyes of the world were upon us, at least to judge from the phalanx of *Time* reporters who invaded the office in November.

Michael Krantz, the magazine's San Francisco bureau chief, requested an interview with Kerry and me. By now the department had moved again, to 520 Pike Street, and it was in the little kitchen, which had turned into a dumping ground for unwanted books, that we sat down to chat.

He began with the customary queries about education, background, our circuitous route to Seattle. How did we know each other? "I inherited James, so to speak, at the *Voice*," Kerry recalled. In connection with Amazon's nomadic atmosphere, I mentioned that I had changed offices nine times since I was hired.

We paused while a fellow employee came in to zap her Chinese food in the microwave. A faint perfume of hoisin hung in the air. Then Krantz said he wanted to ask us a hypothetical question. Go ahead, we told him.

"How does it feel to be rich beyond your wildest dreams?" he said.

Define *hypothetical*, I felt like saying. Instead we did our usual ducking, dodging, and harrumphing.

"This would be a dream job even without the options," Kerry said.

"We get told not to watch the ticker," I said.

Recognizing a certain comfort level with the media, the PR department now allowed Kerry and me to meet the press without a chaperone. We could fend off these spitballs about our funny money in any way we pleased. Yet the things we said were true: neither of us had come to Amazon expecting to strike it rich, and all that cash still felt like an arbitrary, accidental phenomenon.

Krantz took notes and taped the whole exchange. He arranged for a photographer to shoot me and Kerry in the office she shared with Alix, who was away: we sat on the floor amidst a carefully orchestrated avalanche of books and galleys, burning up beneath the lights. Then Krantz disappeared along with the rest of the people from *Time*, and we were left to wonder why another run-of-the-mill magazine story required so many helping hands.

As it turned out, there was an excellent reason. Jeff was about to make the cover of *Time* as Person of the Year—joining a select club that included Mahatma Gandhi, Charles Lindbergh, Martin Luther King, and Queen Elizabeth II—and the magazine would be running a lavish, multipart spread on the company and its creator.

This bit of intelligence fell into my lap a little early, as usual. At 4:45 A.M. on December 19, I was sitting in a television studio in downtown Seattle. I had a tiny speaker in my right ear, a microphone clipped to my lapel, and a look of total exhaustion on my face. Outside, it was still dark. Inside, the technicians had propped me in front of an illuminated backdrop, with a bright blue sky and the Space Needle visible over my shoulder. I was about to address the American people on the subject of great holiday books.

From time to time a voice whispered in my ear. This was a CNN production assistant in Atlanta, who sounded much more alert, as well he might: there they were approaching the relatively humane hour of 8:00 A.M. "Six more minutes," the voice told me. "Remember to look at the camera." I took a sip of water, tugged down the back of my jacket the way Albert Brooks did in *Broadcast News*, and whispered back: "Okay."

I had been thrilled with the assignment. True, I wasn't being called upon for a display of critical fireworks. The idea was to discuss our seasonal blockbusters, and Kay Dangaard had eavesdropped on my pre-interview a few days before to make sure I didn't start raving about Paul Celan or the Oulipo School. I did, however, get to pick a wild card of my own: a reissue of Charles Portis's *Norwood*. My aim was to transform that little paperback into Number One with a bullet, even as I sold enough copies of *The Greatest Generation* to build a 300-foot-high effigy of Dwight D. Eisenhower.

My cue was approaching. I had rehearsed my lines and knew exactly what I was going to say to the boy-and-girl anchor team in Atlanta. Moments before I went live, however, I heard some excited crosstalk in my earpiece: Jeff had been anointed Person of the Year!

They would be making the announcement in just a few minutes! At once it dawned on me that this little segment, which would allow me to preach the gospel of books to my biggest audience ever, was simply an appetizer for the main event: a lengthy celebration of my employer. Well, he had earned it.

The red light on the camera went on. Miles in Atlanta, with a full head of gleaming black hair, thanked me for getting up so early: I must have really looked like a cadaver. Then he and I and pretty Kyra talked about books. I blinked too much, and sounded skittish for the first minute, but otherwise did fine. Then it was over. Abruptly I was unplugged from the national consciousness and allowed to stagger home, where I slept for a few hours before starting my abbreviated 2:00 P.M. shift at the warehouse.

On my way to Dawson Street I stopped at the office, where an advance copy of *Time* was already circulating. The cover had a creepy look to it, as if somebody had decapitated Jeff and then stuffed his head in a box. But inside you found the snazziest piece of free advertising in the history of commerce: twenty-two pages of text and graphics, which made Jeff sound like a combination of Thomas Edison, Henry Ford, and Sir Edmund Hillary.

The opening photo spread alone was worth the price of admission. It depicted Jeff in a slouch hat and khakis, swinging from vine to vine through a perilous swamp: an evocation, clearly, of Indiana Jones. At once I recalled his confession two years ago in the bar at Sleeping Lady. *There goes Indy!* He looked awfully pleased, gripping the network cables the stylist had substituted for jungle creepers. Were we witnessing some secret jouissance here? Or merely high spirits? Only Jeff, who was also pictured repairing a windmill, autographing hats, and carrying a large stuffed Pikachu, knew for sure.

At my desk I picked up a single phone message—a friend in Florida had glimpsed me on CNN!—then anxiously flipped through the magazine in search of Michael Krantz's piece. There it was. On the fourth page I came across a nice color photo of Kerry and me sitting on the floor of her office. The carpet was artfully covered with books, and we both looked studious, discriminating, as if we were just then making or breaking a literary reputation. On Kerry's desk, in the foreground, you could see a large bottle of Advil and her glasses, which we no doubt spent some time looking for after the shoot. It was all very satisfying, except for the caption: *Kerry Fried and Alix Wilbur of the editorial group offer opinions on Amazon's book selections.* That was a low blow, and not only because they had spelled Alix's name wrong.

And what about Krantz's piece? For the most part, it was lively and smart. I was quoted a few times, once with a bit of retroactive spin from the reporter: *"We get told not to watch the ticker,"* says Marcus, *a three-year vet who, one imagines, does so anyway.* There were some additional fumbles with proper names. After mentioning Simon Leake and Jenny Brown, both editors in the video department, the article later quoted a two-headed monster named Jenny Simon.

What strikes me now, though, is the sheer ecstasy of the entire issue. In this sense it resembles an artifact dredged from the bottom layer of an archaeological dig. Despite some token attempts at objectivity, the reporters seem as intoxicated by the company as we were, wallowing in the numbers (3 million square feet of warehouse capacity! 13 million customers! 18 million items for sale!) and generally beating the drum for Jeff's vision of a brave new world of retail. And Krantz, like the rest of us, got one crucial fact very wrong:

Amazon isn't about technology or even commerce. Any moron can open an online store. The trick is showing millions of customers such a good time that they come back every few days for the next 50 years. Amazon is, like every other site on the Web, a content play.

In the editorial department this was music to our ears. Finally somebody had recognized our heroic role in keeping the company on its feet! But Krantz's epiphany was about six months out of date: content had already gone from golden goose to stale foie gras. And over the next six months, it would become clear that if Amazon *weren't* about commerce, it was going to make like a virtual *Hindenberg*.

For the moment, though, that magazine was a glorious thing. I still have my copy. At some point my son took a pencil and decorated Jeff's face with a mustache and a Jheri curl, two cosmetic touches I doubt he would mind. I thumb through it now and then, with alternating expressions of comedy and tragedy on my face, and feel strangely furtive, as though it were porn. But no, I'm simply traveling back in *Time*, to the annus mirabilis of 1999. That was the year when I was sitting on the floor of Kerry's office and Jeff was sitting on top of the world.

19

ON DECEMBER 31, 1999, I sat in front of the television with a couple of old friends and watched a giant crystal sphere descend over Times Square. The crowd was enormous, jubilant, drunk. The police had corralled them behind wooden barriers and welded the manhole covers shut. We opened some souvenir champagne my father had gotten at a medical conference—the only bottle I've ever seen with the word *thrombosis* on the label—and drank a toast at midnight.

After all the fuss, the new millennium felt an awful lot like the old one. At Amazon, however, the next year would be darker and drearier than its predecessor, a kind of evil twin. The first premonition came on January 28, when the company canned about 150 employees. Now, this wasn't exactly a freak occurrence: after three years of explosive growth, layoffs were now a staple of the Web economy, as were bankruptcy filings. And Amazon was firing only a tiny fraction of its staff, which then numbered around 8,000. Still, for a business whose very existence was predicated on getting big fast, this shrinkage came as a shock. It was a symbol, at the very least, of diminished expectations.

For the employees who were fired, of course, it was more than a symbolic event. Both Jordana and Alix lost their jobs. Neither was really prepared for the pink slip. Alix, for example, had just returned from an exhausting hitch in the Georgia warehouse: despite her fear of heights, she spent much of the holiday season in an industrial cherry picker, retrieving television sets and DVD players from their storage berths. Surely this display of esprit de corps should have earned her a warm spot in every manager's heart—not to mention the fact that she churned out witty content like a demon. She was an example to us all, wasn't she?

Evidently not. After being summoned to Nick's office to hear the bad news, she and Jordana and every other unlucky employee were escorted directly out of the building. Their ID badges were repossessed. Jordana was told to surrender her parking pass, too, until she pointed out that she needed the card to exit the garage. This was a dilemma: it could have been one of those Zen logic problems posed to potential employees. After a short confab, the HR people agreed to let Jordana keep her parking pass until she left the garage, but *no longer than that.*

As a business decision, the layoffs were certainly defensible, probably necessary. Still, there was something ugly about the way it was done: you gave loyal, even ardent employees the boot, then marched them out of the building like petty criminals.

To be fair, the criminals received generous severance packages. What's more, the layoffs themselves were part of a broader trend, which had first been outlined to us by David Risher under the rubric of GOHIO—i.e., Getting Our House In Order. Evidently our house was a mess. Our sloppy, seat-of-the-pants methodology was no longer going to cut the mustard. We had to start behaving less like a utopian frat house and more like a traditional corporation.

Certainly the arrival of Joe Galli in June 1999 had been a step in this direction. The new president—who resembled a Mediterranean version of Jeff, with an extra dose of Joe Pesci–like volubility—had cut his teeth selling hardware, not software. He had boosted Black & Decker's market share through the roof by dint of energy, innovative zest, and grim efficiency. Granted, he lacked Jeff's magical touch with the media. In an early interview with the *Seattle Post-Intelligencer,* he predicted that the Internet would "pour gasoline on the human imagination." (After that, I assumed, it would rub Clorox in your eyes, then steal your wallet.) But he knew how to run a big retail operation, and he brought a traditionalist's point of view to the table—which made him a paradoxical novelty at a place like Amazon.

One of his initiatives was to push for private label products: in other words, stuff with the Amazon brand on it, which would make us into quasi-manufacturers as well as merchants. In short order we began selling knapsacks, backpacks, briefcases, and messenger bags with our logo. Next we developed a board game called Bookology— a kind of Trivial Pursuit for bibliophiles, few of whom actually bothered to buy it.

If we were going to put our imprimatur on products, however, there was an obvious choice before us: books. There had already been some industry speculation as to whether Amazon would go into the publishing business itself. Certainly we had the clout, the distribution network, and the marketing machinery to make a go of it. With Galli's encouragement, we sent up a trial balloon during the 1999 holidays: the company quietly leased the rights to a defunct imprint called Weathervane, and repackaged a handful of titles for this virtual publishing house. As I recall, the list included a public-domain trifle by Charles Dickens, a collection of Christmas recipes, and perhaps two or three other marginal items.

These were not incipient bestsellers. They were creatures from the black lagoon of the remainder table. No editor would have selected them—and indeed, no editor did, since we were never consulted about the entire project. On the contrary, it was concealed from our department, presumably on the grounds that we would bitch about the selections or fail to keep our lips zipped or both. In retrospect, the situation has a certain screwball charm to it. You can imagine Ernst Lubitsch committing it to film: the oblivious editors, the cynical, pomaded bosses, the furtive shipments of *Plum Pudding, Mincemeat, and Roman Punch: A Victorian Christmas.* At the time, though, we weren't laughing. Kerry, who had worked at three of the most prestigious New York publishing houses, took particular offense at our exclusion. There was nothing to do about it, though. Weathervane was a done deal.

It was also, as I've already mentioned, a cautious testing of the waters. For that reason, the company bigwigs wanted it to remain below the radar. Well, they got their wish, and more: Weathervane's profile was so low that it could have slithered under a limbo pole. And the books themselves stiffed, despite being promoted on the home page and other parts of the site.

Frustrated, perhaps, by our lukewarm record as a publisher, Galli looked for other corner-cutting stratagems. In a widely noted measure, he decided to remove the Advil from various departmental larders. Amazon would provide its employees with coffee, tea, and filtered water, but we would have to supply our own analgesics. Again, there's something intrinsically comical about this penny-pinching. The company was squandering buckets of money—by the end of 2000, we would rack up a net loss of $1.4 billion for the year—even as our partners in the much-touted Amazon Commerce Network continued to drop like flies. Meanwhile, our president fought back by plundering the medicine cabinet. What would be next? No more paper towels? A quarterly disbursement of a single sugar packet for each employee?

To some extent, these are facetious complaints. True, they point to some genuine contradictions, some real specimens of corporate myopia. By the early months of 2000, however, Amazon had a much bigger problem to contend with than the failure of its stealth publishing imprint. Namely: the bubble finally began to collapse.

On March 10 the NASDAQ hit a new peak of 5,048.62, having doubled since the previous summer. This statistic was duly noted by investors, who sat back in the happy expectation of doubling their money once again by mid-July. Instead, the tech-heavy index began to slide. At first the market met this minor correction with a shrug: it was good medicine, and you had to swallow it if you wanted to get better. Then the losses accelerated. On April 10 the NASDAQ dropped by 258.25 points, followed by a further drop of 286.27 on April 12. Two days later came Black Friday, the biggest rout in the short, sweet history of the index: 355.49 points in a single session. Less than a month after the NASDAQ topped out, the jewels in the crown of the New Economy had shed a third of their collective value. And the bloodletting was far from over.

Needless to say, the cratering NASDAQ was merely the symptom of a more profound disorder. I'll let the economists wrangle over the precise nature of the Internet bust. But clearly what Alan Greenspan called our irrational exuberance—a kind of national suspension of disbelief—had finally snapped. Nobody stopped shopping on the Web or sending dirty emails. I never read about a single auto-da-fé of CPUs, modems, and ethernet cables. In other words, we didn't relinquish the Internet as a practical necessity. Yet we did cease to think of it as the mother of all slot machines, pouring a jackpot into the cupped hands of every investor. In fact, people began to lose money—rivers of money, oceans of money—and many hung onto their deflating shares all the way to the bottom.

At first Amazon fared better than most of its peers. The stock had hit its own all-time high of $113 in December 1999: if you factored in all the splits since the company had gone public, you got an adjusted price of $1,356 per share. That made even Henry Blodget's predictions sound flinty and conservative. True, the price had taken a beating toward the end of the year, and plunged again in April when the markets went south. Yet it stabilized during the early weeks of spring, which persuaded us Amazonians that we had ridden out the storm.

We hadn't. What happened next had little to do with the company's performance: instead it reflected the fact that Wall Street had awakened with a terrible, perhaps terminal hangover. The analysts, once our loudest cheerleaders, now sharpened their knives and went to work. On June 23, Mary Meeker—a Morgan Stanley superstar who had probably pumped more air into the Internet bubble than any other commentator—announced that she saw "no upside" for the company in the immediate future. The next month, Holly Becker of Lehman Brothers, another early booster, revealed that she was "throwing in the towel on Amazon." Even Henry Blodget, spooked by the company's second-quarter revenue slump, began backpedaling away from his previous pronouncements. On July 27, after we posted results for the recent quarter, he downgraded the stock, as did a conga line of four other analysts. Not to be outdone, Banc of America Securities issued *two* downgrades in a single week: perhaps *mea culpa* sounded more sincere if you said it twice.

All of this naysaying took a toll on the stock, and put a real dent in company morale. Oddly enough, though, it wasn't the turncoat behavior of our former champions that seemed the most damning. Having spent the last three years running as a pack, they were almost obliged to change course in strict formation, like synchronized swimmers. No, the most damaging slap on the wrist was issued by a convertible debt analyst at Lehman Brothers named Ravi Suria.

Unlike his peers, Suria had never talked up any Internet stocks. He had never appeared on television yammering about killer apps or disruptive technologies. In other words, his hands were clean. That suggested he could be taken more seriously than his colleagues, who seemed to be stampeding into the media equivalent of a sheep dip. And what did Suria say? In his opinion, Amazon's credit was "extremely weak and deteriorating." What's more, we were faced with a triple-whammy of "negative cash flow, poor working capital management, and high debt load," which would prevent us from clawing our way back to solvency. According to Suria's analysis, the company would start running out of money within the next six months. Then it would experience a credit squeeze—meaning that suppliers would refuse to ship us goods without immediate payment—and shortly thereafter lapse into a fiscal coma.

Suria issued this doomsday scenario on June 23, cheek-by-jowl with Mary Meeker's gloomy comments. In response, the stock plunged 19 percent that very day, to a new fifty-two-week low of $32.50. It's important to note that Suria wasn't merely lowering targets or trimming his sails: he was predicting the company's demise, and soon. Nor was he dismissed as a Chicken Little type, which is what would have happened just a few months before. His analysis got a wide hearing, and persuaded many people that Amazon, the invulnerable engine of e-commerce, was now on the ropes.

The fact that he was wrong—dead wrong—is beside the point. What mattered was the climate of opinion, which no longer operated in the company's favor. As the public saw it, we had morphed from David to Goliath: a clumsy giant who couldn't even balance his checkbook. The Federal Trade Commission was casting a cold eye at one of our recent acquisitions, an outfit called Alexa Internet, which was also the target of two different privacy-related lawsuits. Even our cachet on the Web itself had begun to evaporate; tech purists didn't like it when we enforced our patents for one-click shopping or the affiliates program. We were stifling innovation, they claimed, behaving like the bullies who dominated the traditional corporate landscape. Nobody would cut us any slack, it seemed. The good times—when cutting slack for Amazon had been an international pastime—were over.

At the office, meanwhile, life went on. Joe Galli bailed on July 15, leaving a gigantic pile of worthless, underwater options on the table. This abrupt departure might have rattled many a company. At Amazon, though, we were already so rattled that most employees greeted the news with indifference. Meanwhile Galli's subsequent career offered another lesson in turn-of-the-century economics. His first stop was VerticalNet, a bright light of the business-to-business sector. When B2B went down in flames a few months later, Galli dusted himself off and decided to give the Web a wide berth: he ended up at Newell Rubbermaid, a nice old-fashioned manufacturer of brooms, trash cans, and other kitchen paraphernalia.

Were we bowed and bloodied by the economy? Sure. Did we stop expanding? Of course not. Certain overseas initiatives were put on a slower track, but others plunged forward as if the company were as hale and hearty as ever. On August 29, just after Faye Landes of Sanford Bernstein shot another analytical arrow into our flank, we launched our French site. A little more than two months later, the Japanese site went live as well. These were both enormous markets for books, not to mention the many other products we now sold. They were also tricky environments, where the government regulated prices and frowned on commercial interlopers like us. It could be a while before these latest outposts began to perform. Still, it was cheering to see the company show the flag overseas while we wrestled with our demons at home.

During that summer, in fact, the company flew a clutch of foreign journalists into Seattle for an extended session of show-and-tell. They were largely from Spain, Italy, Holland, and Sweden: nominees for our next round of expansion. Kerry and I attended the reception for them, talking up the company and neatly sidestepping any questions about the stock price, which even the most rudimentary English speakers insisted on asking. Everything was coming up roses, we told them.

Then we were surprised to see Rick Ayre, our elusive vice-president for Editorial, who had been sidelined by a spate of recent illnesses. He approached our little group, brushing back his long hair, and gave us one of those self-effacing smiles.

"What do you do at Amazon?" said a Spanish reporter with a plastic cup of chardonnay in his hand.

Rick mumbled something in return: not an answer.

"No, really," the Spaniard persisted. "What is your job at the company?"

After a minute or so of mysterious reticence, Rick answered the question. To this day I'm not sure why he was stonewalling the crowd: perhaps it was an index of disgust at our diminishing role in the company. Even odder, though, was the tack he now took with another journalist, a Scandinavian woman. Having established (sort of) what Rick did, she asked him whether he enjoyed his work.

"We love our jobs," he said. "Otherwise we wouldn't still be doing them. James here"—he indicated me with a wave of his hand—"doesn't have to work anymore. Not unless he wants to."

Everybody peered at me, a millionaire who loved his job. Actually I did have to work: not only was I supporting two households, but if I opted for early retirement, I would lose most of my remaining options, the source of my supposed wealth. And even if I had been rich as Croesus, I wouldn't have appreciated Rick's comment, which breached our customary decorum. You weren't supposed to flaunt our good fortune. It would make the Europeans twitch with envy and confirm all their ideas about American-style vulgarity.

"*I* have to work," Kerry said with a smile, trying to put things back on track. She steered the conversation over to the Spaniard, asking him how many of his countrymen had access to the Internet. The icebreaker did the trick. Nobody said anything further about my riches. But once or twice I found myself being covertly studied, as if I were a rare specimen on the verge of extinction. God knows what sort of stories later appeared in *El País* or *Svenska Dagbladet*.

As editors, anyway, we did feel like an endangered species. We were menaced on one side by personalization, on the other by co-op requirements, and now we had a third threat to deal with: customer reviews.

This was an unexpected problem. Most of us had come to enjoy the perpetual racket from our customers. A certain percentage of them were dumb as a post, of course, but the same thing could be said of any party I'd ever attended: if you eavesdropped, you heard insight and inanity in equal measure. And remember, we were talking about a big party. Amazon now had upward of 15 million registered customers, and many of them liked to share their opinions. Some of them couldn't *stop* sharing their opinions, as if their existence depended on it: they were nothing if not critical.

At times their contributions seemed to validate all the rhetoric of Internet democracy. Here was an intelligent and articulate conversation about books—about many other things, too—conducted by a group of disinterested, disembodied spirits. There was little of the schadenfreude, the verbal grapeshot, that many professional critics seemed to regard as their stock-in-trade. These were amateurs, in the most honorable sense of the word.

And even when they weren't, they brought something new to the table. I recall, for example, scanning the detail page for one of Nicholson Baker's novels and coming across a customer review written by his Spanish translator. Here was a guy who had studied Baker's prose with a jeweler's loupe. Who better to comment on his mandarin vocabulary and dirty mind? Another example: when Paul Theroux's memoir of V.S. Naipaul, *Sir Vidia's Shadow,* got a thorough drubbing in the press, the affronted author immediately posted a comment of his own. This wasn't so much a review as a tail-gunning reply to his critics. Still, it added yet another dimension to the conversation, which took place as always within earshot of a million kibitzers.

What was the problem, then? Well, at some point a conversation of a different kind took place in the Amazonian corridors of power. The company had a choice. It could continue to pay its editors and freelance writers top dollar for book reviews. Or it could shift the emphasis to its customer reviewers, who numbered in the hundreds of thousands and were happy to work for nothing. What was the decision? Let's just say it was a victory for Internet democracy.

Having thrown in its lot with the vox pop, the company now concluded that a little glorification was in order. Visitors were encouraged to vote on the reviews they read. The scores were then tallied, run through some mysterious algorithmic wringer, and used to rank every single customer reviewer. In no time at all a former librarian named Harriet Klausner was anointed Amazon's Number-One Reviewer. She had already written 3,122 reviews, even as she continued her duties as a freelance columnist for *Porthole Cruise Magazine* and *Affaire de Coeur.* And this mighty output was no flash in the pan. Three years after snagging the top spot, Klausner had notched 5,420 reviews, and received 33,687 positive votes from other customers. She was still leading the pack, and seemed likely to do so for a long, long time.

In her photo, Harriet Klausner looks like a nice woman. For this reason, and to forestall the inevitable charge of sour grapes, I'm not going to dwell on her role as Amazon's Number-One Reviewer—a title I had mentally assigned to myself. But two things do need to be said. First of all, having waded through a great deal of Klausnerian prose, I can report that it's pretty banal stuff. (If pressed, I'd probably give the palm to Amazon's Number-Six Reviewer, a real-estate developer named Francis McInerney who was recently profiled, to my considerable distress, in *The New Yorker.*) More to the point, though, is the patent absurdity of the whole system. It represents the Culture of Metrics at its worst, with a dose of some managerial quackery like Six Sigma stirred in for good measure: the more you write, the better you are. Quantity equals quality. It's the statistical fallacy all over again, applied like a mustard plaster to my own line of work. A reminder: art is not a popularity contest. Taste, talent, and discrimination have nothing to do with numbers. Case closed.

During the early months of 2000, though, I wasn't quite so sanguine about the situation. Harriet Klausner's coronation had gotten some heavy coverage—including articles in *People, Wired, The Baltimore Sun,* and a long, unintentionally comical Q-and-A in *Suck*—and I felt fairly tetchy about online populism. It was clear that being a professional critic at Amazon now constituted the kiss of death. You were an elitist, a snob, a dying breed. What was I supposed to do? If you couldn't beat them, you could join them. I would come up with an alter ego, and fast.

Thus did Jim Kibble enter the scene. This mild-mannered yet opinionated gent began posting customer reviews during the early spring. He had a nice style, not unlike my own, and stuck up for many of my cherished favorites: Albert Murray's *The Omni-Americans,* Czeslaw Milosz's *Bells in Winter,* and Mary Jarrell's *Remembering Randall,* not to mention the unfairly maligned *Ishtar.* Yet he, or I, didn't feel compelled to crank out the paragraphs like sausages. They were a matter of whim, impulse, momentary passion. And Jim, who ran out of steam after thirteen reviews and 146 positive votes, never ranked very high in the pantheon. Three years after his first appearance, he was still Amazon Reviewer Number 1609, in a dead heat with a half-dozen other contenders.

Still, he did accomplish his purpose: he earned me a pat on the head from my employer. On June 14, 2000, Jim Kibble got an email from the company's Contest Administrator—meaning Melissa, who sat down the hall from me. "Your review," I was told, "was selected as an Amazon.com Book Review Writing Contest winner. Well done!" Apparently my squib on *Remembering Randall* had put me over the top. My prize was a $50 gift certificate, which I could redeem for music, videos, toys, electronics, home improvement, or (perish the thought) books.

I found the news deeply, perversely flattering. It would be pushing the envelope, though, to accept the money. Instead I typed out a brief, rather idealistic reply. I decided not to reveal my secret identity just yet. A few weeks earlier, though, Melissa had been filling me in on a favorite collegiate prank at the University of Oregon: doing handstands on a beer keg. Recalling our conversation, I inserted what I thought was a conspicuous clue:

> I'm delighted to have won your Book Review Writing Contest—I nearly did a keg stand in my living room! Alas, I don't feel comfortable accepting any prize money for these reviews. So why don't you give the fifty bucks to some other deserving reviewer? I'm happy with the honor and nothing more.

That was that, I told myself. I expected Melissa to pop her head into my office at any moment, helpless with mirth and insistent that I take the money. Instead there was silence. Then I got another email, addressed to *Dear Jim* rather than *Dear Book Review Contest Winner:*

> Your response was certainly the nicest, if not most amusing, response I've received recently. Do you really have a keg in your living room?

This was getting complicated. I didn't mean to hoodwink Melissa, nor did it seem wise to launch into one of those flirtatious email roundelays. I wandered into Kerry's office and explained the whole mess. "You have no choice," she told me. "You'll have to blow your cover now." Grabbing hold of my sleeve, she escorted me to Melissa's cubicle, where I felt myself at an odd loss for words.

"Hi," Melissa said, making a notation on some mind-numbing spreadsheet. "What's up with you two?"

"The fact is that I'm . . . I'm . . ." I couldn't seem to complete the sentence.

"Are you okay?" she asked.

"He's Jim Kibble," Kerry said. "The contest winner."

After a perplexed moment, Melissa looked amused. "I should have known," she said. "The keg stand."

"Right. I didn't mean to toy with you."

"Right."

"Can I keep the money?"

"Let's not be a greedy guts, shall we?" Kerry said.

I'm still curious about why I found it so hard to confess. I wasn't the only person at Amazon with an alter ego to his name: even Harriet Klausner might have been the creation of some bored and bemused colleague, if only she hadn't been so damn productive. The problem, I think, is that I liked being Jim Kibble. He was a fresh face, a new voice, and hadn't yet been contaminated by the real world. He was happy with the honor and nothing more: in fact, *he* was the idealist Rick had been discussing at the reception. No wonder I was reluctant to spoil the fun. For one bright shining moment, he had made me into a virtual celebrity—and that was something he, or I, or we, would never forget.

20

TOWARD THE END OF 2000, the editorial department was in the midst of yet another reorg. Tinkering with the organizational chart was a favorite hobby in every branch of the company. But the people who ran the books division just couldn't resist one more cut and shuffle of the deck. Earlier we had been slotted into small groups called pods—an apparent tribute to *Invasion of the Body Snatchers*, although it made us sound like zombies. (An accident, surely.) Now we were herded into new configurations called business units. Each unit consisted of several editors and a project manager, and despite the usual tomfoolery about workplace democracy, it was perfectly clear who was in the driver's seat.

My unit consisted of me, Kerry, Barrie, Katherine, and Stefanie. Our project manager, as I observed with a sinking heart, was the Bird. Her very presence was something of a shock: for reasons we would never know, she had fallen from her high estate in cross-product site development and plunged back into the netherworld of books. Given that we still earned more than half of the company's total revenues, you would have thought that we were a *desirable* division. But it had been years since we were the favored child. Nobody ever spent quality time with us anymore.

Then, just as our unit began to show a cozy coherence, Kerry dropped a bombshell: she was quitting. I was crestfallen, but not completely surprised. She had spent the last eighteen months locking horns with various managers—one in particular seemed determined to make her cry uncle—and no longer had the patience to stick it out. Years earlier, she could have pulled a Bartleby Maneuver and done as she pleased. Now that was impossible: Amazon had discovered the fine art of downsizing. So she gave notice, planning to leave right before we were marched off to the warehouse.

At this point, office politics raised its ugly head. I had always assumed that if Kerry left, I would take over management of the literature area, especially now that my home page duties had dwindled. In early December I attended yet another superfluous unit meeting. While I made my latest drawing of the little old man in my latest steno notebook, the Bird made an announcement.

"As you all know, Kerry is leaving us for greener pastures," she said. "That means we have open headcount for somebody to run the literature page. I've got a few people in mind already." At this point she made a deliberate effort to avoid her scan-and-pan head movements, possibly to indicate there were no contenders in the room. "But if you know of any strong candidates, please do speak up."

I said nothing. Neither did anybody else. We concluded a few remaining bits of business—mostly nonsense about our upcoming PowerPoint presentation to Lyn Blake—and the meeting ended. I left the room enveloped in a cloud of rage. Everybody knew I should get the job. But since the decision was hers and hers alone, the Bird was punishing me for this presumption. As I walked back to the office I now shared with Kerry, I realized that my habitual, detached attitude toward all things Amazonian had snapped.

"That cunt," I said, sitting down at my desk. "I'd like to feed her into a wood chipper."

Kerry looked shocked. It wasn't the antagonism that shook her up—she herself had once talked about shoving the Bird down an elevator shaft—but the fact that I was expressing it. She was used to a more tranquil tone from me around the office. Now every bit of suppressed wrath from the past three years was bursting to the surface, as if I had tapped into a regular aquifer of ill feeling.

"I told you," she told me. "She's two-faced. All those rides in the Volvo were a diversionary tactic. She's a bad egg, a very bad egg."

"I can't believe this," I said. I realized I was talking very slowly. My right foot was also banging rhythmically on the carpet like an industrial piston.

"You look like you're imploding," Kerry said. "I'll go and talk to Nick. You're his direct report, right? He'll probably help you out."

She left, then returned two minutes later.

"I told Nick you were imploding down the hall," she said.

"What did he say?"

"Apparently he thought I was on a diplomatic sortie," she said. "He asked if I was throwing your hat into the ring for my job."

In my current state, I simply couldn't understand the metaphor. I tried and failed to imagine Kerry throwing a hat into a ring— no, wait, that must be a *boxing* ring—and was distracted by the jackhammer action at the end of my right leg. I did grasp, however, that prompt action was necessary.

The next morning, after a sleepless night and a meticulous session with the razor, I dropped by Libby's office and asked if I might speak to her. A kind soul, she gave me an immediate appointment. Looking even more tanned than usual, and a little impatient with her landlocked status, she asked if there was a problem.

"There is," I said. I outlined my clash with the Bird, although on this occasion I used her proper name.

"Right," Libby said. "She mentioned she might be looking for somebody with more commercial instincts."

"I've got plenty of commercial instincts."

"Well, what sort of vision do you have for the literature page? What sort of goals would you set?"

"Here's the thing," I said, trying to *become* an MBA the way a Method actor would. "Literature is consistently among the strongest categories in terms of unit sales, yet we're lagging behind in revenue. There are some good reasons for that. We do tons of backlist business, which is great, but that means mass-market paperbacks with low price points and lousy margin. What we've got to do is nudge the customer into buying more frontlist titles. That means targeting market segments more precisely. We have a crazy quilt of constituencies in this category, and it's going to take some real ingenuity to reach them, but I'm the man to do it."

Libby was listening with real interest. I was listening to myself with fascination: it was *fun* to talk the talk, and some of it was perfectly sensible once your ears stopped ringing. I took a deep breath and dove back in.

"I'm sure you're aware that we're working on a Women's Fiction initiative. That's one way to crack the nut in terms of boosting margin: some of the big stars of the genre, like Nora Roberts, are finally breaking out in hardcover. No more Harlequin Romances for these ladies! But I should also mention the Classics initiative I've been developing. It's an obvious opportunity to bundle titles. What's more, I've already talked to three different publishers about co-op opportunities, and they're good to go. Probably they won't pay for placements. Instead they'll give us deeper discounts on selected trade paperbacks if we feature them in an introductory mailing."

I went on in this vein for several minutes, pausing as little as possible. Finally my ideas, or the available oxygen, ran out. Libby drummed her fingers on the desk.

"Clearly you have some skill sets we weren't aware of," she said.

"I think so."

Libby then posed me a ticklish question: Did I trust the Bird? It struck me as a curveball, one of Jeff's Zen brainteasers. And the horrible thing was that I could already feel myself forgiving the Bird for her crappy little trespass. This was the ideal moment to shiv her in the back, after all. I should have answered, honestly, that nobody in the entire department trusted her—that *Garfunkel*, her miniature Jack Russell terrier, didn't trust her. Instead I went the cryptic route.

"Forget about trust. Let's just say I'm very unhappy with the way she's handled this situation."

"I'll talk to her," Libby said. "It's still her decision. But you've been very impressive, I'll say that."

Since this was a special occasion, I went off to the Dahlia Lounge with Kerry. She demanded a blow-by-blow account of the meeting, then interrupted me during my aria about Women's Fiction. "You're scaring me," she said. We drank most of a bottle of wine, feeling our concentration ebbing away during the final glass, and lurched back toward the office. The unspoken question was whether Libby would crack the whip over the Bird. If she didn't, I would be following Kerry out the door sooner than I had anticipated. To delay any bad news, we stopped on the way back and examined many pairs of boxer shorts. I bought two pairs—one with polar bears, another with a blue pinstripe—and when I returned to my desk, I was delighted to find a groveling phone message from my nemesis. Did I know how much she valued my contribution? Would I mind dropping by so she could tell me?

I didn't. I wouldn't. I got the job.

Even this victory, however, couldn't salvage an increasingly dreary year. The holidays rolled in and the top brass set up a War Room, where they could scribble on the whiteboard and look at pie charts. Half of the department was airlifted to Nevada or Georgia or Delaware for the Christmas rush, fully aware that they might be canned upon their return. The lucky few, me included, stuck around Seattle and did our shifts down at Dawson Street.

Since there was now only a skeleton crew at the office, I was assigned temporary stewardship of e-books, awards, Oprah, and a few other odds and ends. I seemed to spend most of my life driving to and from the warehouse, and always at strange hours. At dawn I zipped past the Costco on the way home and wondered what time it opened. At dusk, or later, I cruised around Dawson Street looking for a good parking space, and found one near the florist. In between I dropped by 520 Pike to update dozens of inconsequential XML documents.

Finally there was a break in clouds, at least as far as my personal funk went: CNN wanted me to do another holiday segment. I would be chatting with Miles and Kyra again. The idea was so cheering that I didn't even mind the 4:30 A.M. rendezvous at the television studio.

I spent the previous evening going over my spiel. Then, after another in a long line of sleepless nights, I slipped on a jacket—black wool with a crepe finish, which I imagined would look very suave on television—and headed for the studio in my car. It was dark, and the fine drizzle outside had turned into a downpour. That made it all the more enchanting when I strolled up to my destination, which seemed to be surrounded by a high, chain-link fence. I peered through it as the rain pattered down on my shoulders: where the studio building had stood the year before, there was now a big hole in the ground. A stationary, mud-splattered backhoe testified to a work in progress, as did various construction materials piled on pallets. But something told me that the new facility wouldn't be done within the next ten minutes, when my segment was scheduled to begin.

Clearly I hadn't noticed the new address on my information sheet. I groped for it in my pockets: no luck. The important thing was to avoid panic, I told myself, feeling that jackhammer impulse in my right leg again. Although I knew the segment could be cancelled at the drop of a hat, I kept seeing a nightmarish image of Miles and Kyra cutting away to my remote feed in Seattle: an empty chair, a glass of water, a pathetic backdrop of the blue sky. What was I going to do? I sprinted up to Denny, where everything was dark. At the end of the block, though, I noticed a Seven Eleven with the lights on, and burst directly inside.

"Where's the television studio? What happened to it?" I asked the clerk. "I'm supposed to be on television in *five minutes!*"

He gazed at me, evaluating. I sounded very much like a crazy person: I might just as easily have announced my impending departure for Mars. My hair was soaking wet and sticking up at odd angles, and I'm sure my eyes had that alternating look of exhaustion and frantic energy. Yet I was wearing a respectable raincoat, and underneath that, a snazzy tropical wool jacket with wet lapels.

"They're putting up a new one," he said.

"I know! I know! But where's the temporary studio?"

"Somewhere around here. I think it's the big square building behind the construction site."

I ran across Denny—across four empty lanes, daring the Seattle PD to ticket me for jaywalking—and made my way upstairs to the studio, my heart pumping. The technician plopped me in my chair, hooked up my microphone and earpiece, and gave me a handful of paper towels to dry my hair. I was still grooming when I got the one-minute warning from Atlanta.

The segment? Oh, that went well enough. I stumped for *The Beatles Anthology,* which was our top holiday title, and for Stephen Ambrose's history of the transcontinental railroad. I put in a plug for Philip Pullman's *The Amber Spyglass,* and risked being incinerated by a bolt of lightning when I ranked him above J.K. Rowling. My wild card this time was Charles Baxter's *The Feast of Love.* But we spent the lion's share of our conversation on *Maestro*, Bob Woodward's new biography of Alan Greenspan. At this point you couldn't find a more topical book: Americans of every political stripe were hoping and praying that the Fed chairman would prop up the collapsing economy. He was a potential savoir, although you would never know that from my penetrating banter with Miles and Kyra:

Me: Greenspan is a legendarily inscrutable figure. These days, he's a sort of monetary Wizard of Oz for the United States. But according to Woodward, he was just as inscrutable during his youth, and when he proposed to his wife, she evidently had no idea what he was talking about. He mumbled something about stagflation, I think.

Kyra: It's almost as confusing as the interest rates.

Me: Well, the *second* time he proposed, she understood.

Miles: As Andrea Mitchell would say, it was a case of rational exuberance.

Me: He wanted to have a thirty-year bond with her.

What lingered in my mind later on wasn't the segment itself: it was my panicky circuit of the deserted streets, the discouraging rain on my shoulders, and the big hole in the ground. It would be hard to find a better encapsulation of the year 2000. As for the next one, well, we would be digging ourselves in a little deeper, but I didn't know that yet.

It didn't take long to find out. On January 30, 2001, which happened to be my birthday, the company announced another round of layoffs. True to the principle of sequential decay—which decreed that each year must now be a more depressing version of the one before—this purge made its predecessor look like child's play. We were giving

1,300 people the pink slip. This amounted to about 15 percent of the total payroll. We would also be closing our Georgia warehouse and our customer-service operations in Seattle. Longtime CS veterans were given the option of moving to Grand Forks, North Dakota, or Huntington, West Virginia, but few of them seemed fired up by the idea.

At 520 Pike, we sat in our offices and waited for the summons. You didn't even want to peek into the hallways, for fear of encountering some HR person in a Grim Reaper costume. I watched the clouds blowing west to east in my corner office: they were tall, gray, and elaborately crenellated. I could see the renovated high school where my wife now lived on the summit of Queen Anne Hill. I thought of various things that had gone wrong since my arrival at Amazon— focusing, for some reason, on the time a teenager had plowed into our car just two blocks from home, and the old black VW had spun around twice before coming to rest with a bent axle. It was the *spin-ning* I kept thinking about. My phone rang: it was Kerry, checking in. She wished me good luck, not for the first time, and I sat back to wait for the knock at the door.

It didn't come. Other members of the department, however, were being evicted from their offices. Perry Atterbury got the bad news: his hands shook, according to his roommate, while he packed up his papers, his expensive single-malt whiskey, the fiddle I always wanted to try and never did. Over in the video division, both Simon Leake and Anne Hurley were discharged. Employees telephoned each other every few minutes for damage reports. There was a sense of dread in the air, and it definitely didn't feel like Day One.

In shifts we were now called to a conference room upstairs, where Jeff and David Risher were trying to rally the troops. It was crowded, and the only spot I could find was a perch near the back. To my surprise, David approached me immediately and shook my hand.

"Mister Marcus!" he said briskly. "What are you reading these days? What's the book I can't live without?"

"Get yourself a copy of *The Feast of Love*. It's by Charles Baxter. A tremendous novel, and very funny, too."

David repeated the title with great enthusiasm. In the midst of all this corporate bloodletting, his attempt at bookish conversation sounded a little desperate, but it was touching, too. He needed a friend, or a friendly face, or at least a non-unfriendly face. Even in my new, sullen mood, I was willing to be his Bob Cratchit for just a moment.

Jeff called the room to order. He looked less assured than usual—hell, he was perspiring, having already delivered this speech two or three times—but his famous, goofy calm had yet to abandon him.

"This is an upsetting situation for all of us," he began. He went on to explain that various reversals in the economy had made the cuts essential if the company was to survive. He reiterated the good news from the previous quarter ($972.4 million in sales) and the bad news (net losses of $545.1 million). These numbers came so fast that there was no time for cheering or booing: just stupefied silence. But Jeff knew better than to end on a down note. There were some future initiatives he wanted to share.

At this point a slide appeared on a screen behind him: it depicted some sort of rustic Barcalounger, impossible to pack and ship in less than fifteen minutes. This, Jeff promised, was not an item we would continue to sell.

"We will *fiercely* manage our inventory in order to cut costs and lift margins," he declared. The catalogue would be purged of its insane home-improvement products: the bag of concrete, the fifty-pound barrel of assorted nails. Another slide appeared. This one seemed to depict a box filled with several rocks and some broken glass.

"We won't be selling that one either," Jeff said with a chuckle. You could hear a sigh of relief going around the room. Our boss hadn't thrown in the towel: he was still cracking jokes and pursuing the vision thing. His perspiration wasn't a bad omen after all. He introduced a couple of new initiatives and wrapped things up. Slightly encouraged, we filed back downstairs and returned to work. There were empty offices, empty cubicles, everywhere you looked. But if you hadn't yet been accompanied down to the lobby by an embarrassed security guy, you were a survivor. Another natural disaster had passed you by.

Or so I thought. Barely a month later, I was asking Barrie whether she planned to leave when she hit her five-year mark. She didn't seem sure: she liked her gig as mystery and thrillers editor, even though the Bird got on her nerves. Maybe she would stay on, at least until (obligatory joke) they fired her.

"How would Miles feel about that?" Miles was her husband, and a former Amazon employee.

"Oh, he's perfectly willing to let me—" There was a loud bang, as if the building had been punched in the solar plexus, and the floor began to ripple. Then the room, and all the adjacent rooms, shook violently back and forth. It was 10:54 in the morning, and the Nisqually Earthquake of 2001 was now underway. "Shit!" Barrie said. We ran out into the hallway to brace ourselves against a structural column.

Objects of every description were experiencing a kind of wanderlust: books, lamps, staplers, coffee cups, pads, and pencils flew back and forth. In the hallway we found many companions, all of them methodically leaning against one vibrating column or another. The building made scary noises. "I don't want to die here," I said to Barrie, or to myself, as we waited for the ceiling to come down. I thought of my loved ones. And then, less than a minute after it started, the quake was over. Except for the debris on the floor and the terrified staffers in the hallway and the blinds that were still trembling in the windows, it might never have happened.

Since the elevators hadn't yet been checked for damage, we all evacuated the building via the stairs. Here and there you saw new cracks in the walls, but nothing a little spackle couldn't fix. Down we went, flight after flight, and I realized I hadn't looked out the window before we fled. I half-expected to see the city in ruins when we hit the lobby. Instead, there was hardly any evidence of the disaster, aside from a giant crowd of office workers in the street, like a procession in honor of Secretary's Day. I did see an upended garbage can near the corner Starbucks. And across the street in F.A.O. Schwarz, a million or so pieces of candy had vacated their bins: gummy worms, lollipops, twizzlers, gumballs, caramels, and those little necklaces made of Sweet Tarts.

I found a working payphone. I called Nat's school, where everything was fine, and Kerry, who had been showering when the quake struck, and then ran out of change. I began to worry about the cat: what if Al had been pinned beneath a falling shelf or halogen lamp? Retrieving my car, I drove home. There I discovered a slightly spooked animal and a single compact disk with a broken jewel case.

As it turned out, the Nisqually Earthquake had registered a very respectable 6.8 on the Richter scale. Indeed, if the epicenter hadn't been so deep underground—about thirty miles below the surface— it would have inflicted horrendous damage on the entire region. As it was, the temblor had cracked the dome of the capital building in Olympia. It did some minor structural damage to Tod's new house: to my amusement, FEMA eventually sent him a check to help with the repairs. And it seemed to zero in on the enormous Starbucks headquarters on First Avenue, where I had lunched with the crew during my initial interview. Pieces of the cornice tumbled to the ground. Inside, some of the elevator shaft walls buckled and collapsed. Luckily there were no major injuries. But it made you wonder: did God have it in for the high-end coffee merchant and its yuppie clientele? Did He prefer instant?

Nor was Starbucks the only New Economy stalwart to be called on the carpet. That morning, Bill Gates had been addressing a technology conference at the Westin Hotel. At 10:50, while the orangutans and elephants at the Woodland Park Zoo began howling with anticipatory angst, he was deep in a demonstration of the new Microsoft XP operating system. Four minutes later, the chandeliers in the ballroom started to sway. Audience members hit the floor or ran for the exits, and Gates himself was whisked offstage, presumably to the same reinforced bunker where he kept Leonardo da Vinci's notebooks. It was the day of judgment! The richest man in the world would now be brought to heel for his quasi-monopolistic domination of the marketplace, and for sponsoring all those terrible MSNBC talk shows!

I know, I know. An earthquake is meaningless, a geological sneeze. There's no divine intent, no punishment. Half the time, as Emerson knew, these agitations are hardly worth noting. Awakened out of a sound sleep at 5:25 A.M. on October 22, 1869, he later wrote in his journal:

I got out of bed, lit a match, & looked at the clock. I heard no other noise than the wave-like shaking of the house would make. At breakfast, I found that Mrs. Small had also observed it, & thought it an earthquake.

He and Mrs. Small had it right. But after nearly five years at Amazon, with an increasing sense of drift and disconnection, I was eager for a sign, and can hardly be blamed for latching on to this one. The earth moved, the ground shook. Wasn't a message being sent? Sure, I was succumbing to that absurd thing: the pathetic fallacy. But as I listened to the news that night, and absorbed the dire prophecies of landslide and liquefaction, it seemed no more pathetic than the next one.

21

I SURVIVED THE LAYOFFS, and I survived the quake. But there was now a third biblical plague to contend with: our annual reviews. For the first couple of years, under Susan's regime, this had been a simple and relatively decent process. You sat down with your boss, discussed your professional vices and virtues, and shook hands at the end. Since Amazon tended to give miniscule raises or none at all, you seldom haggled over money. It was a progress report, and at the beginning, everybody seemed to be progressing quite nicely.

By around 1999, though, this chummy protocol ended up on the junk heap. An elaborate system of numerical rankings was imported from Microsoft. It, too, had a veneer of anticorporate humanism: you and your supervisor were both required to comment on your performance, then produce a grand synthesis, preferably while you shared a hot tub and a wine cooler. What mattered, though, was your grade. Superstars, who delivered "precedent-setting results," might qualify for a 5.0. A 3.0 indicated that the employee met "position requirements and expectations." If you had "numerous performance deficiencies," you were looking at a 1.0 and an imminent pink slip.

None of this was so unusual. What stuck in my craw, though, was the notion of ranking all employees on a bell curve. This Darwinian practice had probably been part of the package all along. But nobody really enforced it until the beginning of 2001. The reason, I would guess, was to prepare a paper trail for future firings: if you had already earmarked one third of your staff as statistical mediocrities, who could argue with the idea of getting rid of them?

In any case, I was downgraded. I had asked Barrie, now my quasi-official supervisor, for a 4.5. (In 1999, I had asked for a 5.0, and was told that this was an index of Platonic perfection: even Jeff, who was only human, failed to qualify. Henceforth I would be more realistic.) Barrie countered with a 4.0, my current score, and I figured the negotiations were over. When the document finally returned from the powers-that-be, however, my grade had been lowered to 3.5.

I sat in my office, barricaded by a thousand books and by numerous cardboard boxes of bluegrass CDs that Kerry had left behind, and seethed. In my heart of hearts I knew the whole process was a charade. I knew I shouldn't give it a second thought, that it had no real bearing on my performance. But the very thought of some geek in management plotting my position on a curve—and nudging me from the upper, precedent-setting slopes to the undistinguished foothills—made me crazy.

I trotted down the hall to Barrie's office, the document in my hand. She smiled and shrugged, with what I'm sure was a genuine sense of helplessness.

"I'm sorry," she said. "They lowered everybody's grade."

"There's no reason to lower mine. My work is better than ever."

"Well, you do have to keep in mind that you're a senior editor now," she said. "You're competing with all the other senior editors."

"I've always been a senior editor," I said, which was true. Still, titles had never meant anything at Amazon—at one point, Jeff had been on the verge of abolishing them entirely and calling us all "associates"—and people seemed to put whatever they liked on their business cards.

"It's the bell curve," Barrie went on.

"What about all those layoffs? Should that theoretically leave only the upper end of the curve?"

"It doesn't work that way. They just start over with a new curve. You know that."

"Yeah. It pisses me off anyway."

"Make a note of that on the form. You can sign it and stipulate that you don't agree."

"Maybe."

I left. I signed the form without stipulating anything. The truth is, I was lapsing into a defeatist funk. In six months, when the last of my options vested, I would leave the company. This would be no surprise to my employers. Not long before, in fact, I had found a staffing memorandum in the printer—still the most reliable source of departmental dish—which predicted my departure in September due to "natural attrition." That sounded fatal, didn't it? Yet it was only an acknowledgment of an elementary truth: Amazon employees of my vintage operated on a five-year cycle. By the time their vesting periods came to an end, most were too frustrated, burned out, or bored to consider staying on.

I couldn't, on the other hand, *admit* I was planning to leave. That would make me a prime candidate should Amazon decide to throw some more ballast overboard. Instead I did my impression of a zealous company man for the remainder of my career—and my bosses, putting on a stylized performance of their own, accepted it.

It wasn't as difficult as you might think. I still got a residual thrill from the place. I still recalled the early years, when we had reinvented the wheel on a daily basis. (By contrast, the official 2001 Amazon.com Competencies chart frowned on such seat-of-the-pants innovation: *Does not reinvent the wheel* was listed as a strength rather than a weakness.) At times, I still loved my job. This may have been the biggest challenge of all, because editors now amounted to a kind of fifth column within the company, striking tiny, ineffectual blows against their own obsolescence. Reviews, articles, interviews: these were now black ops, to be hidden from your supervisors.

That wasn't too difficult, though. They weren't paying attention in the first place. They were focused on the most recent wave of automation, which was bringing all of us one step closer to our ultimate role as corporate lawn jockeys.

I'm not talking about my former pride and joy, the home page. No human being had laid a finger on that for many months. The new frontier for the personalization department—which one disgruntled manager had described to me as "Jeff's cowboy team"—was the category page. The editors, you see, still spent a disgraceful amount of time fiddling with content. That was a proven time sink and a money pit. The obvious solution: automate the category pages, add a host of personalization widgets, and liberate what remained of the editorial staff from its drudgery. Given this mandate, the software elves retreated to their lair for a long interval. Bulletins, depressing ones, emerged—mostly small questions about functionality. Then it was time to meet our new master: Amabot.

The name said it all. Content was dead. Oh, there were still certain levers and switches you could pull to post an actual essay or interview, as long as you kept your head down. But the category pages—originally conceived as every reader's home away from home—were pretty much extinct. They now ran on automatic pilot. That left us editors with time on our hands. We wouldn't be idle for long, however, thanks to another miracle of automation called Mercury.

Except in passing, I haven't said much about the company's targeted email program. Back in 1996, it was actually a great innovation: you sent a monthly newsletter to readers via email, filling them in on new releases and relevant stuff on the site. It wasn't spam. These people had signed up for the program and could stop it any time they liked. They often wrote back, as if they had received a personal letter. And indeed, that was the desired effect: an intimate conversation on the Transcendentalist telephone. It had that barrier-smashing allure of all the early Internet gimmicks. It was also a direct-marketer's wet dream, since you could address an unlimited audience without paying a dime for postage or printing.

Within a couple of years, of course, every website under the sun was peppering its clientele with email. The thrill was gone, or at least the novelty. At Amazon, meanwhile, the program had been sucked into the usual black hole of hyperbole: the word got out that each email was generating an average of \$100,000 in revenue. Since we editors kept a close eye on the books we featured, we knew perfectly well that this was a fiction. Yet we weren't going to argue with the numbers, nutty or not. If we could summon a million dollars out of thin air simply by jotting ten mash notes to our customers, we were truly wizards of e-commerce. As such, we kept our mouths shut.

This was a mistake. Dazzled by the prospect of all that cash, the managers doubled the number of mailings, then doubled *that* number. We also stepped up the flow of PBMs, or Past Buyer Mailings: in other words, when John Grisham published his latest indictment of our flabby legal system, we contacted every customer who had ever bought a previous Grisham title. It didn't occur to our bosses that the law of diminishing returns might soon kick in. Overkill didn't concern them. Instead they challenged the programmers to come up with a semi-automated tool, which would allow us to carpet bomb the entire planet with email. The result was Mercury, named after the winged messenger of the gods and patron saint, incidentally, of thieves.

Now we spent entire days cranking out newsletters or PBMs. The latter had been rechristened SNPs, or Single New Product Mailings—nobody knew why. In any case, hundreds or perhaps thousands of emails were soon going out each quarter. If they brought in $100,000 a pop, we would swiftly become the most successful company in human history. Hell, at that rate we could shut down most of our operations and just send messages to our customers. The editors could correspond with them on a 24/7 basis, kept awake with amphetamines and nourished through a feeding tube. O brave new world, that has such people in it!

Luckily it wasn't quite that bad. When nobody was looking, I still did my old job. In February I persuaded Richard Holmes to write a witty guide to the Romantic essentials, which struck me as a happy fusion of art and commerce. Over the next few months I reviewed a couple dozen titles, ran brief essays by Richard Russo, James Wolcott, and Sheila Kohler, interviewed both John Grisham and Czeslaw Milosz, and assembled features on W.H. Auden, Eric Newby, and J.D. Salinger. This amounted to a very respectable output for a literary journalist. If I shut my eyes and covered my ears, it was possible to ignore the fact that I was among the living dead. But as soon as I poked my head out of the office I now shared with Tim, there were plenty of reminders.

There was, for example, my business unit. After weeks of meditation, the Bird had decided that the royal road to profitability was paved with romance novels. Why? A couple of industry studies suggested that women would now be the fastest-growing demographic on the Web. Since we needed to grab some of that business—some of that *wallet share*, as the Bird called it—we had better zero in on Harlequin Heaven.

Now, I had already done a song-and-dance for Libby about the likes of Nora Roberts, who was selling truckloads of hardcovers to the same audience. But the mass-market paperbacks were a different story. These disposable items—which featured Fabio or his bleach-blond epigones on the cover and sold for a measly five bucks—had rotten margins. What's more, it was hard to see why any customer would want to be dinged for the shipping fee, which almost equaled the price of the book. That didn't prevent people from buying them, of course. During my sojourns in the warehouse I had picked many a copy of *Love's Tender Rhapsody* or *A Rogue's Rough Pleasure*. But were we really going to hitch our wagon to this dubious star? After our long-awaited PowerPoint presentation, the idea was quietly abandoned.

You couldn't say the same thing for Project Shift, which Jeff had introduced during his post-layoff sermon. The basic concept was that we would eliminate shipping charges on orders of two or more items. This was certainly a sound experiment, at least to see whether the upsurge in business would compensate for lost shipping revenues. Alas, somebody got the bright idea of raising prices at the same time. When we rolled out the initiative the second week of June, our bestsellers retained their deep discount of 40 percent—but several hundred thousand additional titles quietly reverted to list price. Who would ever notice?

Oh, only our entire customer base. The complaints came thick and fast over the next few days, and the company got reams of bad press for its double dealing. Meanwhile, *The Book of Hope* began its meteoric ascent. This slender biblical tract clearly had much to recommend it, with one customer paying particular mind to "its investigation of Job's earlier misdeeds." Most shoppers, however, were attracted to its 99-cent price tag. Droves of them tossed it in the shopping cart with a second, more expensive item and made their shipping charges disappear: a miracle on par with the loaves and fishes. We also did suspiciously brisk business in Dover Classics, which sold for a dollar each. None of this was doing wonders for our balance sheet.

Before Jeff pulled the plug, however, I was witness to a wonderful piece of managerial comedy. The Bird, still chafing at her exile from

the corridors of power, somehow attached herself to the panicky de-
liberations over Project Shift. Every now and then she scuttled into
our office with an update. On this particular day, though, we saw her
run past the door several times: first in one direction, then the other.
We got just a glimpse of her short, frazzled, energetic figure, like a
single frame isolated from a movie. There was a certain elegance to
the whole effect, like something Buster Keaton would have dreamed
up. Then she finally burst into the office, her eyes bright.

"Guess what?" she said.

"What?" I asked. I saw that Tim, on the other side of the partition,
had put down the biography of Zsa Zsa Gabor he had been reading
and cocked an ear.

"They're going to eliminate everything under five dollars from
the catalogue! That way nobody will be able to beat the system with
free shipping!"

"That's crazy," I said. "We're supposed to be Earth's Biggest
Bookstore. How can we stop offering all those items? We'll look like
morons."

"I'm telling you what they said," the Bird countered. "There's
supposed to be an emergency build this evening. Anything with a
price point below five bucks will disappear. In some cases they may
slap on a big surcharge, which comes to the same thing in the end."

"Why don't they simply exclude those items from the free shipping offer?"

"No can do!" The Bird was still out of breath. She seemed
affronted that we didn't share her excitement. "I'll keep you in the
loop!" she said and ran back out the door to another confab. Sounder
minds must have prevailed, because I never heard another whisper
about this proposal. The cut-rate titles remained. And a week later,
when Project Shift came to a halt, *The Book of Hope* resumed its position at the bottom of the heap.

All of these things made me mad. Again, I should have been indifferent. I should have been doing my impression of a bobble head, nodding complusively until September 19. Yet I couldn't seem to cultivate the proper attitude of lofty contempt: the job still mattered to me, which is why I cobbled together my Classics initiative before I left.

In a sense, this was a no-brainer. Anybody could see that a huge fraction of our literature and fiction sales came from backlist titles: here as elsewhere, depth of catalogue was the store's real strength. So why not capitalize on the fact? With little consultation—and in a hush-hush atmosphere worthy of *Mission Impossible*—I arranged to add a Classics bestseller list and a monthly e-mailing. The list I compiled myself, because the BISAC coding for Classics tended to overlook anything not written by Ernest Hemingway, Ayn Rand, or Hans Christian Andersen. I wanted *The Federalist Papers* in there, and *The Elements of Style,* and that recent reissue of the Marquis De Sade's *The 120 Days of Sodom.* Beginning in February, I posted the list on the site and sent out the first of the mailings.

The response was tremendous. Having heaped abuse on the company's statistical fixation for the last few chapters, I may have forfeited my right to relish the numbers. No matter: by June, my hand-compiled Classics list was outselling every other part of the literature area. Between June 4 and July 16, for example, it got nearly 25,000 hits and sold 3,956 books. This amounted to a conversion rate of 15.98 percent, which was almost unheard of. Even the Bird gulped when she examined the figures, and told me I was now set for life at the company. Hooray! Yet there was, as always, an epilogue. As soon as I left in the September, the whole shebang was dismantled. No more mailing, no more personal touch. Amabot stepped in with its customary, silicon-based suavity and restored BISAC to the throne. It also sent the naughty Marquis back to the erotica browse tree, where he belonged.

• • •

The Classics thing cheered me up. Very little else did. Those final months I felt myself in a void. In March I had walked down to the courthouse with my attorney, where a bored-looking judge in an office the size of a powder room stamped some papers for me: I was divorced. This final sundering of my marriage had been a long time coming. Still, it felt like a shock, an amputation, and I could hardly make sense of it.

Tod, now retired, told me I was "Seattle's second-most-eligible bachelor." He offered a few tips on short-term intimacy. Luckily I had met somebody more than a year before, who made me feel as if I had awakened from a long, sad, bad dream: who made me happy. Yet she lived in a city far away. That happiness was at some distance, then. It would be my prize for getting through the next few months, an impossible task.

Spring came. For the last time I bought pansies and petunias and planted them in little pots on the patio. One plant from the previous year made a comeback: an indestructible survivor with rubbery stems and reddish blossoms, whose intricate system of burst capillaries made it look as though it had a drinking problem. I watered them and spooned fertilizer into their pots. I cut them back when they got too leggy. And by the time they began to drop their petals, it was summer. The light was sparkling, transient, white and gold, blue. Tim and I grew bored in our exorbitant office and regularly would sneak down to the garage, where he kept his Miata. With the top down we headed off to Alki Beach, two grown men playing hooky.

Usually he powered up the subwoofer and we listened to *Rubber Soul* while the little sports car zipped over the West Seattle Bridge. We ate fish and chips, then got a gin-and-tonic, then had a valedictory beer before strolling along the sand. A few courageous bathers ventured into the freezing water. Most sat on the beach and studied the rippling immensity of the bay, which every so often whipped itself into a frenzy against the seawall.

.   .   .

The last time I saw Jeff was at a barbecue that summer. Maryam Mohit was pregnant, and several people had thrown a bash to celebrate her impending maternity leave. Once she had the baby, she wouldn't come back. In fact most of the dramatis personae of this book had already made their exits: Tod, Barrie, Kerry, Susan, Eric, Jonathan, and so forth. But Jeff remained. We stood by a table, within striking range of the raw vegetables and mushroom dip, and had a chat about parenting.

"I'd love to have another child," he said, the proud father of two infants.

"Bravo," I said. "I find that one really keeps my hands full."

Jeff guffawed loudly: he didn't scale his laugh down for domestic use.

"The other thing is," he continued, "I still have a fairly short attention span for kids. I'm going to have to push it beyond ninety minutes. I'm working on it, though."

I nodded and we talked some more. Jeff had aged in some minor respects. His hairline had receded—about the same degree as mine, in fact—and his skin looked more weathered, as it well might after five years of exposure to the ultraviolet rays of celebrity. Yet he still seemed like a normal guy. He didn't emit the static charge of a multibillionaire, didn't put on airs, didn't speak in the carefully cleansed periods of a press release. Of course, his entire biography had a prodigious stamp to it. He did everything earlier, and with more intensity, than most of his peers, and perhaps Amazon wouldn't even be the Bezonian culmination. Still, his normality seemed part and parcel of his gift. He wasn't a mad scientist, just an ordinary citizen in khakis and an Oxford shirt, with a modest car and a family to support.

Before I get too carried away with this, though, I should mention the Hawaiian grass skirt. Jeff climbed into it, I was told, just as I was leaving. After a few tentative hula moves, which made an audible swishing sound, the great artificer of the e-commerce revolution left his skirt on for the remainder of the party.

I flew to New York in early September, to get Nat settled in his new home before the school year began. I had a return ticket to Seattle on September 12: a flight that was scrubbed for obvious and excruciating reasons. A few days later I made it back. My final week I did little but pack up my stuff, a task that had been simplified for me shortly before, when Tim and I were evicted from our big office and dumped into tiny cubicles. The great culling had already taken place. Now I sat tight at my desk, wrote emails, and waited for Friday.

I didn't expect a big farewell. For one thing, the department was now too small to mount a major party. Nor was the mood conducive to good times. We had moved to US1, an office complex near the Amtrak station, and our little warren of desks—the final resting place of the mighty editorial machine—felt like a ghost town. You almost expected to see tumbleweeds collecting by the xerox machine. Meanwhile, some of the vacant offices and cubicles had been filled by MBAs. They left their doors open and talked constantly about pure product margin and revenue velocity, as if to remind us that this was Amazon's *real* lingua franca. Content was a dead language: the dialect, in Milosz's phrase, of a village high upon inaccessible mountains.

Well, these things happen. On Wednesday Nick sent out a Meeting Maker alert for Friday, September 21 at 3:30. He included a rather touching message:

It's time to bid farewell to our beloved James Marcus, king of Literature & Fiction. He's off to the Big Apple, and we're going to miss him terribly. Join us for some cookies, and please pass this invitation along—I'm sure I missed a bunch of people.

My first thought was: *cookies?* Surely the department could do a little better than that. How about a Sara Lee cheesecake? But Nick had called me the king, which I appreciated, and at this point I was lucky we weren't simply meeting by the Coke machine. At the appointed hour I showed up in the conference room. There was a plate of cookies on the table—oatmeal and chocolate chip—along with two pints of milk and some plastic cups. I was the only guest. Trying hard not to feel hurt, I sat down and waited.

People showed up: Nick, Karin, Therese, and a few others. We sat at the long table and had our milk and cookies. It looked as if Mister Rogers were staging his own version of the Last Supper. At some point, though, one of the newer hires said to me, "What was it *like* here in the beginning?"

If I weren't playing by the rules, I would now clear my throat and address myself to the new hire: *One fine spring day in 1996, I took off from Portland, Oregon, in a prop plane the size of a toy, which seemed to touch down in Seattle only minutes later.* It would give such an elegant circularity to this entire story! But that's not what happened. Instead I told a string of wandering, disconnected anecdotes. Prompted by additional questions, I kept going. My fear was that if I stopped, the guests would leave and I'd be stuck sweeping up the crumbs. So I strung together incidents, numbers, factual embellishments, trying most of all to convey the atmosphere of those days, which had vanished for good.

I shook hands and promised to stay in touch. Back at my desk, I looked at the computer for a long time. Although I never admitted it, I had always been proud of my email address: james@amazon.com. The minimalist ring of it identified me as a member of the first wave, the elect, the virtual sodbusters of the New Economy. The moment I shut off my computer, that would be over. My name would be stricken from the company directory by Monday afternoon, my email address retired. My visibility would be nil. Natural attrition would do me in. I found that hard to contemplate.

I put a finger on both power buttons and pushed. The CPU fell into an instant sleep. The monitor sounded its daily death rattle—that faint susurration of static electricity—and went blank. Did I feel any different? Well, I knew one thing for sure: for me, at least, Day One was finally over.

EPILOGUE

ON AUGUST 22, 2003, I strolled through the summer heat down to Grand Central Station. In my pocket I had a freshly laundered handkerchief, which I used to mop my brow every block or so. In my shoulder bag I had a thick manuscript—a copy of this very book—and my intention was to hand it over to Jeff Bezos. Did I have an appointment with my former boss? Not exactly. But Jeff was scheduled to play tennis with the alluring Anna Kournikova in one of the cavernous waiting rooms, and I hoped to catch his eye between volleys.

What he would think of the book I had no idea. When I began it, nearly two years before, I envisioned an exercise in self-flagellation: I would record the universal hubris of the era, including my own, and then administer some satirical comeuppance. At that point, anyway, the moral of the story seemed perfectly clear. We had gone on a national bender. We had surrendered our good sense for a quick buck—for many, many quick bucks—and were now paying the price. Most of the Internet powerhouses had collapsed, taking several trillion dollars in equity with them, and the rest of the economy fell into a major slump. There was a plague of finger-pointing, much of it justified. But there was also a sense of universal folly: *In NASDAQ's fall, we sinnéd all.* If you ended up in a sucker's paradise, you had nobody to blame but yourself.

Amazon, of course, never went out of business. But the stock continued its swoon throughout my final year on the job, and by September 28, 2001, it closed at an all-time low of $5.97 per share. To be fair, this was in the wake of the terrorist attacks, which demoralized the entire market. Yet it was a reasonable moment to wonder about the company's future. And as I began this book, the attacks seemed to throw our speculative frenzy into even sharper, more shameful relief: the fat years, the good times, had prevented us from noticing our precarious perch on the edge of a volcano. My mission—my moralistic mandate—was obvious.

And then it wasn't. Events caught up with this rather cut-and-dried vision, then overtook it. Amazon, left for dead by most of its former boosters, refused to go gently into that dark night. During the fourth quarter of 2001, the company finally posted its first profit. And throughout the next year, while the economy lingered in the recessionary basement, my former employer showed an amazing resilience.

How did this happen? For one thing, our first visible flop, the auctions site, had now morphed into Marketplace, a highly profitable clearinghouse for used goods. For another, the company continued to expand, although the pace had slowed to a more sensible trot. In September 2002 Jeff announced a new partnership with Office Depot. Two months later, the company waded into the apparel business. From there it was just a hop, skip, and a jump to sporting goods, which is where Anna Kournikova came in.

It seemed that the racket-wielding siren had now designed the Multiway Sports Bra, and for the first few weeks, Amazon would be its exclusive American distributor. Earlier that morning, Jeff and Anna had opened the trading day at NASDAQ headquarters: yet another index of the company's public rehabilitation. Two years earlier, Jeff might well have been pelted with fruit by a horde of disenchanted investors. Now, with another tech minibubble underway and his own stock at a heartening $45.22, he had resumed a heroic role. Indeed, according to friends who still worked at the Seattle HQ, Jeff spent part of each morning making a high-spirited circuit of the hallways on his Segway Human Transporter. He had invested a chunk of his own money in the lawnmower-like vehicle, and another chunk in some kind of space-travel initiative. Happy days were here again!

No wonder the waiting room at Grand Central was so jammed. When I arrived, the guests of honor were about to begin a press conference at the far end of Vanderbilt Hall. I pushed through the crowd: there were more guys than gals. Half of them, it was clear, were aroused by the sight of a sexy woman in a scanty top, which exposed her belly button and presumably hid one of those flagship bras. The other half were aroused by the sight of a grinning billionaire in tennis whites. Yes, the two groups overlapped.

I finally got close enough to see, and to hear. Jeff was wearing an Amazon T-shirt. His hairline had continued to recede, a fact he made no effort to hide with a cowardly comb-over, and he appeared slightly thinner. Otherwise he looked like the same guy who had interviewed me seven years before, diagramming the workings of a hedge fund on a piece of scrap paper. He stood close enough to Anna to indicate their commercial alliance, but not so close as to suggest any physical intimacy. It reminded me of the way Walter Mondale used to indicate his professional distance from Geraldine Ferraro: it was stiff but humorous, somehow.

"Hey Anna," shouted one reporter, looking for some salacious copy. "What do you look for in a sports bra?"

She paused, then said: "Support, I guess."

Jeff laughed. Clearly he was having a great time.

"A question for Jeff," said another journalist, holding a tiny recorder above his head. "What do you think of Intel's revised revenue forecast?"

Again: Jeff was now an oracle rather than a laughing charlatan. But on this occasion he made some inaudible comment and affirmed that he was here to play tennis. The two players now left the floodlit stage and made their way toward the fenced-off court on the other side of the room. The crush grew more intense. Still, this was my chance to get his attention, so I squirmed through the crowd and reached into my bag for the manuscript. No doubt I resembled an assassin: I was lucky not to be tackled by some civic-minded spectator. I had to try, however.

No such luck. Jeff and Anna were surrounded by a flying wedge of cops, MTA officers, National Guardsmen, and a cadre of serious-looking African-American men in dark suits, who looked exactly like the Fruit of Islam. I wasn't going to get within ten feet of my subject. Downcast, I shoved the manuscript back into my bag and made my way to courtside, where I had to stand on a bench to see.

You had to hand it to Jeff. Most men might daydream of volleying with the world's foxiest tennis player (although the Williams sisters surely gave Anna a run for her money). Jeff simply *did* it. Of course it was a publicity stunt, with clear commercial benefit for both parties. Yet he still seemed to have reality at his beck and call, still seemed capable of manipulating it like taffy, which is what had allowed him to sell the Amazonian dream to so many people in the first place.

The two batted the ball back and forth. Clearly Anna was lobbing little pattycakes to Jeff, who nonetheless swatted several of them into the net. Then, just as the initial game was ending, she applied a wicked forehand to one shot, which zoomed past Jeff's shoulder at a lethal clip. Much laughter erupted from the crowd. Jeff made a frightened face for the cameras and declared: "My life just flashed before my eyes!" More laughter. Still dejected over my failure to make contact, I left. There was little doubt as to who won the match, although I'm sure Jeff extracted precisely the right sort of triumph from this delicious defeat.

And so it goes. If I had set out to write this book in early 2000—when a journalist named Robert Spector published the first account of Amazon, the celebratory *Get Big Fast*—I would have produced the equivalent of a victory lap. In 2001, with Jeff's brainchild seemingly on its last legs, I prepared to deliver a guilty sermon on our rise and fall. And in 2003, as I type out these very sentences, that version too has fallen into obsolescence. Art, to the extent that this book is artful, simply can't keep up with life.

What's the moral of the story, then? Let me put it this way. Emerson famously noted: *Every day is a god.* Jeff countered him with: *Every day is Day One.* At the time I left Amazon, I was a confirmed Emersonian and felt little sympathy for Jeff's vision of a perpetual clean slate. But now, having been outdistanced by events—having observed the company rise from the dead and violate every rule of the narrative I had in mind for it—I'm no longer sure who's right. Until the last word is in on Earth's Biggest or Largest or Most Transcendental Bookstore, I'm willing to split the difference.

AFTERWORD TO THE
PAPERBACK EDITION

IN THE SUMMER OF 2003, when I was putting the finishing touches on *Amazonia*, my former employer was on a roll. In recent months, Jeff Bezos had signed new deals with a posse of partners, including Target, Foot Locker, the National Basketball Association, and Google. The company was quietly shoring up its credit, redeeming $264 million worth of bonds it had issued at the height of the Bubble. And let's not forget the Multiway Sports Bra: with its molded cups, inner support sling, and ultra-wicking fabric, this was merely the tip of the sporting-goods iceberg.

There was, of course, the occasional cloud in the sky. Amazon had been harried by two recent lawsuits, one by Pinpoint (which accused the company of stealing its personalization technology) and another by the Corbis Corporation (which accused the company of stealing images of Cameron Diaz and Vin Diesel). A good many analysts—even those with a sunny picture of Amazon's long-term prospects—still thought the stock was obscenely overvalued. Meanwhile, Jeff was the darling of NASDAQ once more, and the poster boy for the Segway Human Transporter, which was projected to conquer the entire nation over the next five years.

Well, the Segway hasn't kept to that schedule. Amazon, on the other hand, has rolled forward with the kind of relentless energy that the Segway was *supposed* to deliver. In October 2003, the company launched a gourmet food store: just the place to go when you had a midnight craving for foie gras in aspic and a handful of peppered beef sticks. In May 2004, Jeff formed an alliance with the Bombay Company, and a few months later, he bought Joyo.com, China's biggest online shopping site. Then came the beauty products store, the jewelry store, the musical instrument store, some kind of hand-holding agreement with Diane von Furstenberg, and a deal with Macy's—the world's biggest department store and a major bastion of bricks-and-mortar retail.

This madcap expansion reminded me of *something*. Oh, I know: the good old days of the Bubble, when Amazon was wolfing down new partners like so many salted peanuts. At certain moments, it's possible to believe that we're still in that era. An example? On May 4, 2005—the very day I started to write this afterword—the company announced a deal with Wine.com, an Internet booze merchant. This inevitably brought to mind Jeff's previous dalliance with Wineshopper.com, which had cost about $30 million back in the palmier days of 1999. Everything old is new again! But this wasn't merely a case of déjà vu: it was more like a square dance, where the same partners keep lining up for an additional do-si-do. You see, Wineshopper.com had merged with Wine.com in August 2000, citing high customer-acquisition costs. Then eVineyard.com absorbed Wine.com, kept its more quaffable domain name, and was now rolling the dice with Jeff once again.

The drive to add more partners and product lines is impressive enough. Establishing a beachhead in China is a shrewd move. But it's the starry-eyed initiatives, with their mad scientist overtones, that still seem the most Amazonian to me. One is the A9 search engine, which the company unveiled in September 2004. Jeff had spun off this subsidiary nearly a year before, and based its offices in Palo Alto, supposedly to take advantage of the large pool of software engineers. Initially the engine depended on Google's algorithms, combined with Amazon's own, oceanic database. There were personalization features galore—including the ability to access all of your previous searches, along with any notes you took at the time—and the company soon added a sort of Yellow-Pages-on-steroids, which encompassed not only 14 million local businesses but actual, street-level photographs of their locations. To date, A9 has taken only a microscopic nip out of its nominal rival (and current partner) Google. As of January 2005, the site was ranked behind twenty-nine other search engines, and Google alone had a lock on 60 percent of the market. Still, search is the new Klondike for online commerce, and Jeff is clearly determined to stake his claim. In fact, he's plowing mountains of cash back into technology—a course of action that has both enchanted and enraged investors over the years—and I suspect he'll find some way to make A9 pay its way.

Even more imperial in its breadth and ambition is the Search Inside the Book initiative: basically a digitized library of several hundred thousand titles, searchable down to the last paragraph, sentence, and word. Amazon rolled this one out in October 2003, beginning with 120,000 books from nearly 200 publishers. I see that I've been bitten once again by the metrics bug, so let me toss out another mindblower: at launch, the database included some 33 million pages.

Now, the initial rationale for this project, and the obvious allure for publishers, was that customers would be able to make more informed buying decisions. Or to put it succinctly: they would buy more books. The company has already produced figures to back up this argument. But it would take a very stunted imagination indeed to overlook other uses for this trove of digitized texts. Amazon was quick to hook up the whole kit-and-kaboodle to A9, so that the search engine could not only dole out results from the Web but delve into every page of an enormous virtual library. The developers also integrated the database into the regular search box on the Amazon site, then rapidly backpedaled from this customer-unfriendly blooper: as it turned out, people who typed *The Da Vinci Code* into the box didn't want a list of thousands of books in which those words occurred. They just wanted to buy the damn novel.

In any case, it's obvious that this Alexandrian initiative—which already has a formidable competitor in the wide-ranging Google Print project—may have other uses down the road. What if, for example, Amazon were to enter the print-on-demand business? The company would instantly have a wealth of public-domain texts at its fingertips, ready to be delivered to shoppers via download or, who knows, some sort of freaky kiosk at your local Foot Locker or Diane Von Furstenberg skin-waxing joint.

Speak of the devil: on April 4, 2005, Amazon announced that it had bought BookSurge LLC, a Charleston-based operation specializing in "inventory-free book printing and fulfillment." The initial focus, according to Amazon, would be on restoring out-of-print rarities (a service that archrival Barnes & Noble had begun offering five years ago). The new subsidiary could also function as a vanity press. There was little discussion of the company's textual treasure chest, possibly to avoid spooking publishers, who don't exactly relish the thought of being cut out of the supply chain. But sooner or later, once the logistical and legal hurdles have been cleared, I'm confident that Amazon will become a de facto producer of books. It's a no-brainer, if you're wearing your visionary spectacles.

Ah, the V word! It's bound to come up in any discussion of Amazon, because one of the main questions at this point is whether the company will now settle into a long, comfy existence as the online equivalent of Wal-Mart—no small accomplishment, that—or continue its rule-breaking, icon-smashing reinvention of commerce-at-large. This is more than an academic dispute. At the moment, Jeff's brainchild has a market capitalization of $14.2 billion (less than Sears, but more than U.S. Steel, in case you're keeping track.) If investors were to apply the same, stodgy yardsticks they use to size up traditional retailers—let's say, the forward price-to-earnings ratio, which is now 15.84 for Wal-Mart and 38.43 for Amazon—that lofty valuation might well be slashed in half. But if you believe that Jeff has yet to exhaust his visionary capital, then there's no reason not to factor that into the stock price. Hell, the shares are currently close to a fifty-two-week *low*. It could be Day One after all.

In this thumbnail sketch of Amazonian life since 2003—and it *is* a thumbnail, with no mention of numerous initiatives, alliances, and lawsuits—I have omitted a key item, at least from my own selfish perspective. That would be the publication of *Amazonia*.

There was a time when the appearance of a potentially muckraking kiss-and-tell might have sent chills up and down the managerial spine: especially during the early days, when the company leaned so heavily on its reputation as the hip, smart, freewheeling spearhead of the New Economy. Now things were different. Amazon had shucked off its atmosphere of civilized bibliophilia, and morphed into an e-commerce leviathan that just happened to sell books. Nobody expected spotless behavior from such a heavyweight. Short of implicating Jeff Bezos in a child-slavery ring, then, *Amazonia* was unlikely to bring down the corporate temple, or even cause a mild tremor.

Still, I thought Jeff should see the manuscript prior to publication. So did my publisher, eager to nip any potential litigation in the bud. My first attempt to pass it along—at the Bezos-Kournikova smackdown at Grand Central Station—was a failure. Instead I bundled it up and stuck it in the mail, with a friendly note and a premonitory shudder. And I heard . . . nothing. I knew it had arrived in Seattle, because a friend of a friend who still worked at the company told me the manuscript had been vetted by the legal department, then passed along to some of the dramatis personae for a quick read. But neither I nor The New Press heard a peep of protest from Amazon, which seemed like a very good sign.

A happy fact: Amazon was eager to promote and sell the book. What's more, they were willing to host a small reception for me when I came out to Seattle as part of my two-city author tour. I agonized over this proposal. Wouldn't such festivities suggest that *Amazonia* was, well, a little *too* complimentary—that it verged on an author-ized, airbrushed account of the company's rise and fall and rise? After about five minutes of agony, though, I decided there was no problem. It would be fun to march back into the PacMed fortress, to make a prodigal return. Maybe there would be champagne. Maybe Jeff would let me ride his Segway.

As it turned out, Amazon's enthusiasm was shot through with just a little ambivalence. A few days prior to my Seattle trip, while I was packing my Gore-Tex and tongue studs, I got a call from my publisher. My wine-and-cheese blowout had been scuttled. Why? According to the company spokesperson, it would violate a rather tautological rule in the corporate playbook: *Amazon was not allowed to give a party for a person who had written a book about Amazon.* No doubt the ink was still wet on that regulation. Still, I wasn't too hurt. And my conscience remained clean. And Amazon, whatever doubts it may have harbored about my nostalgic, good-natured spitballs, went on to sell more copies of *Amazonia* than any other bookseller. (In this regard the company has been narrowly trailed by the inde-pendents, who soon recognized that if the book was no assault on Amazon, it was certainly no advertisement, either.)

And what of the reactions from my former colleagues? Those too have been positive on the whole. Some ex-Amazonians have issued small caveats, or put a different spin on certain events, which is only natural, given the erosion of memory: theirs *and* mine. At least one person (I was going to say, *character*) was unhappy to be identified as a practitioner of the Bartleby Maneuver. For this I'm inclined to apologize—and also to point out that my goal in explicating the Maneuver was to highlight Amazon's early, bizarrely elastic corporate culture. If I hadn't loved my job as much as I did, I would have gladly pulled a Bartleby myself.

Still, when my old comrades-in-arms *did* complain, they didn't limit themselves to nitpicking: they condemned the whole enterprise as a myopic mess. One individual, whom I won't identify here, posted his piss-and-vinegar summation right on the Amazon site. In his own words: *What the early days of Amazon.com looked like to someone who didn't understand it very well.* Ouch.

I confess at the very least to the charge of myopia. I understood my narrow slice of the company quite well indeed, and that's what I undertook to describe in *Amazonia*. But as The Little Bookstore That Could was transformed into a sprawling (and sometimes brawling) operation spread out over three continents, there was no way for anybody but Jeff Bezos to keep the whole whirlwind in focus.

Even now, I'm told, the company is suffering from an enfeebled institutional memory. This may be the inevitable outcome when most of the employees bail on a five-year cycle. Still, there's a signal irony to the fact that a high-tech bellwether like Amazon must depend on what one current Amazonian described as an "oral culture"—a corpus of folklore about data mining and merchandising techniques—to pass along its collective wisdom. *Listen my children and you shall hear, / Of our revenue goals for the preceding year.* I like to think of *Amazonia* as my limited contribution to the memory bank.

Myopia is, in any case, the writer's occupational hazard. I won't evoke Emerson, whose abundant presence in this book nearly lost me a few friends. But I can still turn to his disciple Thoreau, who wrote about the entire universe as if it were merely an adjunct to the tool-shed he happened to be occupying on Walden Pond. "We commonly do not remember that it is, after all, always the first person that is speaking," he wrote. "I should not talk so much about myself if there were any body else whom I knew as well. Unfortunately, I am confined to this theme by the narrowness of my experience." As are we all. Amen!

James Marcus
May 2005

A CONVERSATION BETWEEN HENRY BLODGET AND JAMES MARCUS

ON JULY 27, 2004, James Marcus sat down with Henry Blodget at the Housing Works Used Book Café in New York City for an extended conversation about *Amazonia*, e-commerce, and Internet fever. Blodget, of course, witnessed Amazon's spectacular rise at very close quarters: covering the company for CIBC Oppenheimer in December 1998, he set the famous $400-per-share target, which the split-adjusted stock obligingly hit only two weeks later. But the former analyst, who now writes for *Slate* and other publications, also brings some welcome historical and economic context to the table. He began the exchange by explaining his own role in the story, and comparing the Internet Bubble to the speculative frenzy of the Roaring Twenties.

BLODGET: I began covering the Internet back in the Netscape days, around 1995. I picked up on Amazon in 1998—and for reasons that James goes into in the book, I probably will be forever linked to some degree with the company. I followed it all the way up and all the way down. By way of disclosure: I've owned the stock since, I believe, 1999 and continue to own it now. I should also say that I'm a character in the book. Sometimes I'm treated favorably, sometimes not so favorably, or so it seemed to me as I read it.

But I should also say that I think this book is far more important than just somebody's experience at Amazon. What we *really* experienced—and what James went through—is an incredibly important period, both for the Internet and for the stock market in general. In twenty-five years, I think people will look back on the bubble of the 1990s the same way we look back on 1929. It will seem like the same sort of historical moment.

Now, I've read a lot of the books about 1929. Very few of them are actually written from an honest perspective of what it looked like *at the time*. Everything is obvious in hindsight, of course. It's easy to look back and say, oh, we were all such idiots, all these stupid things happened, and so forth. What's much more interesting is to get into the meat of it: to see how it felt, how decisions were made, why they were made. And that comes through in this book very well. I think there is some hindsight, which we'll talk about, but *Amazonia* really does convey the experience of the era.

From my perspective on Wall Street, obviously, we watched Amazon from the outside. You had this image of incredible experimentation, and hyper-growth, and this brilliant freak at the helm. You were never quite sure if Jeff Bezos was going to go off on some tangent and blow the company up. One interesting discovery for me in reading the book was that Bezos was viewed the same way *within* the company— meaning that we weren't totally misperceiving things on Wall Street.

Anyway, to begin the conversation, let me go back to my earlier point, that everything is obvious in hindsight. James, you were employee number fifty-five, which is extraordinarily early in Amazon's history. When you joined, what was your expectation, if any, of what the company could become? And was that expectation shared by your colleagues?

MARCUS: I have an oddly bifurcated response. On one hand, my immediate reason for joining was simply that somebody was offering me a job. It seemed to me that the company might well detonate and explode a year later, because e-commerce was so much in its infancy. It wasn't that I thought e-commerce was a bad idea, or that nobody would buy books from the company. It seemed likely, however, that Amazon would be shoved out of the way as big players like Barnes & Noble entered the marketplace. So in that sense, my expectations were low. I thought, well, I'm getting a job at a very interesting operation, and I'll just see what happens.

On the other hand, the excitement of the place—the weird sense that you were making history as part of your job—was so palpable! Of course, all those people could have been kidding themselves. But in fact they were correct to sense that they were onto a huge thing, an enormous socioeconomic ripple, and that feeling was extremely contagious. So I showed up there with modest expectations. And within a few weeks, I drank the Kool-Aid—for what it's worth—and became enormously excited, even though I didn't know exactly where we were going.

BLODGET: If you weren't excited at that point, you were probably dead. Amazon's growth, for twenty or so quarters from inception, was astronomical. It got to $100 million in revenue faster than almost any company in history, and this was in an industry that was not growing: the book business. Meanwhile, all of these sales were coming right out of the pocket of Barnes & Noble, smaller bookstores, and so forth.

Now, on Wall Street, the conventional wisdom was that as soon as B&N threw together a website, Amazon would be toast. This happened all the time during the Internet boom. People assumed that the industry incumbent would steamroll the upstart. In Amazon's case, however, B&N effectively got nowhere. As you note in the book, you were able to protect your turf.

MARCUS: I've always thought that B&N, the biggest bookseller in the United States, made a terrible mistake by not getting into online commerce six to twelve months earlier. If they had, I think things may have played out a little differently. Because although Amazon enjoyed periodic infusions of capital, B&N had infinitely more money and resources than we did. Jeff stayed ahead by means of brilliant PR, and by being more inventive—because Amazon wasn't hobbled by the Old Economy way of doing business. Still, if B&N had jumped in faster, they might have grabbed a bigger slice of the market.

BLODGET: I would say that's probably true. But one of the reasons they *did* jump in was the spectacular success Amazon was having. If you look at B&N's core competency—what they knew how to do—it was incredibly different from what you were figuring out on a daily basis, in a kind of Internet laboratory. True, Amazon was sometimes criticized for its kindergarten atmosphere of experimentation. Yet I don't think the business would have survived if it hadn't been running at 150 miles per hour during the initial phase. In fact, I would argue that this is what *has to happen* for a new industry to develop.

MARCUS: I totally agree. The number of initiatives that Amazon rolled out and quickly folded is basically unknown to the public. They threw a lot of stuff at the wall, some of it almost invisibly. At one point, for example, Jeff became very enamored of the way Yahoo was presented, with everything stacked in these subject-based browsing categories. He thought that was the future. Amazon, with its storefront-like appearance, was going to be a dinosaur. So he had the company design a Yahoo-style front page, and said: Look, the switch is going to hurt, but we're going to have to suck it up, because this is where the future is. They put it up for fifty percent of all visitors during a given day—and the revenue began to tank. As I recall, it dropped by 2 or 3 percent over the course of a single afternoon! And that was the end of it. I give Jeff credit for not insanely sticking to his guns and insisting that we follow this idea straight to the bottom.

BLODGET: When you have such rapid growth, of course, very weak ideas can sometimes take hold—just because there's so much opportunity. Which of the things that Amazon did during this period were internally viewed as mistakes right from the start? Did some of these turn out to be home runs?

MARCUS: Let's see. Amazon's first couple of acquisitions included Planet All, essentially an online address book, and a software company called Junglee. The latter did a number of things, but what Amazon really wanted—the plum of the transaction—was an engine that would allow customers to come to the site and search the entire Web for merchandise. Now there are plenty of what are called shopping bots, but back then, there was nothing like (as it was called) Shop-the-Web.

For various reasons, people at the company didn't think much of Planet All. Amazon paid some enormous amount of money for the operation, and it didn't really seem like such a big deal. What happened, in fact, is that PDAs really hit the market about six months later, and wiped out the whole business. So here was an initiative that people perceived as a mistake from the beginning—and indeed, it never went anywhere.

On the other hand, we all thought Shop-the-Web would be either a big disaster or a giant success. Why? Because it was so counterintuitive: sending customers out of the store to buy cheaper versions of the product you might be selling struck most retailers as pure suicide. Jeff's feeling was that it would bring traffic into the store, and that we would heighten *customer ecstasy*—which was a particular focus of his at that point. Well, they poured a lot of effort and time into it, and the surprising result was that nobody could care less. Nobody used it. It kept being moved to a smaller and more obscure part of the site—by the end, as I noted in the book, you practically needed another search engine to *find* it. And finally it just disappeared.

BLODGET: Any others come to mind?

MARCUS: Well, we all thought that auctions would be a big success. There was a perfectly sound rationale at the time. EBay was gaining on us at a frantic pace, and they could have easily launched a fixed-price operation. In other words, there was nothing to stop them from launching their own Amazon, so we'd better launch our own eBay and beat them to the punch. There were many arguments to support the idea. Yet it flamed out completely.

BLODGET: As James notes in the book, apparently *I* thought it was going to be a big success as well.

MARCUS: Again, with good reason. You have to recall that the company had this zeal for expansion: every three weeks they were announcing another deal, many of which I didn't even mention in the book. Some of that stuff seemed insane. But by 1999, Amazon had very deep pockets for acquisitions, partially because the stock was priced so high and they could use it to pay for companies, but also because they had done these bond issues and raised hundreds of millions of dollars in cash.

Jeff wanted to get into every market at once, before we were too identified as a bookseller. By 2000, in fact, Amazon seemed to be working very hard to *conceal* the fact that it was a bookseller. The company would buy four-color inserts in the newspapers, and there would be the garden hose, the asparagus pot, the salad spinner, but not a single book in sight. In the editorial department, we were very hurt. We weren't the favorite child anymore. But Jeff really felt it was expand or die.

BLODGET: It's interesting to see how the model has evolved. You talk early on about Amazon's initial efforts to rent space to other sellers. The first time around, that wasn't so successful. But now it's an incredibly profitable business for them.

MARCUS: That's right. The first time around, most of the partners went under. Then Amazon moved toward a different partnership model—the kind they have with Toys'Я'Us—where Amazon basically runs the front end of the online store in exchange for a commission. And now they've moved back to renting space in the mall as well, to thousands of third-party sellers.

BLODGET: Amazon always had this cult feeling from the outside. There was certainly an atmosphere of secrecy: unlike Yahoo and some of the other Internet companies, they wouldn't tell the Street anything. Things were developed and suddenly sprung on you. Well, according to your book, it felt the same way inside the company. There would be Project X, and you would find out about it accidentally the day before launch.

MARCUS: Exactly.

BLODGET: But it comes out in an interesting way in your book. You seldom use the word *we*—as in, "We fifty-odd employees built this incredible company." You talk about these events as though they're just happening *around* you. To what extent is that a literary device, and to what extent was there really a kind of inner cabal at the company, from which almost everybody else was excluded?

MARCUS: Two things. One, I made up my mind to do the book from memory. Having taken up that formal challenge, I was forced to have a fairly myopic (or let's just say narrow) focus.

But I think it's also an accurate reflection of what it was like at Amazon. As I said before, we at the bookstore tended to feel resentful, because even though we were still generating more than half the revenue, and essentially paying for the early-stage businesses like wine, tools, or cell phones, we were left to fend for ourselves. We weren't told about things. You overheard conversations in the elevator, or you took something out of the fax machine you weren't supposed to take, or you saw it in the newspaper—another popular channel for intracompany communications. There was an undeniable element of secrecy, of cloak-and-dagger behavior, in the corporate culture.

BLODGET: I think that was one of the reasons there was such a backlash in the press against Jeff Bezos. In just five years, he went from having started the company in his garage to being the Man of the Year in *Time*. Then, a year and half after that, he was just *excoriated* by the very same journalists and pundits. The company was going to go out of business! It was all over!

It's been interesting to watch how Jeff has dealt with that. Clearly this is a maturation process for him, now that he's a world-famous entrepreneur and CEO. But as you point out so effectively in the book, it's very difficult to make the transition from a garage-style business to a global corporation, where you're offending half your employees every time you make a move.

MARCUS: Yes, that was a tough hurdle to jump over. As for Jeff, he may have had his moments of sitting bolt upright at three in the morning, covered with perspiration, but he always seemed very convinced of what he was doing. And he remained quite accessible, even after becoming a billionaire: he didn't have the billionaire's static field of repulsion. And let's face it, he's done OK. The company is here to stay, I think, and it's his creation.

BLODGET: Absolutely. The company is ten years old, and I think we're really looking at the equivalent of Wal-Mart in 1970, in terms of the trajectory from here. And all of this early stuff will be forgotten—which is why I think this book is not only a great read, but very important from a historical point of view.

A NOTE ON SOURCES

Amazonia is a faithful account of the five years I spent at the company, reconstructed from my own memories and a handful of fugitive and intermittent notes. All events and conversations took place as reported. No names have been changed. From time to time I have turned to secondary sources—newspapers, magazines, and Robert Spector's ebullient *Amazon.com: Get Big Fast*—to confirm certain figures and dates. Indeed, most of the statistics cited throughout are matters of public record. Only a few—such as the earth-shattering conversion rate for the Classics Bestseller list—have been extracted from internal documents.

There is, of course, one obvious exception to this statement of documentary purity: the Bird. Yet even this fictional Frankenstein was cobbled together out of factual parts. Just about everything she says and does was said and done by *some* managerial type at the company. In that sense, she's as true to life as anybody else in the book, including the author.